The Methuen Drama Anthology of Contemporary Italian Plays

The Methuen Drama Anthology of Contemporary Italian Plays

Nalini Vidoolah Mootoosamy
Davide Carnevali
Magdalena Barile
Emanuele Aldrovandi
Ubah Cristina Ali Farah
Francesco Alberici
Valentina Diana
Pier Lorenzo Pisano

Edited by MARGHERITA LAERA

methuen | drama
LONDON • NEW YORK • OXFORD • NEW DELHI • SYDNEY

METHUEN DRAMA
Bloomsbury Publishing Plc
50 Bedford Square, London, WC1B 3DP, UK
1385 Broadway, New York, NY 10018, USA
29 Earlsfort Terrace, Dublin 2, Ireland

BLOOMSBURY, METHUEN DRAMA and the Methuen Drama logo are trademarks
of Bloomsbury Publishing Plc

First published in Great Britain 2025

© Italian Cultural Institute in London - London 2025
The Foreigner's Smile © Nalini Vidoolah Mootoosamy, 2025; translation © Nalini Vidoolah Mootoosamy and Margherita Laera, 2025
Portrait of the Artist as a Dead Man: Italy '41 – Argentina '78 © Davide Carnevali, 2025; translation © Margherita Laera, 2025
Gentleman Anne © Magdalena Barile, 2025; translation © Margherita Laera, 2025
The Fattest Woman in the World © Emanuele Aldrovandi, 2025; translation © Marco Young, 2025
Antigone Power © Ubah Cristina Ali Farah, 2025; translation © Atri Banerjee, 2025
Bidibibodibiboo © Francesco Alberici, 2025; translation © Flora Pitrolo, 2025
Big Fright © Valentina Diana, 2025; translation © Margherita Laera, 2025
Carbon © Pier Lorenzo Pisano, 2025; translation © Atri Banerjee, 2025

The authors have asserted their right under the Copyright, Designs and Patents Act, 1988, to be identified as authors of this work.

For legal purposes the Acknowledgements on p. ix constitute an extension of this copyright page.

Cover design by Matt Thame

All rights reserved. No part of this publication may be: i) reproduced or transmitted in any form, electronic or mechanical, including photocopying, recording or by means of any information storage or retrieval system without prior permission in writing from the publishers; or ii) used or reproduced in any way for the training, development or operation of artificial intelligence (AI) technologies, including generative AI technologies. The rights holders expressly reserve this publication from the text and data mining exception as per Article 4(3) of the Digital Single Market Directive (EU)

Bloomsbury Publishing Plc does not have any control over, or responsibility for, any third-party websites referred to or in this book. All internet addresses given in this book were correct at the time of going to press. The author and publisher regret any inconvenience caused if addresses have changed or sites have ceased to exist, but can accept no responsibility for any such changes.

No rights in incidental music or songs contained in the work are hereby granted and performance rights for any performance/presentation whatsoever must be obtained from the respective copyright owners.

All rights whatsoever in this play are strictly reserved and application for performance etc. should be made before rehearsals to Permissions Department, Bloomsbury Publishing Plc, 50 Bedford Square, London, WC1B 3DP, UK. No performance may be given unless a licence has been obtained. No rights in incidental music or songs contained in the Work are hereby granted and performance rights for any performance/presentation whatsoever must be obtained from the respective copyright owners.

A catalogue record for this book is available from the British Library.

A catalog record for this book is available from the Library of Congress.

ISBN: HB: 978-1-3503-7047-0
PB: 978-1-3503-7045-6
ePDF: 978-1-3503-7050-0
eBook: 978-1-3503-7048-7

Series: Methuen Drama Play Collections

Typeset by RefineCatch Limited, Bungay, Suffolk
Printed and bound in Great Britain

For product safety related questions contact productsafety@bloomsbury.com.

To find out more about our authors and books visit www.bloomsbury.com and sign up for our newsletters.

**FABULAMUNDI
PLAYWRITING
EUROPE
NEW VOICES**

To my multilingual family, con amore infinito

Contents

List of Illustrations viii
Acknowledgements ix

Introduction: Beyond Stereotypes by Margherita Laera 1

Nalini Vidoolah Mootoosamy, *The Foreigner's Smile* 11
Translated by Margherita Laera and Nalini Vidoolah Mootoosamy

Davide Carnevali, *Portrait of the Artist as a Dead Man: Italy '41 – Argentina '78* 55
Translated by Margherita Laera

Magdalena Barile, *Gentleman Anne* 83
Translated by Margherita Laera

Emanuele Aldrovandi, *The Fattest Woman in the World* 109
Translated by Marco Young

Ubah Cristina Ali Farah, *Antigone Power* 151
Translated by Atri Banerjee

Francesco Alberici, *Bidibibodibiboo* 169
Translated by Flora Pitrolo

Valentina Diana, *Big Fright* 231
Translated by Margherita Laera

Pier Lorenzo Pisano, *Carbon* 269
Translated by Atri Banerjee

Contributor Biographies 313

Illustrations

The editor and Bloomsbury Publishing Plc are grateful to the following copyright holders for granting permission to publish the following images.

Disclaimer: Every effort has been made to contact copyright holders for their permission to use material. The publishers would be grateful to hear from any copyright holder who is not here acknowledged and will undertake to rectify any omissions in future editions of this title.

1. Maurizio Cattelan, 'Bidibidobidiboo', 1996.
   Taxidermied squirrel, ceramic, Formica, wood, paint and steel.
   45 cm. × 60 cm. × 48 cm.
   Installation view: *Italics. Arte italiana fra tradizione e rivoluzione 1968-2008*, September 26, 2008 to March 22, 2009, Palazzo Grassi, Venice, Italy.
   Fondazione Sandretto Re Rebaudengo, Turin.
   Photo © Zeno Zotti. Courtesy: Maurizio Cattelan's Archive.   172

2. 'Western Australia's Jack Hills'. Image by Robert Simmon, based on data from the University of Maryland's Global Land Cover Facility, captured by the Landsat satellite on July 27, 1999. © NASA's Earth Observatory.   275

3. 'Diagram of vertebrate evolution' © John Lomberg.   279

4. 'Sprinters' © History of the Olympics, Picturepoint, London.   284

5. 'Demonstration of licking and eating' © Cornell University.   288

6. 'The Great Wall of China' © Dana Andreea Gheorghe.   292

7. 'Skeletons' © unknown.   296

8. 'Climber' © Gaston Rébuffat Archive, Cinémathèque d'Images de Montagne.   300

9. 'Golden Record' © NASA / Alamy Stock Photo.   305

Acknowledgements

This book is a collective labour of love and I owe a debt of gratitude to all the people who made it possible. Firstly, the staff at the Italian Cultural Institute who supported the project from its inception as an idea in 2020 to its practical delivery in 2024: Director Katia Pizzi and cultural attachés Nicola Locatelli and Maria Teresa De Palma. This book would not have been possible without their support. Secondly, I am grateful to Claudia Di Giacomo and Valentina De Simone of PAV / Fabulamundi Playwriting Europe for supporting this book, and for involving me in the project, Playground London, which inspired the editing of this anthology. I want to thank all the authors and translators for their essential contribution, and all the theatre-makers who were involved in workshopping the plays and their translations for their generosity. Lastly, I want to express my gratitude to Dom O'Hanlon and all at Bloomsbury Methuen Drama for believing in the value of this book.

Introduction: Beyond Stereotypes

By Margherita Laera

Italy is home to a vibrant contemporary playwriting scene, yet Italian dramatists are little known to English-language readers and audiences, with only a handful of notable exceptions in recent times, such as Stefano Massini and Dario Fo.[1] Of course, the struggle to 'make it' in Britain is not a challenge faced by Italian writers only, but by many, if not most, writers who work in a language other than English. As I have argued elsewhere (see Laera, 2019; 2022; 2024), the marginalisation of plays in translation on British stages is made possible by a number of interconnected factors, including, above all, the formidable strength of the playwriting field and its traditions at 'home', which stifle curiosity and openness towards other ways of writing for the stage. This is coupled with an ingrained sense of geopolitical self-importance and cultural dominance on the world stage, which supports huge structural omissions in the school and HE curriculum, leading to unfamiliarity with, and therefore mistrust of, cultural difference. Ultimately, this value system underpins a view of translated texts as inferior to their 'originals', but also supports the assumption that stories that are originally written in a language other than English are irrelevant to English-speaking audiences. Add to this the fact that the British theatre industry receives very little subsidy, in percentage terms, relative to the yearly budgets of venues, festivals and companies in mainland Europe, which forces British programmers to avoid risks. However, the exclusion of translated plays from British stages says more about the British theatre industry, and the attitudes of British theatre-makers and gatekeepers, rather than about the artistic merits of international plays themselves.

This anthology presents a selection of eight outstanding plays by award-winning playwrights, whose work explores complex characters and stories that go beyond enduring cultural stereotypes about Italy. The core of the book emerges out of a project, called Playground London, which I co-curated with Fabulamundi Playwriting Europe – a network of European venues, festivals and producers of contemporary playwriting based in ten European countries. Supported by the Italian Cultural Institute in London, the aim of the project, which took place in 2021 and 2022, was to introduce a selection of Italian dramatists to British directors and actors, creating connections and establishing a space where different ways of making theatre could meet. Playground London was also part of a wider research project investigating the circulation of contemporary plays in Europe, which I carried out in partnership with Fabulamundi, exploring the conventions, best practices and challenges to the staging of plays in translation in European theatre systems. The wider research project culminated in the publication of my monograph, *Playwriting in Europe: Mapping Ecosystems and Practices with Fabulamundi* (Routledge, 2022; Franco Angeli, 2023), exploring how playwriting and theatre translation work in 15 European countries. With Playground London, the spotlight was more specifically on the British capital's theatre scene, and on the perceived resistance of British creatives and institutions to foreign-language plays.

With the aim of eliminating the cost barrier associated with translation, the Playground London selection committee read and considered many unpublished, yet-to-be performed plays by mid-career and emerging Italian playwrights for inclusion in our programme of translations into English. We then selected three plays per year, which we thought had a particularly good chance to resonate with British audiences, and proposed them to a number of directors who regularly work with living dramatists. Translations were commissioned specifically for Playground London and then tested through week-long R&D workshops with creatives on Zoom, followed by online public readings on day five. In the UK, R&D workshops are a popular way to try out new plays, before a venue or a director decides whether to put on a full production of it, so we used the format to establish connections between London-based creatives and Italian theatre-makers. Each director recruited actors for their play, with whom each text and its translation were dissected and tested, word choices discussed and challenged in a collaborative creative setting with the translator and dramatist. A final sharing of each play, with a new and improved translation, was presented at the end of each workshop. Five of these translations are included in this book. Three additional dramas by leading writers Ubah Cristina Ali Farah, Davide Carnevali and Emanuele Aldrovandi, were subsequently added to the anthology, complementing the rest of the volume through thematic and stylistic expansion.

This book is motivated by what I perceive as a growing necessity to make space for plays in translation in English, which I developed as part of my research over the past 15 years. Through my explorations of the attitudes of British creatives and gatekeepers towards international plays, I have developed a belief in the ethical imperative of honouring and respecting stories that emerge in different languages, especially within the lingua franca of the western world, to foster understanding between cultures. As this is one of very few collections of this kind available in English, the selection of authors and texts for this book carries a lot of responsibility.[2] This anthology sets out to present the work of a generation of Italian writers for the first time to a global readership in English, and yet it is impossible to be representative of such a wide-ranging and active field in the space of a few pages. Despite the variety of performance genres and styles that Italian stage authors have experimented with in the twenty-first century, especially the of post-dramatic kind, the texts in this anthology align fairly closely with British taste and expectations, favouring plot-driven stories, clearly delineated characters and fast-paced dialogue. Many excellent plays by influential and emerging writers, especially by those who tend to work with more performative, self-reflexive paradigms, such as Emma Dante, Deflorian/Tagliarini, Liv Ferracchiati and Jacopo Giacomoni, are not included in this selection, as they would deserve a volume and a research project of their own. However, my selection process has sought to be inclusive and diverse in several other ways, especially with regards to gender and race, but also on a thematic level.

I am delighted that four out of eight plays in this collection are written by women, and five out of eight are translated by women. Moreover, this collection is, to my knowledge, the very first to include two plays by Black Italian women, the Somali-Italian writer Ubah Cristina Ali Farah, who is better known to English-language readers for her award-winning novels, and the Mauritian-Italian dramatist Nalini Vidoolah Mootoosamy, whose contribution to the current landscape of Italian playwriting cannot be overstated. Two plays in the collection are also translated by theatre director Atri Banerjee, whose family is of Indian heritage and who lived in Italy as a child, moving back to Britain in his teens. Considerations around inclusivity are far from common sense in Italy, and I hope my editorial decisions can inspire more activism against current levels of gender and race discrimination in the Italian theatre industry. For anyone seeking hard evidence of sexism in Italian theatre, the lack of equal opportunities for women, non-binary and female-identifying artists and theatre practitioners is well documented by two recent reports commissioned by the feminist activist organisation, Amleta. The report, authored by a team of researchers at the University of Brescia, gathered data on the percentage of women employed in some of the country's most prestigious professional theatre venues in the years 2020–24, divided by role. Unsurprisingly, women playwrights were under a third of the total at 29.1 per cent, while women adapters fared even worse at 26.8 per cent. However, the most exclusive role for women is that of director, where only 17.4 per cent were women. Women actors fared marginally better at 39.7 per cent of the total.[3] The report also stresses that women are less likely to be employed in bigger venues, and that the length of the average run of productions by women directors and playwrights is generally shorter, so their capacity to reach audiences is further diminished.[4]

Things are not dissimilar in other fields, but the theatre is also, surprisingly, lagging behind parliamentary politics, where around 33.6 per cent of MPs in both chambers and in government are women.[5] In October 2022, Italy elected its first-ever female Prime Minister, 45-year-old Giorgia Meloni, leader of the far-right party, Brothers of Italy. A few months later, the centre-left opposition, the Democratic Party, elected its first woman leader, Elly Schlein, who incidentally had just come out as bisexual. Seeing two young women at the centre of Italian politics, despite their diametrically opposed views on immigration, abortion and LGBTQ rights, is unprecedented for a country permeated by patriarchal and heteronormative values. In contrast, none of the eight prestigious National Theatres in Italy are run by women. One can only hope that parliamentary politics might contribute to the development of a more complex representation of women in the theatre, both in terms of character portrayals and in the numbers of women employed in positions of power and prestige.

However, when it comes to equity, diversity and inclusivity in terms of race and ethnicity, Italy lags well behind the UK and other nations: Italians of Global Majority heritage – so-called 'New Italians', or 'seconde generazioni' (second-generation migrants) – who were either born in Italy or moved to Italy as children, are scarcely represented in the theatre field, but are emerging strongly as crucial voices of hope and change in a deeply racist country, especially in the fields of sport, literature and music, but also within the performing arts.[6] Although more work is needed in this area, my early research findings indicate that the Italian theatre sector is far less inclusive than it would like to believe itself to be. As part of another project that I co-curated with Suq Festival in Genoa, called Performing Italy (2021 and 2022), also supported by the Italian Cultural Institute in London, we interviewed fourteen Italian theatre-makers of migrant background to highlight and disseminate their work, in order to end the harmful prejudice held by white Italian theatre-makers that 'there are no Global Majority Italian theatre-makers'. The collective message delivered by these video interviews tells the story of a theatre system still deeply unfit to represent the voices of the multicultural Italy that is steadily emerging in the twenty-first century.

The stories and perspectives told in this volume are diverse, representing multiple identities through different value systems, aesthetics and genres, from comedy to tragedy via science fiction, tragicomedy and post-dramatic explorations of history. The plays in this collection were first performed in various Italian contexts between 2018 and 2024 and written in the aftermath of a period of consecutive 'crises' and intense change for both Italy and the world – such as the 2008 financial crisis, the 2015 migrant 'crisis', the #metoo movement, the 2018 Black Lives Matter protests, and the Covid pandemic in 2020. They document a theatre culture not only preoccupied with the inward-looking dimension of intimate and family relationships, or with the hedonistic indulgence of a stereotypical *dolce vita* that still persists in depictions of *italianità* in the media, but with deeply collective, socially engaged matters of global resonance. Taken together, the plays offer a snapshot of public sphere discourses around the most pressing problems and debates of our times: migration, racism and colonialism (*Antigone Power* by Ubah Cristina Ali Farah); race equality and citizenship rights (*The Foreigner's Smile* by Nalini Vidoolah Mootoosamy); the climate emergency (*The Fattest Woman in the World* by Emanuele Aldrovandi); rising fascism, state-backed violence and the spectres of history (*Portrait of the Artist as a Dead Man* by Davide Carnevali); labour, mental health and relationships in late capitalist times (*Bidibibodibiboo* by Francesco Alberici); LGBTQ+ identities and the role of women in society (*Gentleman Jack* by Magdalena Barile); social isolation and the search for companionship and purpose (*Big Fright* by Valentina Diana); grief and imagining life beyond Earth (*Carbon* by Pier Lorenzo Pisano).

There are many other connections between the themes and poetics of the plays presented here that one could highlight. For instance, metatheatricality links Carnevali's *Portrait of the Artist as a Dead Man* to Alberici's *Bidibibodibiboo*: both dramas function as games of mirrors inviting audiences to explore the distinctions between reality and fiction, theatre and everyday life, memory and fabrication, history and propaganda. Strong women – Antigone and Tiresias, Anne Lister and Jo – are at the heart of Ali Farah's *Antigone Power* and Barile's *Gentleman Anne*, and their feminist re-readings of the past complement a vision of history that repeats itself in Mootoosamy's *The Foreigner's Smile* and Carnevali's *Portrait of the Artist as a Dead Man*. Mental health, depression and grief is central in Diana's *Big Fright*, Alberici's *Bidibibodibiboo* and Pisano's *Carbon*, while a sense of anxiety towards the future of humanity animates both *Carbon* and Aldrovandi's *The Fattest Woman in the World*.

My contribution to this volume as a curator, editor, scholar and translator began through my encounter with Nalini Vidoolah Mootoosamy's multilingual play *The Foreigner's Smile* (*Il sorriso della scimmia*, 2 F, 3 M), which I read as a jury member for the Fabulamundi Playwriting Competition for Italian authors of Migrant Background in 2020. The play was subsequently performed in Italian by the author's company, Ananke Arts, opening at Milan's Teatro 89 in December 2022. As one of the competition organisers reading this play in 2020, I immediately saw the ground-breaking relevance of Mootoosamy's writing. *Il sorriso della scimmia* was written by the author in response to the Fabulamundi competition brief and is, to my knowledge, the first play by a Black Italian dramatist that centres on the life experiences of a family and community made up of first- and second-generation migrants living in Italy. Mootoosamy, who migrated to Palermo as a child, beautifully encapsulates the plight of millions of multilingual, multicultural, second-generation migrant residents in Italy who have been denied Italian citizenship by an outdated legal framework.

In the play, Raoul is a young man of Mauritian heritage based in an unnamed Italian city, who moved there as a child. Raoul's Father is about to be sworn an Italian citizen in a public ceremony, after seventeen years living and working in Italy. Raoul's Mother, however, has heard that some Italian Mayors have denied citizenship to those migrants who were unable to read the oath in correct Italian pronunciation at the ceremony, and has asked her fluent Italian-speaking son, Raoul, a university student revising for a Roman History exam, to help his dad memorise it at the last minute. The generational clash that ensues is explored with bitter yet sensitive humour, highlighting the human consequences of a citizenship law that is no longer fit for purpose. Mootosamy's play was performed as a Zoom reading in English as part of Playground London in June 2021, translated collaboratively by the author and myself, and subsequently adapted after the workshop led by director Omar Elerian with a cast of British-Mauritian actors.[7] The translation published below was reworked following two more R&D workshops carried out with English-speaking creatives: firstly, at the Casa Italiana Zerilli Marimò New York City in February 2024, directed by Phillip Christian Smith, and subsequently with Good Chance Theatre Company in London, directed by Ammar Haj Ahmad in April 2024. Both Smith and Haj Ahmad, along with the cast in both workshops, were very generous with their time and allowed the translation to reach the more polished version offered here.

My other two translations as part of Playground London were of Magdalena Barile's *Gentleman Anne* (2 F), a play that pursues the author's fascination with exploring queer identities in Western history, and of Valentina Diana's *Big Fright*, a drama developed through improvisation with actors, starring five middle-aged characters in search of a meaning in their own lives. In *Gentleman Anne*, Anna is a University Professor of English Literature whose research focuses on the Brontë sisters and other gothic novel writers of the nineteenth century. Anna's student, Jo, arrives at her tutor's home to discuss her dissertation about the nineteenth-century lesbian writer and diarist, Anne Lister. While Anna and Jo debate whether Lister or the Brontës are the real revolutionaries, Jo makes it apparent that she is sexually attracted to her tutor yet is ready to blackmail Anna in order to get her support for her own literary ambitions. Mirroring their mysterious, opportunistic relationship, a historical cameo shines a spotlight onto Anne Lister's courtship and eventual marriage to Miss Walker. Infused with hints of gothic horror, this play explores the enduring echoes of literature and history on the present. It was first performed in Italy at the Teatro dei Filodrammatici in Milan in May 2021, and then at Milan's Elfo Puccini Theatre in February 2022. My translation of the play was workshopped with British creatives under the direction of Mingyu Lin and performed as a Zoom reading as part of Playground 2021.

In Diana's *Big Fright* (3 M, 2 F), a group of middle-aged people are attending a bogus mental health support group aimed at connecting participants to their inner selves by establishing a relationship with plants and by developing a sensitivity to their plants' 'vibrations'. The characters are named after their plant species – a creative intervention that emerged out of the translation workshop – and come from very different social and cultural backgrounds, yet they rub shoulders by politely accepting each other's idiosyncrasies, habits and beliefs. Their mundane chats about simple, often inane topics, betray a deep sense of loneliness, trauma, and a search for companionship. Over the course of several years, they get closer to each other while remaining perfect strangers. This is a tragicomic, a meditation on the meaninglessness of life that ends as unexpectedly as it had begun. A production at the Cantieri Teatrali Koreja in Lecce was staged in October 2023. The translation presented here is the result of collaboration with director Omar Elerian and the actors who took part in the Playground London workshop, which I then edited following the final draft used by the author for the Koreja production. Feedback obtained by participants to a play reading held online as part of a CambioScena table read was also useful in finalising this version.

Extracts from both Diana's and Barile's plays, directed by Atri Banerjee and Nastazja Domaradzka, were presented at the Royal Court Theatre in October 2022, as part of a week-long in-person residency with the dramatists who had taken part in the Playground London's online residencies, further supporting opportunities for exchange and discussion. As part of an afternoon programme of six staged readings, Francesco Alberici's *Bidibibodibiboo* and Pier Lorenzo Pisano's *Carbon* were also staged, directed by Domaradzka and Alessandra Davison respectively. In Alberici's *Bidibibodibiboo* (4 M, 1 F, 1 N) a playwright named Daniele approaches his brother, Pietro, to ask if he wouldn't mind having his recent unfair dismissal from a multinational company turned into a stage play. With the brother's permission, Daniele sets out to write up the highly personal story of his brother's rise and fall within the not-to-be-mentioned company. The play, which constantly interrogates the distinction between fiction and reality, does not spare us the details of how Pietro was treated by his bosses, but later the permission to share his personal story is withdrawn as Pietro gets cold feet about going public. Runner up for the prestigious Premio Riccione in 2021, this is a metatheatrical comedy about life in neoliberal times, questioning the role that theatre should play in relation to injustices. A full stage production opened in La Spezia in January 2024 and then transferred to Milan's Piccolo Teatro. The Playground London R&D workshop and reading was directed by Omar Elerian on Zoom, in a translation by Flora Pitrolo, which was subsequently edited to match the final draft presented in Udine and Milan.

Pier Lorenzo Pisano's *Carbon* (1 F, 1 M, 1 N), presented here in a translation by Banerjee, won the prestigious Premio Riccione in 2021. It was also selected for the 2022 Berlin Theatertreffen and won the Eurodram competition in 2022. First performed in Italian as a stage reading in Rome's Teatroeuropa Festival in 2021, it was translated into English for the first edition of Playground London, with a Zoom reading in English directed by Omar Elerian. A full-scale stage production opened at the Piccolo Teatro in Milan in June 2022. In the play, a man – called B – has had an encounter with an extraterrestrial creature that has warped his sense of self and distorted his perception of time and reality. A woman – a state authority of some kind, named A – interrogates him to try to understand what happened. Their conversation takes us on an entirely unexpected journey through grief, alternative realities, and what it means to be human. The alien, as we gradually discover, is a creature that is not based on the main component of life on Earth: carbon. Playing with dramatic and post-dramatic conventions in equal measure, this extraordinary science fiction play also reflects on the future of our civilization by looking back at how it represented itself in the Voyager Golden Record images sent to outer space in 1977.

Similar concerns for the future of life on Earth animate *The Fattest Woman in the World* by Emanuele Aldrovandi, presented here in a translation by Marco Young. This play, which opened at the Piccolo Orologio theatre in Reggio Emilia in December

2018, reimagines the climate emergency debate as a dispute between two neighbours relating to a crack in the floor/ceiling of a house. The crack, caused by an absurdly overweight woman who spends her time sitting on a sofa and eating, is intended as a metaphor of overconsumption rather than a realistic discussion around women's bodies. The Woman – who does not move from her room because of her weight, and whose body covers the whole stage – is fed and cared for by her Husband, who challenges the Downstairs Neighbour's complaints about a crack which threatens to kill him and his family. The Downstairs Neighbour is on a mission to persuade the Woman to lose weight, while the Husband considers this an insult and an example of a body-shaming attitude. The play concludes rather tragically, with the Woman wanting to lose weight and not being able to. In the play's epilogue, we see a family of dinosaurs visiting a museum of humanity, and commenting on the stupidity that determined the extinction of the human race. The play, which was staged several times in Italy and France between 2018 and 2022, is a perceptive satire of the current situation of impasse that humanity finds itself in, pointing the finger on our wasteful lifestyles and overconsumption of resources. While some might understandably perceive the play's premise as perpetuating harmful fattist attitudes, Aldrovandi's approach to political correctness underpins an anti-realist, metaphorical treatment of the climate crisis, which in his view is more direct and impactful than realist representation.

A similar use of metaphor is enshrined in Ubah Cristina Ali Farah's *Antigone Power* (3 M, 3 F, 3 N). In this highly poetic adaptation, Ali Farah reimagines Antigone's myth in light of the 2015 'refugee crisis', yet opts for depicting timeless characters that defy the fast-paced rhythm of everyday life. The play was commissioned by Sutta Scupa, a theatre company based in Palermo, who staged an adapted version of it in 2018 and 2021, featuring white Italian actors, as well as refugees and asylum seekers from across Africa. The production opened at the Cantieri Culturali alla Zisa, a reclaimed ex-industrial site in a city shaped by a history of cross-cultural co-existence, where migrants who cross the Mediterranean arrive on boats nearly on a daily basis. Published here in an English translation by theatre director Atri Banerjee, this deeply lyrical rewriting starts with the announcement that Eteocles and Polynices have killed each other, Eteocles defending the city against the migrant 'invaders' and Polynices siding with them. Antigone, supported by her lover Haemon and warned by her sister Ismene, defies Creon's edict to leave Polynices unburied, but the King is determined to impose his law and close the borders to foreigners. The chorus of anti-migrant citizens sides with their authoritarian leader, Creon, while the female seer, Tiresias, advises Creon to end his mad rejection of fellow humans if he wants to avoid a future of unending war. Ali Farah's writing breathes new life into Sophocles' drama by setting the myth in Sicily, whose waters, beaches and ports are the backdrop to so much tragic loss of life, as well as hundreds of thousands safe arrivals to Europe via the Mediterranean route every year. Inscribed in this version of Antigone we can glimpse a snapshot of Italian political discourses on refugee arrivals by sea, with Creon bearing clear similarities with the then Home Secretary, Matteo Salvini, a far-right politician who threatened to defy international law by closing Italian ports and criminalising non-governmental search and rescue ships operating in Sicilian waters.

Also reckoning with the rise of far-right discourses is Davide Carnevali's investigations of the legacies of fascist histories either side of the Atlantic Ocean, through a man's search for his true identity and heritage among the rubble of the Argentinian dictatorship. *Portrait of the Artist as a Dead Man: Italy '41 – Argentina '78* (1 M) was commissioned by the Munich Biennale in co-production with Berlin's Staatsoper Unter den Linden, and staged in German as *Ein Porträt des Künstlers als Toter* at the Schwere Reiter in Munich in 2018, and linked Argentinian dictatorship with Germany's Nazi past. Rewritten for a French context for the Comédie de Caen, Comédie de Reims, Théâtre de Liège and Le Quai CDN d'Angers in 2023, the play was then adapted into an entirely new site-specific Italian version for actor Michele Riondino at the Piccolo Teatro in Milan in March 2023. It is the latter version that is presented here, in my translation for the Piccolo's performances which featured English subtitles for international spectators. In the play, a man named Daniele welcomes the audience into the theatre. He assures the audience this is not a play, but a true story and told in his own words – it is his own story. The ensuing monologue revolves around a puzzling letter the man had received not long ago from Argentina's Federal Court. The letter implied that Argentina's Human Rights Commission had examined the case of a flat in Córdoba, of which he would be the rightful heir through a distant uncle, and which appears to have been unlawfully repossessed from a desaparecido, to whom the court is now returning the property. Daniele seeks assistance from his playwright friend, Davide Carnevali, who has some knowledge of the Argentinian context. What follows is a mysterious rollercoaster search for the truth, evocatively moving between doppelgangers, mistaken identities, and historical hauntings, which are adapted to suit every new context that the play travels to.

Popular media, such as TV, continue to be rife with stereotypical, romanticised and glamorous portrayals of Italy, exploiting international audiences' fascination with it as the beautiful land of *la dolce vita*, good food and good fashion, or as the sinister hotbed of criminal organisations (two faces of the same coin?).[8] On stage, one of the very few portrayals of Italy that has gained any traction in recent years has been the adaptation of Elena Ferrante's *My Brilliant Friend* by April de Angelis, which took the Rose Theatre in Kingston (2017) and the National Theatre (2019) by storm, following the Neapolitan novel's success. While Ferrante's novels are about a lot more than Camorra, exploring friendship, womanhood and class in post-war Italy, the 'exotic' setting has definitely played a role in its popularity across the world.[9] Instead, with this collection we explore stories that revisit history's enduring influence in present times, and confront some of the most pressing challenges of our globalised world from an Italian perspective, without the plays ever being reducible to any definition of *Italianness*, and without the authors ever banking on the multiple clichés about *italianità* available to them. The order in which they are presented would make for a compelling dramaturgical concerto, full of dynamic crescendos and diminuendos, opening and closing with a bang, but they can be accessed in any other order. I do hope that, one day, these plays can see the limelight in a theatre near you. For the time being, please enjoy reading them.

Notes

1   Dario Fo's *Accidental Death of an Anarchist* has enjoyed a number of productions in the UK, most recently a version by Tom Basden played at the Lyric Hammersmith in 2023, and the play is currently one of the set texts for the Edexcel A Level Drama curriculum (component 3). Directed by Sam Mendes and adapted by Ben Power, *The Lehman Trilogy*

by Stefano Massini has enjoyed a series of notable runs, beginning in London's National Theatre from 2018 and touring to New York's Park Avenue Armoury in 2019. The production won numerous awards, including the Tony Award for Best Play in 2022, and toured internationally with different casts, returning to London in 2023 and 2024.
2. The only other comparable volumes are the 4 anthologies, *New Plays From Italy, volumes 1-4*, edited by Frank Hentschker, featuriung plays by Lucia Calamaro, Fausto Paravidino, Michele Santeramo, Daria Deflorian/Antonio Tagliarini, Elisa Casseri, Giuliana Musso, Armando Pirozzi, Fabrizio Sinisi, Mimosa Campironi, Giuliano Dammacco, and Tatjana Motta.
3. Bannò, Mariasole, et. al., 2024, p. 21.
4. Ibid. p. 22.
5. Openpolis, La rilevanza delle donne nel governo e in parlamento', 21 March 2024.
6. In sport, see for instance Marcel Jacobs and Paola Egonu, who have become household names. In music, see for instance Ghali, Mahmood, Amir Issaa, and Tommy Kuti. In literature, see Igiaba Scego, Ubah Cristina Ali Farah, Djarah Kan, and Antonio Dikele Distefano. In theatre, see the artists presented in the series of video portraits curated by Alberto Lasso, Carla Peirolero, Oliviero Ponte di Pino and I, entitled 'Performing Italy', Series 1 and 2, see links in bibliography. The artists featured in the two series are: actor-author Shi Yang Shi, dancer Bintou Ouattara, director Thaiz Bozano, actor-author Abdoulaye Ba, producer Alberto Lasso, director Marcela Serli, actor-author Miriam Selima Fieno, director Omar Elerian, writer Nalini Vidoolah Mootoosamy, actors Rabii Brahim, Alberto Boubakar Malanchino, Cristina Parku, and Deniz Özdoğan.
7. I wrote about the process of this R&D workshop in my monograph, *Playwriting in Europe*, pp. 1–15. Notably, the title was changed from *The Monkey's Smile* to *The Foreigner's Smile*, to soften the racist tropes appropriated by the characters in the play.
8. *The White Lotus*, Season 2, 2022, set in Sicily; *Emily in Paris*, Season 3, set in Rome (2022); and *Ripley*, 2024, set in Campania' with '*The White Lotus*, Season 2, 2022, set in Sicily; *Emily in Paris*, Season 3, 2022, set in Rome; *Ripley*, 2024, set in Campania; *My Brilliant Friend*, 2018–24, set in Naples; *Gomorrah*, 2014–22, set in Naples.
9. See De Francisci, 2023.

Bibliography

Bannò, Mariasole, et. al., 'La Disparità di Genere nel Settore Teatrale: Analisi dei Teatri Nazionali e dei Teatri di Rilevante Interesse Nazionale', March 2024, p. 21, available at: https://www.amleta.org/wp-content/uploads/2024/03/Report-AMLETA-PER-MARTEDi-.pdf
De Francisci, Enza 'Translating and rewriting Ferrante's *My Brilliant Friend* at the National Theatre', *The Translator*, 29.3 (2023), 281–296.
Hentschker, Frank, ed. *New Plays From Italy, volumes 1–4*. New York: Martin E. Segal Theatre Center Publications, 2018–2024.
Laera, Margherita, 'Language, Translation and Multilingualism in Contemporary European Theatre'. In Ralf Remshardt and Aneta Mancewitz, eds, *The Routledge Companion to Contemporary European Theatre and Performance*. Routledge, 2024.
— *Playwriting in Europe: Mapping Ecosystems and Practices with Fabulamundi*. Routledge, 2022.
— *Theatre & Translation*. Bloomsbury, 2019.
Openpolis, 'La rilevanza delle donne nel governo e in parlamento', 21 March 2024, available at: https://www.openpolis.it/la-rilevanza-delle-donne-nel-governo-e-in-parlamento/
Performing Italy: Seven Theatre-Makers of Migrant Background on Contemporary Italian Stages, Series 1 (2021) and Series 2 (2022), available on Vimeo at: https://vimeo.com/showcase/7957682 and https://vimeo.com/showcase/9497444

The Foreigner's Smile
Il sorriso della scimmia

By Nalini Vidoolah Mootoosamy

Translated by Margherita Laera and Nalini Vidoolah Mootoosamy

First staged at Teatro i, Milan, on 28 September 2021.

Characters

Raoul
Father
Mother
Vikram
Laura

The action takes place in a small living room of a Mauritian immigrant family in Italy. The decor is sketchy, but very colourful. An image or statue of Ganesh must not be missing.

Content warning: strong racism and racial slurs.

Scene 1

Father, **Mother** *and baby* **Raoul** *are sitting on the ground.* **Father** *and* **Mother** *are teaching* **Raoul** *to speak Mauritian Creole.*

Father   Fro-maz.

Raoul   Froo-mas.

Mother   Fro-maz.

Raoul   Froo-mas.

Father   Fro . . .

Raoul   Froooo . . .

Father   . . . mazz.

Raoul   . . . mazzz.

Father   Fro-maz.

Raoul   Froo-mas.

Father and **Mother** (*laughing and singing*)   Fro-maz. Fro-maz! Fro-maz! Fro-maz! Fro-maz.

Silence. Many years have passed. **Raoul** *has grown up.*

Raoul (*stands*)   Froumaz. (*Beat.*) Fromaz! Fromaz! (*Beat.*) Formaggio! Formaggio! Formaggio!

Father (*gets up and goes towards the exit*)   Fromagio.

Raoul (*to* **Father**)   Not Fromagio. Formaggio! Formaggio!

Father   Fromagio.

Father *leaves.*

Raoul (*to* **Mother**)   Formaggio! Formaggio!

Mother (*gets up goes to the kitchen*)   Fromagio.

Raoul   Not fromagio. Formaggio! Formaggio!

Mother   Fromagio.

Mother *leaves to the kitchen.*

Raoul   Formaggio! Formaggio! For-maggio! For not fro! (*Points to himself and the various parts of his body.*) Me! Myself! I! My! Mine! My body! Foot. Hand. Hair. Head. Face. Nose. Mouth. Lips. Tongue. Mother tongue! (*Points to objects around him.*) Lamp! Light! Mirror! Elephant! Chair! Table! Pen! Book! Notebook! Pillow! Sofa! Sofa bed! Living room! (*Indicates the object.*) Kitchen! Home! Roof! To go! To sit! To eat! To look! To pray! To study! (*Beat.*) Who / What / Where / When / Why. Left! Right! Over! Under! Good! Bad! Very bad! Terrible! Terrible mood! (*Beat.*)

(*The speech becomes more reflective.*) Immigration. Confusion. Exclusion. (*Beat.*) Wherever he goes, he's excluded. (*Silence.*) I don't think he should smile anymore.

Scene 2

Change of atmosphere. **Raoul** *goes to sit at the table and starts reading a book, taking notes.*

Raoul 'The great social changes'. (*Writes.*) The great . . . social . . . changes. (*Reads.*) 'The third century is a very dramatic period in the history of Rome, the very survival of the Empire appears in doubt amid recurring civil wars, and great social, institutional and religious changes. Against the danger of disintegration, the Severi dynasty promoted a rigorous centralization policy . . .'

Mother *enters from the kitchen. She has a round tray in her hands. On the tray are some colourful flowers, a small bell, a banana on which she has stuck several burning incense sticks. She goes to the altar of Ganesh, rings the bell and begins to mutter a mantra with her eyes closed, moving the tray in a circle around the image of Ganesh.*

Mother Om, Gam Ganapataye Namaha. Om, Gam Ganapataye Namaha. Om, Gam Ganapataye Namaha.[1]

Raoul Maa! (**Mother** *continues to pray.*) Maa! . . . Maaa!

Mother *Kwa?*[2]

Raoul You're polluting the air with all this incense!

Mother What?

Raoul Can you use less incense?

Mother No, no!

Raoul Why?

Mother My *pooja*[3] must come from Ganesh.

Raoul But you can't breathe here!

Mother I call Ganesh with the scent of incense.

Raoul Yes, you'll call him, but you'll knock me out!

Mother Don't say that. This *pooja* is for today. You forgot?

Raoul How can I forget? You've been talking about *today* for days.

Mother *Today* is very important day!

Raoul So very important!

Mother Why do you say that?

Raoul Nothing will change for you anyway.

Mother   I don't understand what you saying.

Raoul   Nothing, nothing.

Mother   What doesn't change us?

Raoul   Maa, can you stop praying, I have to study.

Mother   I pray for you too, for your exam tomorrow! I hope Ganesh listen to me!

Mother *quickly mutters the mantra a couple of times, rotating the tray just as quickly in front of the image of Ganesh.* **Raoul** *looks at her impatiently, putting his hand in front of his nose so as not to breathe.*

Mother   Om, Gam Ganapataye Namaha. Om, Gam Ganapataye Namaha.

Mother *finishes praying, rings the bell and goes back to the kitchen.* **Raoul** *snorts to try to breathe better, then gets up, takes the notebook and waves it around him to clear the smoke.* **Raoul** *sits down and resumes studying.*

Raoul   So . . . then . . . the great social changes . . . here . . . (*Reads.*) 'The *Constitutio Antoniniana*, enacted by Caracalla in 212, granted Roman citizenship to all free residents of the Empire'. There, that's a good policy. (*Reads.*) 'This policy resulted in the acquisition of new taxpayers and, consequently, the State's cash reserves rapidly increased: taxes, which were previously paid by Roman citizens only, would from then onwards be paid by all the inhabitants of the Empire'. I knew it was just about money! It is always about money . . .

Re-enter **Mother**.

Mother   Raoul.

Raoul   What is it Maa? Maa, I have to . . .

Mother   . . . Do you think it's okay today?

Raoul   Yes!

Mother   Heart on hand?

Raoul   Well, I think so.

Mother   If something is wrong?

Raoul   He will try again!

Mother   My friend Karishma says no. This is what happened to Gopal!

Raoul   Who?

Mother   Gopal! The cousin of the husband of my friend Karishma. The one that when we went to the market once . . .

Raoul   Maa, get to the point.

Mother   The man . . . What is his name, the one who makes us sign documents?

Raoul   The mayor?

Mother Yes, him, mayor! Mayor said it's not good.

Raoul What is not good?

Mother Gopal! Gopal is not good!

Raoul And why?

Mother Gopal wrong and mayor said 'Come back next time'.

Raoul Exactly, as I told you! They send you back, but it's not all over!

Mother Yes, *mon dire twa*.[4] When Gopal asks for a new appointment, the mayor says that the document expired and that he cannot have appointment. Never again. Never again! I fear it happens the same with your dad.

Raoul I didn't know the document had an expiration date.

Mother I call Karishma and you ask her if you don't believe me.

Raoul Forget about Karishma. Let me check online.

Silence. **Raoul** *takes his cell phone and checks.*

Mother Found?

Raoul One moment Maa!

Silence.

Raoul (*reads*) The oath of loyalty to the Italian State must take place without delay within six months from the date of notification of the decree granting Italian citizenship. Once this term has expired, the decree loses all effectiveness.

Mother You read too fast, I don't understand anything.

Raoul Here it says he must swear within six months of the day he receives the letter. Fucking hell, there's always something.

Mother Which something?

Raoul Nothing! (*Beat.*) Do you remember when he got the letter?

Mother Two months . . . No, maybe three months gone.

Raoul Better check. Go get it.

Mother *leaves.* **Raoul** *goes back to his book.*

Raoul 212 AD Caracalla *Constitutio Antoniniana, Antoniniana, Antoniniana.* Fuck, I'll never finish in time!

Mother *comes back with a letter in her hand.*

Mother Letter arrived 15 December.

Raoul Show it to me! (*He takes the letter and reads it.*) Why did you let all this time go by?

Mother I don't know. Office made appointment then.

Raoul More than four months for an appointment?

Mother They do it on purpose, so they don't give documents.

Raoul Maa, it has nothing to do with it.

Mother Yes, *mon dire twa*. See how much he waited.

Raoul The problem is not the appointment, the problem is that after all these years, one shouldn't be making mistakes . . . one can't get it wrong!

Mother What we do if he makes mistake?

Raoul I don't know!

Mother Can't you help him *today*?

Raoul Why do you think I stayed home?

Mother I know . . .

Raoul . . . but as you can see he is not here!

Mother Dad doesn't want bother you. He knows you have exam tomorrow.

Raoul Maa, stop the bullshit! Just say that he did not want to disappoint his masters.

Mother Don't say that about dad.

Raoul I heard him, you know, on the phone this morning. (*Imitating* **Father**.) 'Yes, ma'am . . . What, now ma'am? . . . Okay ma'am! . . . I will come immediately ma'am.'

Mother He went to Signora Mirabella.

Raoul He could have said no. At least today!

Mother She is very old.

Raoul Stop it! As soon as they call, he runs.

Mother It's his job!

Raoul Being a slave?

Mother Your father not a slave!

Raoul You say it too. You always complain when they call.

Mother Because they disturb us when we eat and also on Sunday.

Raoul You say they treat him like a *dhobi*![5]

Mother They treat him as *dhobi*, but he not *dhobi*! He don't wash dirty clothes.

Raoul You're right, for those there is a washing machine, but he is the one who cleans their dirty houses, their dirty dishes, their dirty bathrooms, their dirty bodies . . . There isn't a day in the week that he does not touch their filth.

Mother You ashamed of dad!

Raoul You still going on with this story? I can't stand that he is always at their service, never protesting, never standing up for his rights.

Mother If he stand for rights, they don't make him work, if he don't work, how do you get beautiful clothes, cell phone, computer, books, university?

Raoul I never asked him for anything.

Mother Because your dad always give you what you want, before you want! (*Beat*) Are you really sure you cannot do something else?

Raoul Maa, I am not your Ganesh. I don't know how to do miracles yet. Maybe after graduation, maybe . . . Maa, I can't get inside his head. I can't speak for him.

Mother So we been waiting all this time for nothing?

Silence.

Raoul Let's do it like this: call him, explain the deadline thing and tell him to come back as soon as possible. Maybe I can still get him ready for this afternoon.

Mother Do you say it works?

Raoul There's no harm in trying!

Mother What arm?

Raoul Harm, ma, harm . . . with an 'h'. It means that it won't hurt!

Mother Ahhhh, trying don't hurt anyone! I like it!

Raoul Great! But now let me finish reviewing this chapter at least.

Mother I'm going to call!

Mother *is about to leave.*

Raoul Maa, a classmate of mine is coming here. She'll be here soon.

Mother Here at home? Today?

Raoul She has to give me some important notes. For the exam.

Mother You not see her outside?

Raoul If I go to uni and then he comes back, what are you going to do?

Mother She come and then go soon?

Raoul Just long enough to review a couple of things together.

Mother She stay for lunch?

Raoul I don't know, is that a problem?

Mother I not want to. I nervous and yes . . . I don't cook Italian well.

Raoul Why not cook something else, then?

Mother They always not like when they eat our food.

Raoul Maa, it happened once, come on. Once! Not all Italians are the same, you know. There are also those who appreciate our dishes and . . .

The doorbell rings.

Raoul Here she is!

Mother I go to kitchen.

Raoul Look, she won't eat you!

Mother I have to call dad.

Raoul Sure Maa, sure!

Mother *goes to the kitchen. The doorbell rings again.*

Raoul Coming! One moment.

Raoul *exits.*

Scene 3

Vikram (*voice over*) About fucking time bro! Were you sitting on the toilet or something?

Raoul *and* **Vikram** *enter.*

Raoul No, I was . . . What are you doing here?

Vikram What is this stench?

Raoul An attempt to kill me!

Vikram Jeez . . . aunty went a bit over the top, mate!

Raoul She's trying to bribe Ganesh.

Vikram We'll be dead before that happens . . . Have you seen how comfortable he is sitting on his throne? He wouldn't come to Italy for all the incense in the world. Too much bother!

Raoul Want to tell that to my mother?

Vikram No way! Don't want to miss out on her *samosas*! By the way, is aunty here? I have to run an errand for my old lady.

Raoul I'll call her! (*Screams.*) Maa . . . Maa . . . Maa . . . (**Raoul** *leans over to look into the kitchen.*) Wait a minute. I think she's on the phone.

Vikram (*looks at the book on the table*) So, you're getting ready, bro?

Raoul Yes, I have to finish a couple of chapters . . .

Vikram I mean for your father! Today is the big day, bitch!

Raoul Ah, you mean that . . .

Vikram So it's party time tonight!

Raoul I don't think so.

Vikram Why not? Your father is becoming an Italian citizen and you don't wanna celebrate?

Raoul He's the one becoming Italian, not me!

Vikram Once you have an Italian dad, you become Italian too, bro!

Raoul That's not how it works Viki!

Vikram But Maya became Italian just the other day!

Raoul Because she was born here.

Vikram So she was already Italian!

Raoul Technically.

Vikram Technically? Fuck does that mean?

Raoul If you are born in Italy you can apply for citizenship when you turn eighteen.

Vikram And before?

Raoul Before you are a foreigner like your parents.

Vikram What kind of bullshit is this, huh?

Raoul It's the law. How do you not know these things? You know, that thing printed on pages . . .

Vikram Hey buddy, we're not all swots like you, bitch!

Raoul You're an idiot!

Vikram Do you know you have the same smile as your father?

Raoul Will you stop saying that please?

Vikram When you smile you have little dimples here and here. (*He touches both sides of* **Raoul**'s *cheeks with two fingers and pulls them up to make him smile.*) You look like an emoji. You know the one that smiles with the pink cheeks . . .

Raoul (*removes* **Vikram**'s *hand*) I don't look like him that much.

Vikram You're his spit, when you smile . . .

Raoul The spit of him, I'm not his spit . . .

Vikram Whatever, I like saying it that way!

Raoul (*screams*) Maa . . . Maa . . . (*to* **Vikram**.) She's coming, so you can go.

Raoul *sits down and goes back to studying.* **Vikram** *wanders around the hall and suddenly whirls towards* **Raoul**.

Vikram What you said before is bullshit by the way! Samir was not born here, but now he is Italian. His whole family has become Italian. Take that!

Raoul Because his parents earn a lot of money, and Samir works too!

Vikram I work too, bro!

Raoul But your mother hasn't got citizenship.

Vikram I know, I know, but as soon as I turn eighteen, I'll apply for it on my own!

Raoul You can't!

Vikram Why? Maya applied for it though!

Raoul She was born here, you were not!

Vikram What the fuck does that mean?

Raoul Oh, Holy Ganesh! Viki, it's simple: you weren't born here, so you can't apply for citizenship until you work here for three years in a row.

Vikram But I've been working since I was fifteen . . . (*Counting on fingers*) fifteen, sixteen, seventeen . . . I've been working for three years, bitch!

Raoul With a regular contract Viki. Not cash in hand!

Vikram Are you telling me that I have to have a regular contract and then work three years to apply?

Raoul You also need to earn at least nine thousand euros a year. Otherwise, bye bye.

Vikram Then what else? Do I have to hold my breath, put a foot in my mouth and jump like a gorilla?

Raoul Who knows, but if all goes well, in five years you can become Italian.

Vikram You just said three, bitch!

Raoul Three years of work to file the application, about two to get an answer. They like to take their time.

Vikram Fuck, I can't do that. Look, you know this stuff, isn't there another way?

Raoul If your mother gets citizenship and earns a lot of money on a *regular basis*, maybe you have a few more chances.

Vikram So I'm right, you're lucky, you'll soon become Italian.

Raoul Technically yes, but it depends . . .

Vikram . . . on how much you earn, bro! Ok. Then you'll get your citizenship for sure. Uncle works a lot.

Raoul That's all he does.

Vikram We're not all like you! Always there on your books, doing I don't know what . . . How boring!

Raoul I'm studying.

Vikram I know . . . My old lady just pisses me off and says 'He's so good Raoul', 'What a clever boy Raoul', 'Yes he will succeed in life Raoul'!

Raoul You and I are not that different.

Vikram We come from the same country, but apart from that . . . You study and I work.

Raoul You could study too!

Vikram To become like you? No thanks! I want to have fun! I want to become rich like Berlusconi and so everyone will fall at my feet.

Raoul Bah! Unfortunately, for those like us, no matter how rich and well dressed, they'll always look at us like we're were shit and tell us to go back to our own country.

Vikram (*imitating*) 'Go away. Go back to your own country!' It's just a few bigots.

Raoul Just a few? I don't know where you live, but where I live there are a lot!

Vikram We live on the same street!

Raoul Yes, Vikram, chill out: I just meant that we don't see the same things.

Vikram I was right: we are different.

Raoul (*screams*) Maa . . . Maa . . . How long are you going to be?

Mother (*voice over*) One minute.

Raoul She'll be here soon, if she hasn't started praying to Ganesh on the other side as well.

Silence. **Raoul** *goes back to studying.*

Vikram Anyway, I have a plan! (*Beat.*) Do you want me to tell you? (*Beat.*) But don't tell my old lady . . . okay?

Raoul Sure. What plan?

Vikram I want to do like Krisna did!

Raoul You want to open a grocery store?

Vikram No! Get married! To an Italian! I can immediately become Italian and then leave her. What do you say? Clever, no?

Raoul Are you out of your mind? It's illegal!

Vikram It's not like I'm selling drugs. Just so I don't have to make nine thousand euros or jump like a gorilla, you get me?

Raoul It's a scam!

Vikram Then it's perfect.

Raoul If they catch you, they'll say we're the usual criminals.

Vikram   You worry too much.

Raoul   What if you end up in jail? Don't you think about your mother?

Vikram   So I move on to plan B.

Raoul   If it's like Plan A, I don't want to know!

Vikram   Plan B: As soon as I can, I'll leave this place. I'm going north to look for a real job. Cool, huh!

Raoul   But you already live in the North!

Vikram   So what? I don't know, I can go more north of the North! . . . Abroad. France! England! They told me that you can find many jobs there that give you (*traces the shape of a banknote in the air*) many square coins.

Raoul   If you leave Italy, you will no longer qualify for citizenship.

Vikram   Fuck I don't care. If I have the money, I don't need that! The point is money, not citizenship!

Raoul   Don't you understand that . . . (*Screams.*) Maa . . . Maa . . . For fuck's sake!

Vikram   Quiet! I'm not in a hurry.

Raoul   I am!

Vikram   I would like to be in your shoes: all day sitting in front of your books, reading . . . What is it that you're reading?

Raoul   A textbook! I'm studying for a Roman history exam.

Vikram   . . . studying Roman history, while I feast on my aunty's delicious and crunchy *samosas*. Mmmhhh.

Raoul   You said earlier that you think it's boring to be 'always there on my books, doing I don't know what'.

Vikram   Well, I don't know, maybe not in the end. Of course, you're always there, you're very serious, you're thinking all the time. What is it that you think so much about?

Raoul   I have a lot of thoughts. (*Screams.*) Maa! Maaaaa!

Mother (*voice over*)   Yes?

Raoul (*screams*)   There's Viki! Can you come?

Mother (*voice over*)   I coming!

Scene 4

Mother *enters.*

Vikram   Hi aunty!

Mother Hi Vikram.

Vikram Aunty, how many times do I have to tell you to call me Viki! Viki!

Mother Too bad, Vikram is so beautiful name. Your name means good and strong man.

Vikram Great, aunty! But I like Viki! It's cooler.

Mother (*to* **Raoul**) Your friend has already gone away?

Vikram What friend?

Raoul She hasn't arrived yet. It was Viki before.

Mother Ah, it was you.

Raoul (*to* **Mother**) Did you call?

Vikram What friend?

Mother Yes. He says he comes back.

Vikram Who comes back?

Mother When is your friend coming?

Raoul This morning. What about him?

Mother Says come back as soon as possible, so you get ready for today.

Vikram What do you need to prepare?

Raoul If he arrives on time!

Mother I hope he come soon.

Vikram Ah, I understand! You're planning the party for tonight!

Raoul You are obsessed with this party!

Mother What party?

Raoul Nothing, Maa. Viki's always joking!

Mother I understand, you know!

Vikram But I wasn't joking . . . If you invite me . . .

Raoul Viki, what is it that you needed?

Vikram Ah, yes. Aunty, my mother asks you if you can lend her some cloves.

Raoul Here, I'll leave you to your things and go back to studying, okay?

Raoul *goes back to studying.*

Mother Cloves. All right.

Vikram And a little cumin . . .

Mother   Okay, Vikram.

Vikram   . . . and also a little cardamom and then some cinnamon. Only two sticks. But not too small, please!

Mother   Your mother think my house is grocery shop?

Vikram   Aunty, you know what mum is like! As soon as she comes up with something, she has to do it right away.

Mother   What is she making?

Vikram   *Briyani* . . .

Mother   Chicken or meat?

Vikram   Fish.

Mother   Tastes better with lamb.

Vikram   I know, but she doesn't listen to me.

Mother   You must tell her cook the fish well.

Vikram   She tries, but your *briyani*, aunty, is so unique.

Mother   Because I always cook the meat well and . . .

Raoul   Maa, can you please hurry up?

Mother   Yes, yes, I going!

Mother *exits.* **Vikram** *approaches* **Raoul**.

Vikram   So what? (*Beat.*) You don't say anything, huh! (*Beat.*) Come on, you can tell me, right?

Raoul   Say what?

Vikram   What does she look like?

Raoul   Who?

Vikram   Your *friend*!

Raoul   She's a classmate.

Vikram   Classmate, huh! And then?

Raoul   Classmate, period.

Vikram   Italian?

Raoul   Yes.

Vikram   Is she hot?

Raoul   What's that got to do with anything?

Vikram   I want to know. So? Is she hot?

Raoul Viki, you're annoying, come on.

Vikram Jeez, why are you always so serious?

Raoul I have to study!

Vikram Studying hurts you! Shit, have a laugh every now and then, bro.

Raoul I'm not a monkey!

Vikram What's your problem with monkeys?

Raoul I have many. You don't even get it!

Vikram We poor monkeys don't get it.

Raoul Yeah, yeah, yeah.

Vikram *laughs and acts like a monkey moving around* **Raoul***, touching and annoying him.*

Raoul Look, next time you watch a game on TV, I'll come and piss you off with the whole zoo. Let's see if you like it.

Vikram You don't know how to have fun! (*Beat.*) Fuck, why don't you just relax, bro?

Raoul . . . the *Constitutio Antoniniana* was the progressive loss of importance of the status of *civis Romanus*, the Roman citizen.

Vikram (*peeking at the book*) Civis Romanus . . . what language is it? Romanian?

Raoul It's Latin.

Vikram Latin . . . It's a shame you don't like having fun. We'd have something in common.

Raoul I think we have nothing in common at all.

Mother *enters with a package in her hand.*

Mother Who not coming to Hall? What happened?

Raoul What Hall?

Mother Town Hall. You said now 'Someone not coming to Hall'.

Raoul You didn't get what I said, Maa.

Mother I always understand wrong! *Tuzur!*[6] (*Gives* **Vikram** *the package.*) Here: *Laiti, cannelle ek ti lani.*[7] I also added sticks of incense. Tell your mother to pray to Ganesh for us today. I am so worried.

Vikram What about, aunty?

Mother Today is very important day, because . . .

Vikram I know, I know.

Mother   I'm afraid uncle fails!

Raoul   Maa, stop it!

Vikram   What are you talking about, aunty? Uncle is too strong. Nobody's going to stop him.

Mother   We hope everything is fine.

Vikram   If you want, aunty, I'll come too, so if you need to . . .

Mother   You coming to the Town Hall with us?

Raoul   No thanks. We don't need gorillas!

Mother   Raoul!

Vikram   Leave him alone, aunty. Today he is in a foul mood.

Mother   Fall moon?

Vikram   Mood! It means he's in a bad mood, aunty!

Mother   I always learn new words from you! You really are a *bon garso*![8]

Raoul   Are you done? Because I should be studying here . . .

Mother   Yes, Raoul. Sorry Vikram.

Vikram   No worries, aunty. I have to go anyway. Will you come with me to the door?

Mother   Yes, I'll open up for you.

Vikram (*to* **Raoul**)   See ya King Kong!

Raoul *grunts.* **Mother** *accompanies* **Vikram** *to the exit. She goes out with him for a moment and then comes back.*

Mother   Raoul why you doing this?

Raoul   Maa, I don't understand you. You pretend you are worried for today and then hang out and chat with Vikram. I have to study for tomorrow, but I have to stay here and wait for dad to come back!

Mother   Vikram so good boy, so . . .

Raoul   Maa, we know that 'Vikram is good. He is beautiful. He's funny'. I've had enough!

Mother   Vikram is right, you just have fall moon.

Mother *shakes her head and goes back to the kitchen.*

Raoul   Moon? The fuck does 'fall moon' mean? (*Beat. Screams to* **Mother**.) You say 'foul mood' or more simply 'in a mood!' How do they live like this? Their language is inaccurate, this house is inaccurate, our life is inaccurate! (*Puffs. Silence. Resumes reading.*) 'The direct consequence of the *Constitutio Antoniniana* was the progressive loss of importance of the status of *civis Romanus*. (*Beat.*) From this moment onwards, the social position and wealth of each individual will make the difference, not the citizenship status'. (**Raoul** *closes the book, stands up and starts pacing up and down the room testing his memory.*) 285 AD. Diocletian declares himself *Augustus* of the East . . . 303 AD. Diocletian orders the persecution of Christians . . . 312 AD. Constantine converts to Christianity and issues the Edict of Milan, through which he puts an end to the persecutions against Christians and proclaims religious tolerance throughout the Empire . . . 390 AD . . . ah no, 395 AD Theodosius I divides the empire into two parts: *pars orientis* to Arcadio and *pars occidentis* to . . . who does he give it to? Ah yes, to Honorius. Honorius! 410 AD, I know this: The Vandals of Alaric I sack Rome. 455 AD The Vandals of Genseric sack Rome. Why couldn't they stay in their own country? It would have been one less date to learn . . . 476 AD. The Germanic general Odoacer proclaimed himself *Rex Gentium*. Fall of the Western Roman Empire. I'll never learn! (*He sits on his chair. The doorbell rings.*) Here she is, finally!

Raoul *puts the book on the table, stands and quickly exits to open the door.*

Scene 5

Raoul (*voice over*)   Hello . . . There you are!

Father *enters, followed by* **Raoul**. *Both are carrying bags.*

Father (*wrinkles his nose*)   *Encore sa loder-la?*[9]

Raoul   Maa went too far with incense today. What should I do with these?

Father (*puts the bags on the sofa*)   *Poz tu ici!*[10]

Raoul   Where did you get all this stuff?

Father   A *moment*!

Raoul *puts the bags on the sofa.* **Father** *leaves to the kitchen.* **Raoul** *picks up the book again. Silence. Re-enter* **Father** *and* **Mother**.

Mother   *Tu saa?*[11]

Father   *Zur special, cado special.*[12]

Raoul   Can we start?

Father   *Fer kwa?*[13]

Raoul   How do you mean, to do what? To practice!

Father (*takes a large bag*)   *Avan uver sa!*[14]

Raoul   Can't we do it later?

Father   No, *allé. Uver sa!*[15]

Mother   Come on, open bag!

Raoul   We don't have much time to prepare. I also have to study because . . .

Mother   Open fast!

Raoul *opens the bag and takes out a very elegant suit.*

Raoul   What's this?

Father   *En costim!*[16]

Mother   Beautiful!

Raoul   For whom?

Father   *Pur twa!*[17]

Raoul   For me?

Father   *Oui!*[18]

Raoul   To do what?

Father   *Pur al Comun!*[19]

Raoul   For today? There was really no need for . . .

Father   *Essei-li!*[20]

Mother   Come on, try! I want to see new suit.

Raoul   With everything we have to do, I don't think it's the right moment.

Father   *Essei-li, do garso!*[21]

Raoul   When did you buy these things?

Father   *Apré mo travai.*[22]

Raoul   How do you mean, after work? Didn't Maa tell you to come back soon?

Mother   Of course I tell!

Raoul   And you went shopping around?

Mother   Dad wanted to make a special present for you today. He also bought new shoes.

Raoul   Why?

Father   *Pars ki,*[23] I become Italiano!

Raoul   You're becoming Italian, not me. You should have bought a suit for yourself.

Father   I took *costume* for *mwa osi.*[24]

Raoul   Anyway, we told you to come back soon, not to waste time shopping.

Father   *Pa tracass twa!*[25]

Raoul   Maa has been praying all day!

Father Yes, *pa tracass twa!*[26]

Raoul I'm not worried, but we have to practice now! I don't want you to look bad ...

Father Yes, *dakor! dakor! Léss mwa buar en zafair. Mo fatighé.*[27]

Raoul Okay, hurry up though! And from now on I don't want to hear you speak Creole anymore! Understand?

Father Yes, understand!

Father *goes to the kitchen.* **Raoul** *puts the suit on the sofa.*

Mother Raoul, the suit ...

Raoul ... Maa, don't you get started as well!

Mother No, no! I just want to know if you like suit.

Raoul I have to try it first.

Mother And your friend?

Raoul She hasn't arrived yet.

Mother Getting late.

Raoul Yes, I know.

Mother And it's no respect to make people wait so long!

Raoul She must have had a problem.

Mother Maybe she forget.

Raoul I don't think so. We agreed we'd meet this morning.

Mother Italians always make us wait. We wait for work, we wait for documents, for appointments ... we always wait.

Raoul Maa, I can't rush her. I asked her for a favour.

Mother What does this mean? What, she can make you wait all this time?

Raoul No ...

Mother Can you tell her to see you after Town Hall?

Raoul I don't know if she can later!

Mother You call and try.

Raoul Shall I tell her to come here later?

Mother Why don't you go to university?

Raoul Maa, they close at 7pm. The university is not a hotel.

Mother This house is also not a hotel for Italians.

Raoul Yes, but Maa: every time an Italian friend of mine comes, you go and lock yourself in the kitchen.

Mother Difficult for me.

Raoul Come on, don't worry: look, from today, if things go well, you'll have an Italian under your roof every day. Are you ready?

Mother Dad different. He not true Italian.

Raoul Maa, if he gets citizenship, he will be the same as all other Italians.

Mother To all the others? Same, same?

Raoul Same, same!

Mother It make me laugh! Dad like Signor Martino or Signor Rinaldi!

Raoul Doesn't make me laugh that much . . . (*Beat.*) Actually, come to think of it, not at all!

Mother Why?

Raoul Because he will be Italian, while to him, I will be twice as foreign (*Beat.*) I'm going to call my friend.

Raoul *exits.*

Scene 6

Father *enters from the kitchen. He looks worried and tired.*

Mother *To tracassé?*[28]

Father *Aimpé.*[29]

Mother *Tu pu al bien zordi.*[30]

Father *Mo pa tracassé pu zordi.*[31]

Mother *Pu ki to tracassé?*[32]

Father It's about the boy. He worries me.

Mother Why?

Father He has been upset for quite some time, he hardly smiles.

Mother You'll see, he'll get over it.

Father Do you remember, as a child, he used to smile all the time?

Mother You were always looking at him.

Father As if a moonbeam had landed on his face.

Mother All this belongs to another life, another country.

Father You can't say that!

Mother Don't get mad.

Father I did everything, every day, to keep that moonbeam shining in this country too.

Mother Right, so sorry.

Silence.

Father I just don't understand what's wrong with him. Sometimes I'm afraid he's mad at me.

Mother No, that can't be. I guess he's just worried about his exam.

Father Why? He's never had any problems with his studies.

Mother There might be some other thought on his mind.

Father What thought?

Mother Maybe a heartbreak.

Father He is still young.

Mother Is he though? Today he invited a friend here. An Italian girl.

Father What did she look like?

Mother Who?

Father His girlfriend!

Mother Who cares?

Father I was just wondering.

Mother She's not here yet. She hasn't been very respectful towards us.

Father Because she was a bit late? (*Beat.*) You're not jealous, are you?

Mother No way, I just mean, she can't behave like that.

Father Stop it! Women always keep us waiting!

Mother And you men always drive us crazy.

Silence.

Father I even bought him a new suit today.

Mother I'm sure he really liked it.

Father He didn't give a damn. He didn't even want to try it on.

Mother Let it go.

Father I'm not angry with him. I'm just worried about him. What's the meaning of everything I'm doing if he's not happy?

Mother I'm sure he will be. Give him some time.

Father *To sur?*[33]

Mother *Si, pa tracass twa!*[34]

Father *Mo espéré.*[35]

Scene 7

Raoul *enters.*

Raoul I told you to stop speaking Creole. Practice your Italian!

Father Yes, yes, understood!

Mother You called her?

Raoul She's unavailable.

Mother She's doing that on purpose.

Raoul Maa . . . Anyway, I sent her some texts to let her know. She will read them. Let's begin?

Father What do we do?

Raoul Now we're going to pretend to be at the Town Hall. You will practice answering the questions the mayor will ask you and read the oath.

Father I cannot say *formul*[36] and that's it?

Raoul No, you must learn to do everything right in front of him. Do you want to make a good impression or not? Move these chairs over there.

Father *and* **Mother** *remove the chairs.* **Raoul** *takes his books off the table. He takes a notebook, opens it, and places it, together with a pen, on one side of the table; then he takes a sheet of paper from the notebook on which he writes the oath statement and places it on the opposite side of the notebook.*

Raoul From now on, I'm no longer your son, ok, I'm the mayor. Please, ok. While you will play yourself. I will ask you some questions and you'll have to answer as if you were answering him. Ok?

Father Understood.

Raoul Now, you both go out and then come back in. Pretend you are entering the mayor's office.

Father *and* **Mother** *exit.* **Raoul** *stands in front of the notebook.* **Father** *and* **Mother** *enter again.*

Raoul Buongiorno Signor Kumarsingh!

Father Bon giorno.

Raoul (*pointing at the side of the table where the sheet of paper is*)   Please, come here!

Mother   Where do I go?

Raoul   Wherever you want, Signora.

Mother *stands next to* **Raoul**.

Raoul   Signora, you cannot stand next to me.

Mother   You said 'wherever you want'!

Raoul   Yes, but not next to the government officer!

Mother   What is government office?

Raoul   The mayor, Maa.

Mother *moves to stand next to* **Father**.

Mother   Okay here?

Father   Yes!

Raoul   No, you can't stand next to him. Step back please.

Father   But she is wife. Wife always near husband.

Raoul   Not in this case. It's just about you, Signor Kumarsingh. You are the one who has to swear the oath, not your wife! (**Mother** *moves a little back*.) Now, please, stop interrupting me. Stop messing about, will you?

Father   *Dakor*.[37]

Raoul   You must say 'I ag-ree'! You're in Italy here, so you have to really make an effort to speak Italian. Is that clear?

Father   I ag-ree.

Raoul   Signor Kumarsingh, are you ready to become an Italian citizen?

Father   Yes. I ready.

Raoul   You have to say 'Yes, I *am* ready', not 'I ready'.

Father   But when I say 'I ready', people understand same.

Raoul   Signor Kumarsingh, do you realize that you are replying to an officer of the Italian Republic?

Father   We start again?

Raoul   No, Signor Kumarsingh, we can't do it again.

Mother   Why not?

Raoul   Signora, did I grant you permission to speak?

Mother   No . . .

Raoul Then don't interrupt us. So, Signor Kumarsingh, are you definitely sure you're ready?

Father Yes, I *am* rea-dy.

Raoul Signor Kumarsingh, the law is a serious matter. Stop smiling, please.

Father Yes, I *am* rea-dy.

Raoul Good. Now I will proceed with the reading of the act to verify the information provided and then you will have to read the oath. Is that ok?

Father Yes, I ag-ree.

Raoul So, on this 22nd day of April, two . . .

Mother But today is not 22 April!

Raoul Signora, are you perchance suggesting you know things better than I do?

Mother No . . .

Father We start again?

Raoul No! So, stop interrupting me! How do you say 'stop' in your language? And anyway, you can't go back: you never can go back in life. I'm the law here. Just keep quiet and speak when I tell you so, understood?

Father Yes.

Mother Yes.

Raoul So, on this 22nd day of April, at 3 pm, before me, Mario Rossi, the City Council's civil registrar, personally appeared blablabla Kumarsingh, born on the 2nd of May whatever, a foreigner of blablabla, residing in blablabla street. Would you please confirm the truthfulness of the facts declared? (*Beat.*) Will you confirm, yes or no?

Father What I do?

Raoul You need to confirm this information, Signor Kumarsingh! (*Beat.*) Your personal data!

Mother You don't correctly say your dad's name . . .

Raoul Signora, I am the law here and the law is never wrong. This is the last warning, if you interrupt me once again, I'll throw you out.

Mother *Kuyon!*[38]

Raoul I beg your pardon?

Mother I not spoke.

Raoul Ok. So, Signor Kumarsingh, do you confirm or not?

Father I . . .

Mother (*whispering*) . . . con-firm.

Father I con-firm.

Raoul Today, by the prefect's decree issued on blablabla, with which Signor Kumarsingh was granted Italian citizenship, I've been asked to hear your oath. Considering your prompt request, I've agreed, and the appearing party solemnly swears pronouncing the statement . . .

Silence. **Father** *looks at* **Raoul**, *who remains impassive.* **Father** *turns toward* **Mother**, *who points at the sheet.* **Father** *looks at the sheet of paper.*

Father (*slowly*)   Geeuro di essere fedelee.[39]

Mother (*whispering*)   Fedele.

Father (*slowly*)   Geeuro di essere fedele a la republik itali.[40]

Mother (*whispering*)   Repubblica.

Raoul Signora, stop it please.

Mother Raoul, I just try to help dad.

Raoul I'm not Raoul and you are trying to fool the State. You've been warned. Get out of my office. (*Beat.*) Please, get out.

Mother You serious?

Raoul Signora, do you understand Italian?

Mother I understand you rude.

Mother *leaves to the kitchen.*

Father Raoul, don't treat so your *maman*.[41]

Raoul Paa, I treat you both as others would treat you. Get used to it!

Father I got used, *mai*[42] you are our son.

Raoul I'm not your son now, I'm the mayor!

Father (*smiles*)   *Monsieur*[43] mayor don't treat my wife and me badly.

Raoul But weren't you the one used to being treated badly?

Father I tolerate a lot . . . not everything.

Raoul Paa, if I really were the mayor . . . (*Beat.*) I told you to practice the oath!

Father I not read *italien* well.

Raoul Why didn't you memorize it?

Father I try but forget.

Raoul You have to insist. Can't you understand that this is not a joke?

Father I know is not joke. I try now. You don't worry.

Raoul If you make a mistake, you won't get your citizenship.

Father This is not good. I work a lot to have citizenship.

Raoul I'm studying a lot too for my citizenship, but I still don't have it.

Father Because law wrong.

Raoul That's how the law works in this country. You can't change it.

Father I not think I change, I think I make better. I give citizenship to those who work and pay taxes. (*Beat.*) Why do you laugh?

Raoul Citizenship is not just about money.

Father More easy if about money.

Raoul Once, in this country, a long time ago, an emperor granted citizenship to all foreigners in exchange for their money.

Father (*smiles*) Right! What he made of money?

Raoul He used it for several purposes.

Father For make country more good?

Raoul That too. But why are you asking?

Father And his people happy?

Raoul I think so.

Father You see? He intelligent. He makes all become citizen, he takes money, he makes better all people life.

Raoul There's no point in smiling.

Father I don't understand why this wrong.

Raoul Stop smiling! You can't always face life smiling.

Father Why?

Raoul In this world, your smile makes you look like a stupid . . . Just forget about it.

Father I not stupid. I gentle.

Raoul It's not like that!

Father Where I wrong?

Raoul If you speak poorly and just smile, people who don't know you will think you're an idiot. This world isn't made for smiling.

Father Raoul you speak fast. I not understand all words.

Raoul That's the point! You don't understand. (*Beat.*) Forget about it, I told you.

Father I don't want you angry.

Raoul And I don't want . . .

Beat.

Father What?

Raoul ... to waste my time.

Pause.

Father Yes, I know. You help me but you study for your exam tomorrow. I say thank you. (*Beat.*) *Va bien.*[44] You go call *maman*. She helps my *mémoir*.[45] She remembers words better.

Raoul She can't speak for you.

Father You call ...

Raoul (*screams*) Maa ... Maa ...

Father *Pas* like this. Go there ... and ask for-gift.

Raoul Give, For-give, not for-gift. Forgive. When will you learn to speak better? (*Beat.*) And stop smiling, come on, it's serious! Haven't you seen enough in your life?

Raoul *leaves to the kitchen.*

Scene 8

Father Not for-gift. For-give. For-give. For-give ... give up. I give up in this new country. My body too tired to run after your strange words. I give up, a little more every day. I give up, when I follow your lips, what you say so quickly. I give up on confusing sounds that come out of your mouths that never get tired. (*Beat.*) I give up. I give up while I try to get by, but it's never enough! My tongue struggles to bend to use your words. I give up to the clash between the old and the new in my head. I give up and I have no more space (*points to his head*) in here. I give up, a little more every day, when you try to erase the words of my past. (*Beat.*) I'm lost. I'm lost. Lost. For-give. Not for-gift. Forgive!

Scene 9

Raoul *enters followed by* **Mother**.

Raoul He needs to go through that all on his own.

Mother On his own? He bring us here to Italy. He works for everybody. He make shopping. He take care documents.

Raoul It's not enough.

Mother You always say, 'It not enough'.

Raoul I'm not the one who makes the rules. And they don't care about anything else.

Father Raoul, I say make peace, not argue.

Raoul I'm not arguing.

Mother I tell Raoul he put himself behind you and say words slowly, so you can repeat.

Raoul He is the one who will become Italian, not me. He must do it by himself!

Mother He becomes Italian for you.

Father Stop! (*Beat.*) I repeat exercise, be kind Raoul, you tell me what I do . . .

Raoul Yes, we are wasting time! We need to start again with the reading of the oath. (*To* **Mother**.) Please, take a seat Maa. Please.

Mother *goes to sit down.* **Raoul** *and* **Father** *return to their original position on the two sides of the table.*

Father (*slowly*) Gee-uro di essere fidele a la republik itali . . .

Raoul But why do you keep saying Gee-uro? I've told you a thousand times: it's 'Giuro'. (*Articulating.*) Giuro! Giuro!

Father (*articulating*) Giuro di essere fedelee.

Raoul Fedele, with an 'ai', not with an 'ee'. Fedele! Don't get confused with Creole!

Father Giuro di essere fedele a la republik ita-lina.

Raoul No, no, no, no! This one can't be wrong. It's unacceptable!

Father What wrong *encore*?[46]

Raoul You said 'italina'!

Father I read so.

Raoul You misread!

Father (*looking at the sheet of paper*) Ita-lina.

Mother *stands up and peeks on the sheet of paper.*

Mother You wrote so. You wrote 'Ita-lina'!

Raoul It's impossible . . .

Raoul *takes the sheet of paper to check. He realizes his mistake. He takes a pen and corrects his mistake.*

Father (*smiles*) Not important. Everyone can wrong.

Raoul . . . now it's correct. (*He puts the sheet of paper again on the table in front of his father.*) Read!

Father Giuro di essere fedele a la republik italiana, di ozervar fedel/

Raoul /Osservare, two 's'...

The doorbell rings.

Father Who is?

Mother (*to* **Raoul**) Your friend?

Raoul I don't know, it shouldn't be her. I'll go see.

Mother You didn't tell her not to come?

Raoul I texted her.

Mother We go to the kitchen!

Raoul Again? Can you stop running away?

Father I stay.

Mother Ok, I'll stay too.

Raoul *exits to open the door.*

Scene 10

Raoul (*voice over*) Vikram! What do you want now?

Vikram (*enters followed by* **Raoul**) Curb your excitement, bro', I'm touched by your concern! I have to ask something to aunty. Hey, hi uncle, you're home already, huh!

Father Yes, I come back early today to be ready for later.

Mother Vikram, what's going on?

Vikram Viki, Aunty, Viki! Aunty, you forgot to give me the cloves earlier.

Mother Really?

Vikram Yes, mom was preparing the rice but there were none in the package.

Mother But where I put my head today? I go get it right now.

Vikram Ah Aunty...

Mother Yes?

Vikram Mom asks if you have a bunch of coriander to lend her?

Mother Nothing else Vikram?

Vikram No, no, just this! I'm not a mooch!

Mother *leaves to the kitchen. Silence.* **Father** *and* **Raoul** *stare at* **Vikram**.

Vikram Hey, what a nice suit! Is it yours? (**Raoul** *doesn't answer.*) Uncle, did you buy it for him?

Father Yes, I buy for today for Town Hall.

Vikram I wish someone would give me a suit like that. (*Beat.*) So uncle, are you ready for today?

Raoul No, he's not ready . . .

Father I? I ready!

Vikram Are you ready or not?

Raoul No, definitely not.

Father I will ready!

Vikram You're both very persuasive, you know? Uncle, now that you become Italian, you'll have to support only Italy, huh!

Father I support Italy and I support Brézil!

Vikram Oh no, you can't support two teams.

Raoul You're not even Brazilian!

Father (*smiles*) Football belong to everybody. I support Brézil, when I was child and saw Pélé playing and scoring. Oh, good god, he is great! He dribbles everybody, also goalkeeper and scores many goals! Love doesn't end with citizenship.

Vikram Pélé is great! I've only seen him online. But if Italy plays against Brazil, what are you going to do?

Father With one eye I support Italy, with another eye I support Brézil.

Vikram Uncle, you're just like me! You'll never lose this way! But next time we watch an Italy match, we'll sing the national anthem together! (*Sings.*) 'Fratelli d'Italia. L'Italia s'è desta!'.

Father Sure. I sing like footballers! They perfect singers.

Father *moves his lips pretending singing Italian national anthem.*

Raoul We're done.

Vikram Uncle you need to learn to sing it!

Father Too difficult. I can't understand words.

Vikram Now that you're going to be Italian, you should be good at singing. Italians can all sing, bro!

Father Ok, you teach me song, I sing. But easy song!

Vikram An easy one? Wait . . . (*Beat. Sings.*) 'Lasciatemi cantare, con la chitarra in mano, lasciatemi cantare una canzone piano piano. Lasciatemi cantare, perché ne sono fiero. Sono un italiano, un italiano vero'.[47]

Father I know this song.

Vikram Really? Com'on, sing it!

Father (*sings*) '*Nasha ye pyaar ka nasha hai. Yeh meri baat yaaron maano. Nashe mein yaar doob jaao. Raho na hosh mein dewaano.*'[48]

Vikram But you're not singing in Italian!

Father No, Hindi.

Vikram It's not the same.

Father Music same.

Vikram But words are different.

Raoul Bravo, tell him. He thinks in Creole and pretends to speak Italian.

Father How you know?

Vikram What?

Father That words are different!

Vikram I know.

Raoul Oh. Do you speak Hindi then?

Vikram Me? Not at all!

Father I do. And I feel words are same.

Raoul Are they?

Father I hear from spirit of song, from same rhythm . . .

Raoul Even better . . . Now he 'feels' the universe!

Father You don't believe language speaks with heart? I do.

Vikram Anyway, uncle, it's an Italian song! It was born here.

Father Not important where it born . . . Music belongs to everybody, like football.

Raoul I go to university only to hear these things at home . . .

Vikram This time, uncle, I don't know if you're right. I'm sorry to tell you this, but I love you anyway.

Raoul Can you stop calling him uncle? He's not your uncle.

Vikram Bro I call your father uncle because I respect him a lot. We don't need to have the same blood to respect each other, bro.

Raoul Look, Bob Marley has joined us.

Vikram (*sings*) 'One love, one heart. Let's get together and feel all right!' Come on uncle, let's sing!

Father I don't like this music, I like Ennio Morricone songs!

Raoul (*laughs*)   Tell this to the mayor! Can anybody explain to him, please, that Morricone is only music, no lyrics!

Mother *comes in with a package in her hand.*

Mother   Ganesh help me! What racket you making? (*Gives the package to* **Vikram**.) Here Vikram.

Raoul   Listen Vikram, please, you need to go now, we still have to practice his lines.

Vikram   Practice what?

Mother   Statement for swearing.

Father   I read badly . . .

Vikram   Don't worry uncle, they'll listen to you with their hearts. Everything will be all right. (**Raoul** *glares at him*.) Ok, I think it's time to go, mum is waiting for me . . . Good luck!

Father   I walk you out.

Raoul   Stop wasting time!

Father *stares at* **Raoul** *for a moment and exits, preceded by* **Vikram**.

Raoul   I'm trying in every way to help you!

Mother   You too nervous. Can you be more patient with dad?

Raoul   Why can't he be more patient with me trying to teach him?

Mother   Dad is patient. He patient so long, never angry, to get citizenship today.

Raoul   He's not the only one waiting.

Mother   You nervous for exam?

Raoul   Maa, I'm tired, there's always something going on here and it's hard to keep the situation under . . .

Scene 11

Father *enters followed by* **Laura**.

Father   There is surprise! (*To* **Laura**.) Please, please!

Laura   Thank you.

Father   We have company.

Raoul   Laura!

Laura   Good morning ma'am. Hi Raoul!

Mother   Good morning.

Raoul But you're here?

Laura Well, if you can see me . . .

Father I saw her look for our door.

Laura And I saw your father, while I was looking for the right door. Or at least I thought it was your father . . .

Father Think well. Bravo!

Laura It smells lovely in here! What is it?

Mother It's my patchouli incense!

Laura Patciali incense?

Mother Patchouli!

Laura I don't know it! It smells so good! It's sweet!

Raoul You're here . . . but I didn't expect you to come!

Laura Didn't you? Didn't we arrange? For the notes.

Raoul Yeah, I know, but I texted you.

Laura Really? When? My phone died while I was queuing at the Town Hall.

Father You also queue Town Hall!

Laura Yeah! I needed a certificate . . . am I interrupting something, by any chance?

Father No, no bother us!

Beat. **Raoul** *looks at* **Mother**.

Mother No, no bother!

Father (*to* **Mother**) After, you give stick incense to Miss nice.

Laura Thank you, that's so kind. Call me Laura.

Father Lorna?

Laura Laura!

Father Laura! Forgift, I misunderstood.

Raoul (*whispers*) Forgive.

Laura It's fine. I do that all the time . . . (*Beat.*) Anyway sorry. I had a crazy day. You won't believe it, but it took me three hours to get a simple document.

Father We also go to Town Hall after.

Laura Really? I'm sorry about that.

Father No, it is good for us!

Mother We have an appointment at 4 pm!

Father Today I become Italian.

Laura Really? Congratulations! I didn't know . . .

Father Thank you, thank you.

Laura (*to* **Raoul**) You didn't tell me anything!

Raoul I forgot about that.

Laura Are you excited?

Father I so excitement. Joy! After long time. I *encore*[49] don't believe.

Raoul (*whispers*) Still! Not *encore*.

Laura Have you been waiting long?

Father Only seven-ten years. I wait, wait, wait and when I forget to wait, she arrives.

Laura (*laughs*) And here I was, complaining about a stupid queue! How shameful . . .

Raoul Actually, he's been waiting six years for citizenship, not seventeen!

Father Yes, but I seven-ten years here Italy.

Laura That's a lifetime.

They all smile.

Father Miss Laura do you want coffee or tea?

Laura No, thanks.

Father No problem.

Laura I don't want to bother you, you must be busy with preparations . . .

Father No. No bother. It's pleasure! True Maa?

Mother Yes.

Laura Well, I'd really love some tea then. Raoul always talks about your tea. He says it's special.

Mother Raoul speaking well of our home?

Laura Yes, he does.

Mother Oh, I don't think so.

Raoul Mom, I don't think this is . . .

Father My wife prepares really good tea.

Laura Thank you so much. I'm curious, I'd love to try it.

Father (*to* **Mother**) You prepare?

Mother Yes! And *twa vin avek mwa*.

Father Yes, ma'am! We go prepare tea! Then we come! Just a moment.

Mother *drags* **Father** *into the kitchen by a sleeve.*

Scene 12

Laura Your parents are so lovely. Especially your father.

Raoul You think so?

Laura Yes, I think he is a very nice man. But, I don't think your mum likes me.

Raoul She's just a little cautious.

Laura You know, you and your father have the same smile? That's why I recognized him immediately in front of the door. Your smile.

Raoul Great . . .

Laura Yeah, yeah, you have both the same dimples at the corners of your mouth . . .

Raoul Yeah, people say that all the time.

Laura What's that face? Don't you like it?

Raoul If you say so . . .

Laura I got everything done and I brought you the notes as promised. I need to revise the last century before the fall of the Roman Empire. Have you managed to finish?

Laura *rummages in her bag.*

Raoul I'm getting a little bit confused about some key dates.

Laura (*giving him a notebook*) Take these notes, it's all in here. Sorry, can I charge my phone for a few minutes?

Raoul Sure, but . . . The fact is that I don't know if you can stay.

Laura Why?

Raoul Because, because . . . dammit! I wrote it in the text message, but fate is plotting against me.

Laura For the Town Hall appointment?

Raoul It must have been Ganesh. He always looks like he's sitting there doing nothing while in fact . . .

Laura Ganesh?

Raoul Yes, the one there with the trunk. He's mad at me. I mean, forget about it.

Laura If you can't do it, there's no problem. I'm leaving. We'll talk by phone.

Raoul No, no, I don't want you to go. I just have to help my father with the citizenship issue.

Laura Why didn't you tell me that you had this appointment with history today?

Raoul I was embarrassed.

Laura Embarrassed?

Raoul My parents turn everything into a circus. They mess around, they don't understand the details, they don't know anything about the country they are in. It's incredible . . .

Laura That's great, then, that you are here to help them.

Raoul I wanted to finish studying with you, but he insisted on going to work this morning, he came back late and now there's no time left . . .

Laura All this is worth more than a Roman history exam! You don't just become Italian every day!

Raoul Nothing changes for me. He'll get his citizenship, not me.

Laura Aren't you happy for him? If it happens to him, it's like it's happening to you too!

Raoul No, he's him, I am me! (*Beat.*) I keep saying this, but nobody gets it. I'm a foreigner here and you have no idea what it's like to study, speak, eat, play, think and even dream in Italian, and continue being a foreigner. I'll be a foreigner even after my father becomes Italian. (*Beat.*) Sorry, I'm a little upset today!

Laura If it helps, to me, you're Italian.

Raoul I'm an invisible Italian. Invisible! (*Beat.*) I know, it doesn't mean anything. In short: it's paradoxical that my father can get his citizenship, while I, who feel Italian, keep wandering into the unknown. For the State I am nothing, or rather, I am a foreigner.

Laura Why would it be paradoxical that he's becoming Italian? I don't understand.

Raoul He's becoming an Italian citizen but has no awareness of what that means. All he does is work.

Laura Well, it must have been hard for your father to get here and to survive, to find a job and a house, without even being able to speak Italian. Perhaps this will be an opportunity for you all to be happier.

Raoul He does nothing but work and smile. He will always be a servant. That makes me angry. That's how people will always see him.

Laura People judge but they don't know.

Raoul If he'd been savvy, he would have stayed at home to practice.

Laura What should he be practicing?

Raoul This. (**Raoul** *gives the oath sheet to* **Laura**.) The statement he will have to read in front of the mayor.

Laura (*takes the sheet of paper and reads it*) 'Giuro di essere fedele alla Repubblica italiana e di osservare la Costituzione e le leggi dello Stato'. Come on, it's not that hard.

Raoul He can't read Italian well and he hasn't practiced.

Laura He will read it as best as he can.

Raoul No, several mayors denied citizenship to those who turned up and weren't able to read the statement.

Laura They won't grant you citizenship if you can't read the sentence?

Raoul If you can read the sentence, you show that you're integrated, if you read it wrong you're not integrated . . . I could read it upside down and crazy-drunk, but they wouldn't give me citizenship anyway.

Laura Is there anything I can do to help you? With your father?

Raoul What about our exam?

Laura I think he's more important.

Raoul If you can get him to learn it . . . That man is a mess. What we need is a miracle.

Laura Don't give up so easily, he's your father!

Raoul He refuses to listen to me.

Laura Parents are all the same. They never listen to their children, maybe out of pride.

Raoul I am an eternal child to him. But he's the child to me. The child who always gives up and can't defend himself. The one who, as soon as other people ask him for something, immediately puts himself at their service. You should hear him talk to his employers: 'Yes, ma'am . . . Right, ma'am . . .'. His oath should be like this: 'I swear to be faithful to all Italian ladies, to clean the stairs, the toilets, the pots and the windows, to promptly comply with all their requests and to respect the constitutional laws of cleaning with a dust cloth in hand'.

Laura Come on, don't say that about him.

Raoul Why are you defending him?

Laura Because I like him.

Raoul For his smile?

Laura No. Because each time he looks at you, his eyes shine . . . even when you told him off, he was always telling the truth, he's genuine. Maybe you are right: he's like a child, but a child in all his beauty.

Raoul I'm just trying to save him from himself, but my father is such a . . . donkey . . .

Scene 13

Mother *enters from the kitchen with a tray and two cups of tea.*

Mother Sorry for disturb you. I bring tea.

Laura Thank you ma'm, that's so kind.

Raoul Thanks Maa. Let's start over in five minutes, okay?

Mother There is no need. You take your time.

Raoul How come, there's no need?

Mother (*to* **Laura**) Do you want sugar?

Raoul Why are you saying that?

Laura Yes please . . .

Mother I say there is no need you help us. How much sugar?

Laura . . . here, I'll help myself, thank you!

Raoul Maa?

Mother One? Two?

Laura Two please. Thank you. I'm so sorry to be disturbing you today . . .

Mother That's not a problem. (*To* **Raoul**.) There is no need you come Town Hall after. Stay home and study.

Raoul What are you saying?

Mother I say what I thinking. There is no need. I hear right before; you say dad is donkey in front of friend.

Raoul We'll talk about this later!

Mother No, it all right.

Laura I'll drink up my tea and leave.

Raoul No, no, wait a minute. (*To* **Mother**.) Come on Maa, don't do that, I didn't say anything presumptuous.

Mother You not use complicated words with me.

Raoul I'm just upset, like everyone here.

Mother You always think you know everything, but you not know nothing.

Raoul Maa, please, we have a guest.

Mother I'm sorry that I give your friend bad show, but you exaggerate. (*To* **Laura**.) His dad always thinking for him, but Raoul not thinking for dad.

Raoul But I stayed home to help him!

Mother Dad bought new suit for him, but he not interested.

Raoul There was no time . . .

Mother He says he help us, but he not want to help us so much. I see that!

Raoul How can you say that?

Mother He says citizenship does not change anything for us. He doesn't understand! His father suffers lot of things for him. All to realize stupid dream to change, stupid dream to give us better life. If he hears Raoul talking like that, he suffering in heart.

Raoul Maa . . .

Laura I'm sorry, ma'am. I think Raoul just means/

Mother /Raoul do wrong! (*Beat.*) I'm sorry we give bad impression. Sorry. Not a good day today. At least tea is good?

Laura It was delicious, ma'am!

Mother True you like tea?

Laura Yes, Raoul was right, your tea is really special!

Mother I have little secret. I put two pieces of cardamom . . .

Raoul I don't think Laura is interested in the recipe.

Mother . . . with cardamom tea smells good.

Laura I'll try to do it too, but I'm not very good at this.

Mother I teach you if you want.

Laura Sure, maybe next time. Now I really should be going . . .

Mother No, you stay! No problem. I go back there with husband to read.

Raoul Maa . . .

Mother I said no! How do you say 'no' in your language? We not need your help.

Raoul You'll never make it!

Mother We doing as always. We trying . . . and also I ask Ganesh for help.

Laura Ma'am, I'm sure that, with a little practice, your husband will make it! I'm quite confident. It's just like studying for an exam.

Mother Laura, you want to help us?

Raoul Maa, you're embarrassing her . . .

Mother Ganesh arrived in our house. I now understand. Laura is our Akhu.

Laura Akhu?

Mother Yes, clever little mouse helping Ganesh! He replied to us.

Raoul For God's sake! Maa, wait a minute . . .

Laura Raoul, I'm happy to do it. Take it easy. If your mum wants . . .

Mother Sure. You good girl, I feel it. No like others. Laura, you come with me in kitchen?

Laura Yes . . .

Raoul What's going on today? Is it the end of the world? You're even letting her into your kitchen?

Mother No, it's not the end of the world, but beginning of new, if Ganesh wants.

Mother *is about to exit.*

Raoul Do as you want. He never learns anything. Nothing!

Mother Oh Raoul, one last thing.

Raoul What?

Mother Better you go to bathroom and wash your face and think about your words. Stop calling him, him. His name is dad.

Mother *and* **Laura** *leave to the kitchen.*

Scene 14

Change of atmosphere.

Raoul Clarify ideas. Clarify ideas. Clean head. Wash face. Wash. Sink, water, water, water, mirror, image, likeness.
Then God said: 'Let us make man in our image, after our likeness, and let him have dominion over all the earth'.
Earth. (*Beat.*) Land, ground, soil, country, homeland, boundaries, borders, barriers, dividing lines, immigration, confusion, fear, despair.
Start survival process: you breathe, you eat, you sleep.
Start adaptation process: you observe, you listen, you get by.
Start integration process: you talk, you play, you study, you participate, you love.
Start membership process: hybrid subject not recognized.
Imperfect Italian.
Membership rejected. Membership rejected.

Silence.

Restart membership process: wash face. Wash. Sink, water, water, water, mirror.
'Mirror, mirror on the wall, who's today the most Italian of them all?'

'My boy, today your father is the most Italian of them all'.
'Mirror, you lie! You lie!'.

(*Silence.*)
Restart membership process: wash face, wash, sink, water, water, water, mirror.
Recognition process. 90 percent compatibility detected:
'You have the same smile as your father!'
Membership approved. Membership approved.
The same smile as my father . . . The same smile as my father.
Error. Error. There must be a mistake.
This is not my membership. I don't belong to a smile that speaks of weakness, a smile that hides embarrassment, a smile that can't say things, that can't defend itself, that doesn't demand respect.
This is not my face. I'm not going to be the happy foreigner, the compliant foreigner, the humble foreigner. (*Beat.*) I'm not your smiling clown.
I refuse this membership. I refuse this membership.
Game over.
If not this membership, which one? Which one? Nothing, deserted, invisible, neutral. Suspended identity: immigrant, assimilated, fragmented, disconnected, expelled, empty. Restart. Restart membership process. Restart membership process. Restart membership process. (*Screams.*) Restart membership process. Restart membership process. Restart membership process . . .

Raoul *falls to the ground.*

Scene 15

Father *and* **Mother** *enter, bend over* **Raoul** *and stare at him.*

Father   Raoul, Raoul, *mo ti bébé.*[50]

Mother   Vishnu, *less li trankil.*[51]

Father   Raoul, *mo zoli ti bébé.*[52]

Mother   You'll wake him up!

Father   You're right, sorry. (*Silence.*) Lakshmi . . . look, look!

Mother   What?

Father   He's smiling!

Mother   If he wakes up, you look after him!

Father   Look, look at his smile. It looks like a half-moon!

Mother   I've warned you Vishnu.

Father   I'd do anything to see him always smiling like this!

Mother   Start by making less noise then!

Silence.

Father Lakshmi, where do you think his smile comes from?

Mother You and me, no?

Father Surely not from you!

Mother Why?

Father Your nose wrinkles when you smile. His doesn't!

Mother But he doesn't look like you either!

Father No?

Mother You never smile with your mouth, only with your eyes.

Father It's a shame. Look how nice it is to smile like that.

Father *tries to sketch some smiles.*

Mother Vishnu, what are you doing?

Father I'm trying to smile!

Mother Like your son?

Father Who said we can't already learn from him?

Mother Nobody.

Silence. **Father** *tries to smile.*

Father Like this? (**Mother** *shakes her head.*) Like that?

Mother Better! But you need a little more practice.

Father I'm sure I'll get it!

Mother Be quiet now or you'll wake him up!

Father It's okay. We have time!

Mother A lifetime . . .

Beat.

Father Did you see that? He smiled again! It looks just like a half-moon hanging in the sky.

Dark.

Notes

1 Salutations to the remover of obstacles, Ganesh (Hindi prayer).
2 What?
3 Prayer.

4   I told you.
5   Washerman.
6   Always!
7   Cardamom, cinnamon and cumin.
8   Good boy.
9   Still this smell?
10 Put it all here!
11 All this?
12 Special day, special gift.
13 Doing what?
14 Open this first!
15 No, come on, open it!
16 A suit!
17 For you!
18 Yes!
19 To go to the Town Hall!
20 Try it!
21 Try it, son!
22 After work.
23 Because.
24 I bought a suit for me too.
25 Don't worry!
26 Yes, don't worry.
27 Yes, ok, ok! Let me have a drink. I'm tired.
28 Are you tired?
29 A little bit.
30 Everything is going to be fine today.
31 I'm not worried about today.
32 What are you worried about then?
33 Are you sure?
34 Yes, don't worry!
35 I hope so.
36 Formula.
37 Ok.
38 Asshole.
39 I swear to be faithful.
40 I swear to be faithful to the Republic of Italy.
41 Mum.
42 But.
43 Mr.
44 Ok.
45 Memory.
46 Still.
47 *L'Italiano*, Italian song by Toto Cutugno, released in 1983.
48 *Nasha ye pyaar ka nasha hai*, is a song from the Hindi movie 'Mann' (1999) based on the melody of *L'Italiano* by the Italian singer Toto Cutugno.
49 Still.
50 My little baby.
51 Leave him in peace.
52 My beautiful little baby.

Portrait of the Artist as a Dead Man – Italy '41 – Argentina '78

Ritratto dell'artista da morto
Italia '41 – Argentina '78

By Davide Carnevali

Translated by Margherita Laera

Only when someone writes it all as fiction, will it be remembered; will it be believed. Journalism expires after 24 hours and official court testimonies die in the confused memory of archives.

Andrew Graham-Yooll, *A State of Fear: Memories of Argentina's Nightmare*

First staged at Piccolo Teatro di Milano – Teatro Studio Melato, Milan, on 16 March 2023.

What happens beforehand

On stage, a number of technicians are building the set. They are being supervised and helped by the assistant director, Virginia. They are building two walls, a cross-section of what will gradually reveal itself to be a flat.

Meanwhile, the audience enters the auditorium.

Every now and then Virginia turns to Michele and talks to him. Michele is sitting at a desk, in front of a computer; he is doing some research on the internet. He is eating a pizza from a takeaway box with the words GRANDE ITALIA written on it. He plays the guitar, strums a few chords. He gets ready.

Next to him is a large panel or blackboard, which will be used as a work surface. It looks like one of those blackboards used by police inspectors when they are assembling evidence for a complicated case; or by theatre authors, when they are assembling a complex dramaturgical structure.

Every now and then, when an important date or relevant fact emerges from the story, Michele writes on the blackboard.

On the desk lies the script of the show.

Next to the desk, on the wall, a poster of Revolving Bridge, *in which Michele appears on the guitar, accompanying a young man on the piano.*

A number of crates are scattered across the stage.

The technicians bring other crates onto the stage, they move them, arrange them in specific spots. All the crates have the words PICCOLO TEATRO – TEATRO GRASSI written on them. Little by little, the crates will be opened and the objects they contain will find their place in the specially marked points on the stage.

The last prop to be placed in its place is the refrigerator.

Everything reminds one moving houses, or of setting up an exhibition within a museum space.

In order to set up the space, Virginia and the technicians use drawings and plans printed on a series of sheets which, once used, are dropped on the floor.

Thus, little by little, the space fills with papers.

A video camera films everything.

The projection screen is located above the stage space.

A couple of screens are also positioned at the edge of the stage space, the kind that are normally part of a theatre's technical equipment or of a museum's security circuit. When the audience has entered and the walls have been built, the stage manager tells Michele it is time to start. Michele goes to leave the guitar inside one of the crates and places himself at the centre of the stage.

1. Prologue. It all starts with a letter

Good evening, everyone, and welcome.

First of all, I would like to thank you for being here. Thank you also on behalf of those who are not present, on behalf of those who unfortunately cannot be with us today.

I'm going to take a few minutes to explain briefly why we're here and what's going happen now.

It's not easy to find the words. It's not easy for me, because normally my job is to bring before you a text that has already been written, while what I'm saying now, I'm saying spontaneously and informally. And also, the fact that I'm here today in this hall so steeped in history binds me to an even greater responsibility as an actor.

We thought this was the best way to start for two reasons. The first is that, using my own words, we would have created some intimacy, a relationship of trust between us. The second is that in the end what I'm about to tell you is my own – or rather, sorry – *also* my own story.

My name is Michele Riondino, many of you probably know me for a character I played on TV: young Inspector Montalbano. Let's face it, we can say it plainly, if you hadn't watched this series, many of you wouldn't have recognized me. It's not a problem: I'm very fond of Montalbano because he's given me a lot of reasons to be proud. The first was to be able to work with Andrea Camilleri, who gave me all the details to be able to build the character of the Inspector, who is, to all intents and purposes, the author's alter-ego.

To study the character, I moved to Palermo for a while, and there I stole people's gestures, sounds, words... Stealing people's lives around me...

I'm obsessed with the idea of stealing other people's lives, it's a professional bias. For us actors, stealing the real and intimate moments that happen between people is very precious, taking possession, appropriating those moments and then reproducing them on stage. Studying them, like clues. The next time you are at the airport, for example, I invite you to observe people saying goodbye: what happens between them? Observe how they wait for the moment that separates them from departure. Watch how time passes, how they wait for the plane to leave.

Now, *observing* is a bit like what the Inspector does too, this creates an analogy between the Inspector and the actor: both collect clues, carry out investigations that will lead the Inspector to identify the criminal's identity, and the actor to build a character's identity.

The second experience I treasured with the Inspector is the following: the character of the Inspector experiences an internal conflict, a contradiction between the concept of law and his own sense of justice. Where there is law, there is not always justice.

I find this contradiction in many everyday stories that concern me closely, and therefore I have decided to spend and use my own image to support political and social struggles. I also became an activist in my hometown, Taranto, for the environmental issue linked to the Ilva steelwork plant. I am one of the founders, for example, of *Uno Maggio Taranto Libero e Pensante* Festival, which is a musical event using music as a tool to tell certain kinds of stories. Music has always been for me the ideal medium to tell certain kinds of stories, certain kinds of injustices. Music offers us the opportunity to say what we wouldn't be able to say in words.

And it's precisely in Taranto that I was born. I was born on 14 March 1979, I turned 44 two days ago, during the dress rehearsal for this production. Now let's go back nine months before that, to the moment of my conception (I know it's not a beautiful image, but we won't be there for a very long time, I promise) and we get to June 1978. It's during the Football World Cup in Argentina. I did the calculations and the exact day when I was conceived is 10 June 1978, during the match, Italy vs Argentina, 1-0. I'm a romantic kind of guy and I like to think that my parents, following the euphoria of Bettega's goal, celebrated by locking themselves in their room.

Why am I telling you this? Because a while ago – well, it's been a couple of years now – I get this letter by recorded delivery.

Michele shows the audience an envelope.

To: Michele Reondino, Corso Concordia 41, Milan. From: MINISTERIO DE JUSTICIA Y DERECHOS HUMANOS, Avenida Sarmiento 329, Ciudad Autónoma de Buenos Aires, Argentina. I thought: Reondino? Michele Reondino? Misspellings can always happen when typing in haste, but . . .

I open the envelope.

Michele opens the envelope.

I read.

'Dear Mr Reondino, following the resolution issued on 6 October 2021 at the National Commission for Human Rights in Buenos Aires, taken into consideration etc., given the bilateral agreements between the Argentine Republic and the Italian Republic – and a whole series of other articles that we will skip for now . . . where is it? Ah yes, here. Therefore: – the Federal Court has now concluded the re-examination of the reassignment procedure for the flat located in Buenos Aires, Avenida Luis María Campos 726 – 3rd floor. The sentence and relative enforcement will take place within nine months, on a date to be determined, with notification by recorded delivery'.

A telephone number is noted at the bottom of the letter.

I call it.

Once, twice, several times. Nobody answers.

Of course, the first thing I think is that this is a mistake. They spelt my name wrong and mixed me up with someone else. And yet . . . the address of my temporary residence is correct.

Michele pins the letter to the blackboard.

When I receive the letter – this is at the end of November 2021 – I am in Milan working on my film, *Palazzina LAF*. *Palazzina LAF* is the story of collective mobbing, of a special place within a factory: these kinds of places are in dilapidated buildings, sheds inside which are white, bare rooms, without chairs or tables. Some workers are imprisoned there, they're held as prisoners, while they can't do anything . . . A real form of collective mobbing. Usually they are uncomfortable employees, unionized workers, but also managers who oppose the company's internal policies.

In that period I often hook up with one of the screenwriters who is helping me write the film, Davide Carnevali, with whom we built my character, inspired by an informer, a worker who pretended to be a victim and instead spied for the bosses. Davide works at the Piccolo, so we usually meet at the 'Grand'Italia', a restaurant nearby, in via Palermo. I knew that Davide had some familiarity with Argentinian culture: in the past he'd been married to a girl from Buenos Aires and had lived there for a while. So I show him the letter and he offers to help me out.

First of all, he suggests I stop calling the number on the letter, because he says no one will answer: Argentina is even worse than Italy and talking to a public office is practically impossible. Davide sends a WhatsApp message to his ex, who hears from a friend, who calls an acquaintance, who asks his brother-in-law, who has an uncle who works at the Ministry of Justice. I don't speak Spanish, so Davide calls and speaks for me. Finally they answer.

– Bueno, señor Rondino, the letter is for you, there is no mistake – they say from the Ministry.
Rondino? Wasn't it Reondino?
– Bueno, Rondino, Reondino . . . it's the same. If you prefer, I'll call you Reondino, but it sounds to me like a made-up name.
Actually, my name is Riondino.
– So why do you want me to call you Reondino, sorry?
It doesn't matter. Forget it.
What matters, says the guy from the Ministry, is that they're looking for me because of this flat. There are no other heirs.
Whose heirs?
– Of Juan Carlos Rondino.
Look, I don't know any Juan Carlos Rondino, or Reondino, or Riondino.
– In any case, a few months ago the Misiti family requested the opening of a judicial proceeding.
Misiti? Another Italian surname – that's what I think. But that's not what I say. What I say is: what judicial proceeding?

The proceedings concerning the flat in which the kidnapping of Luca Misiti took place, and which was reassigned to Juan Carlos Rondino during the National Reorganization Process.

Music: piece no. 1. The music comes from a piano that isn't yet on stage.

Michele writes on the blackboard the following words: 'National Human Rights Commission', 'Judicial Proceedings', 'Kidnapping', 'National Reorganisation Process'.

2. A New Project

National Commission for Human Rights.

Judicial proceeding.

Kidnapping.

National Reorganization Process.

Suddenly all these words, which until yesterday had nothing to do with me, have come into my life. And I can't get them out of my head; like a piece of music that already sounds familiar to the ear the first time you hear it.

In the evening I call an uncle of mine in Taranto. He's my grandfather's brother, I haven't heard from him for months, because relations with that part of the family aren't exactly idyllic . . . I ask him if we have relatives in Argentina.

Silence.

A silence that I perceive as unnatural.

Why?

I remember that, as a child, my grandfather had told me about two brothers who emigrated to Buenos Aires during the war . . . I prefer not to tell him anything about the letter, the judicial proceedings, the flat.

Until my uncle coughs lightly . . .

Michele coughs, which sounds fake.

. . . Which sounds fake, and he tells me that he doesn't know what happened to them, that he hasn't spoken to his cousin for years, because relations with that part of the family . . . aren't exactly idyllic . . .

I decide I need to know more and start investigating. I do an internet research on immigration to Argentina and the history of the country up to the National Reorganization Process, which is the expression by which the military calls the dictatorship. It is there that I find a page dedicated to Conadep, the National Commission on the Disappearance of Persons. You can look too, it's on Wikipedia.

Michele moves the computer so that the screen can be captured by the video camera.

It seems that in recent years, with the presidencies of Néstor and Cristina Kirchner, and then with Alberto Fernández, many cases have been reopened concerning expropriations of *desaparecidos*' properties, people kidnapped between 1976 and 1983, whose traces have been lost. Political dissidents, uncomfortable journalists but also unionized workers or managers who opposed the government's internal policies. Jews. homosexuals. Unwelcome artists.

In January 2022 I am back in Milan to record the soundtrack of my film and I receive a second letter, this one –

Michele shows a letter. But this time he doesn't read it.

– which states that the sentencing will take place on 10 June 2022. The Commission invites me to be present for the occasion.

There are some photos in the envelope. These.

Music: piece n. 2. It comes from the crate on which a model of the flat will be placed.

Michele takes some photos of the flat out of the envelope. He places them in front of the camera, so that they are visible to the entire audience. At the end, Michele zooms in on a photo of a perfectly tidy flat, as it will appear at the end of the show. However, the image shows a stain where the piano will be located.

At this moment, the stage offers a general feeling of untidiness.

For the first time I see the flat. What strikes me is the tidiness: not one object is out of place. It's weird to imagine that a kidnapping took place here.

Michele distributes the photos to the audience.

The letter concludes by saying that the flat will be available for a visit in the days leading up to the sentence, by appointment and in agreement with the relevant police station.

A few days later Davide and I see each other again at the 'Grand'Italia'. I show him the second letter and the photos. At this point the story is getting interesting not only for me, but for him too: the Piccolo has commissioned him a project for the 2022/23 season, but Davide still doesn't know what to write about. When I show him the letter and the photos, he is convinced that we have the solution to his and my problems.

In February Davide is called in for a meeting with the artistic director of the theatre, to which he presents the project: a documentary play on the Argentinean flat. The project seems interesting to Claudio Longhi and he decides to include this production in the 2022/23 season – the title of which Davide doesn't know yet – with the opening scheduled for 16 March 2023.

Davide and I immediately start working and leave for Buenos Aires.

Michele takes a piano stool out of a crate and places it opposite where the piano will subsequently be located, stage right.

3. Mi Buenos Aires querido

The flight hits a lot of turbulence and I'm restless. So after a few hours I take a sedative pill and finally doze off.

Music: piece n. 3. It comes from the piano, covered by a white sheet, that the technicians have moved in stage left.

I wake up heavy-headed when we're already about to land at Buenos Aires Airport. Below me is the open sea. Then the Atlantic Ocean joins the Río de la Plata. The plane does a half turn to the north and continues its descent. It descends, descends little by little towards the water. I think of the quiet of this great blue expanse, of its beaches, of the tourists who dive into the water. And I imagine my own body diving and letting itself be carried away by the waves of that big river.

In Buenos Aires we rented an Airbnb, not far from the airport. It's nice, but a bit anonymous, artificial . . . you can see that it's designed to be used rather than to be lived in. Cold lights. One wall is taken up by shelves full of books that no one seems to have read. I scroll through the titles, nothing particularly relevant. These books are probably there just to give some colour to the space. As is often the case, the flat doesn't exactly match the photos on the internet. In some places, the signs of a half-finished renovation are still visible. 'It's normal' – says Davide. 'We're in Argentina, they're in a crisis every other week. They must have run out of money.'

I unpack, run a washing machine, arrange my things, trying to recreate a corner of my own home in that strange place.

Michele takes a grey shirt out of a crate and wears it.

The same day we go to the Ministry of Justice, where the uncle of the brother-in-law of the brother of Davide's ex-wife's girlfriend's partner managed to get us an appointment.

The secretary shows us the case files. The name 'Rondino' is written on all of the documents; I point out that it's not my name and she explains that Argentina is a country built on immigration, we Italians should know this well . . . Often in Buenos Aires harbour, with all those people, between those who didn't speak the language and the haste of registration, it could happen that a name would be spelt incorrectly . . . Many Argentine surnames do not really exist: they are Italian surnames that have been misspelt or invented, imagined by those who drafted the reports and inserted them into the archives.

The documents state that the Misiti family has formally requested the reassignment of the flat to them, following the purchase by Mr Juan Carlos Rondino in October 1978. The secretary says she tried to get in touch with the interested party, Juan Carlos Rondino, several times, but never managed to: it appears that he wasn't living at that address.

It seems implausible to me that, with today's technology, no one could find a way to get in touch with this Rondino guy.

And so the woman laughs and says that Argentina is precisely the kind of country where the most implausible things can happen.

And the flat? How did it end up in Rondino's hands? Davide asks.

Expropriated flats were often used as a base for covert operations, or as torture chambers; sometimes they were then resold to private individuals. For profit.

It seems absurd to me that the Misiti family did not report the issue to the police immediately, but the secretary points out that many preferred not to say anything to the police, because it could have been the police itself carrying out the kidnapping. No information was ever provided on the detention and those who went on to complain were always told the same thing:

'This person has never been detained. Their detention is not recorded in this jurisdiction.'

In some cases the families gave up. Better to think they were dead than disappeared. The silence of the dead is different from that of the *desaparecidos*. The silence of the dead is much easier to bear.

Then the secretary opens a box, from which she extracts a model.

This is the model of the flat, on which they studied the case – she says. It makes it easier for investigators and ballistics experts to work.

Ballistics . . .?

A technician takes the model of the stage set from the work table.

I'd seen some photographs, but looking closely at the flat for the first time, even if it's just a reconstruction, has a strange effect. Now it's there, at my fingertips.

I want to touch it, but I only look at it.

With the same curiosity, mixed with fear, with which one observes an exhibit in a museum.

The model is positioned on the crate.

Music: piece no. 4. The music comes from the small piano inside the model of the stage set.

4. A deafening silence

Michele gathers the photos from the audience.

That night, neither Davide nor I can sleep. Davide isn't feeling well and blames his stomach issues on the turbulence of the previous day's flight. I keep looking at the photos of the flat and wonder when they were taken. Why, or for whom, were they taken? How can the tidiness be explained? Was it the agency that put the flat up for sale? Or the police? An unnatural sense of quiet shines through these images. These photos were taken to calm the viewer.

Davide, who was ill all night, needs to rest. I look up the police station on Google Maps and I walk there on my own.

The officer with the keys to the flat is at the door. We shake hands. He is a rough type, in his sixties. He wears a beige cloth jacket, a cream-coloured cotton shirt with a high collar, and a brown tie. We get into the car, an old red Ford with tinted windows, and head to Avenida Luis María Campos 726.

We go up to the 3rd floor and arrive in front of a wooden door; there is no name on the bell. I ask the officer if he's going to stay for the visit.

I already know the flat. Lock up when you're done.

Music: piece no. 5. The music comes from the radio. Virginia removes the white cloth from the piano and drops it on the floor. Little by little, during the show, the white cloth will be stained with red. Virginia opens the window curtains. The stage manager, Eleonora, pushes open the right-hand wall.

Here it is, finally. The flat that until recently I didn't even know existed, that has been building in my imagination through the words of others, photographs, a model . . . it's now a real space, full of objects that bear the mark of real facts.

Michele enters the flat. The flat is upside down. Sheets of paper on the floor. Objects scattered. A washing rack with items of clothing hung to dry.

When the secretary told us about the kidnapping, I'd imagined a messy space, with papers on the floor, scattered objects . . . Instead, the flat is like in the photos: everything is tidy. And it is perhaps that unnatural tidiness that makes me move so cautiously. I have the impression of going into a museum, or of stepping onto a crime scene. From the window I look out towards the street. The officer is smoking, sitting on the bonnet of his car. A note on the fridge reads 'H. M. Central' and a time is marked underneath. Then my attention shifts to the wall on the left. There is a piano. It's the home of a musician.

I approach the piano. It's an Italian piano, a Cherubini. I look at it, in silence. I sit on the stool. But I don't touch the keys, I can't play the piano. I just imagine playing.

Michele imagines playing. He is sitting in front of the stain on the wall. The piano, to the left of the stage, plays on its own. Music: piece no. 6.

The bookshelves are full of books. I scroll through the titles, nothing particularly relevant. I can't see any books on politics or philosophy, I can't see any left-wing authors, nothing like Marx, Engels, Gramsci . . . Nothing suggesting the guy was a subversive type. On the lower shelves, some music scores: Dallapiccola, Scelsi, Petrassi, Castelnuovo . . . Wagner. On the shelf below, all the scores bear the signature of Luca Misiti. I flick through some of them, they are complex. This music sounds contemporary, it doesn't sound like it was composed forty-four years ago.

I sit on the armchair. I stay there, sitting in silence, looking around me. A good ten minutes.

Michele stays there, sitting, silent, looking around him. A good ten seconds.

I lose my sense of space and time, which goes by quickly, as if every minute lasted a second. One last look at the flat. Then I walk out and go back to our Airbnb. When I get home, I knock on Davide's door, but no one answers. He must have fallen asleep.

Michele takes a glass. Then he goes to the tap and turns it on. No water comes out of the tap. But Michele acts as if he were serving himself a glass of water. Music from the radio: piece no. 7.

I turn on the radio, tidy up the house. I look around. Now every detail of this Airbnb reminds me of Misiti's flat, which I visited a few hours ago.

Especially the silence.

Davide once told me that when he first entered his apartment in Buenos Aires, what struck him was the silence. A silence he hadn't encountered before. The silence of those who can't find the words to talk about certain kinds of things.

It's the silence of a voiceless cry.

It's hard to bear.

The music, little by little, transforms into a continuous, persistent sound effect.

It's similar to a voiceless cry.

It's hard to bear.

5. Neighbours

In the morning I find Davide on the sofa. He's had little sleep, keeps being sick and has a high temperature. I offer to get him something from the chemist when I get back.

At the police station, the officer greets me by lifting his eyebrow, lowering his Rayban-style sunglasses, which he holds between the thumb and forefinger of his left hand. When we get into the car I ask him what he knows about Misiti.

Very little. Forty-four years old, comfortable family, secondary education.

Does he have any idea of what happened?

He shrugs. I don't know, this person has never been detained. His detention is not recorded in this jurisdiction.

He parks in front of the house, lights a cigarette and sits on the hood of the Ford Falcon to smoke.

Michele goes to the kitchen tap, serves himself a glass of water from a bottle. He drinks. He moves the curtains to one side and looks out the window. Beyond the window, there is a small model of an Alfa Romeo.

It's strange how today the flat already feels familiar to me. The first thing I do, when I enter, is go to the kitchen to drink a glass of water. I try to imagine how many times Misiti must have done this.

Even my relationship with objects is different: there's more intimacy, more credibility. The piano, for example. Today I get close to it, I touch it. I try to imagine the music Misiti was playing, sitting on that stool. The music he was playing one evening forty-four years ago.

Michele now sits at the kitchen stool and imagines himself as Misiti. It's not him playing, but the piano itself. Music: piece no. 8. Then, suddenly, the music stops.

I try to imagine the words of the police at the time of the break-in. The insults, the shouts, the blows. I wonder if they left any traces, and where these traces may be. Or where they may have been. It seems implausible for me to find them now, forty-four years later. But at that moment the words of the Ministry secretary come to mind: Argentina is precisely the country where the least plausible things can happen.

I go to the bookshelves. I take out Misiti's sheets of music one by one. I flick through the pages nervously. Papers fall down, they scatter on the floor. Among these I find a score in which Misiti's handwriting overlaps a series of annotations in Italian. The name of the author is not Misiti.

It says: Giacomo Schmit.

Silence. Michele freezes. It's like he's seen a ghost. But he speaks as if he were dealing with a real person.

Someone knocks at the door.

Yes?

It's the neighbour.

An elderly woman, with long white hair which may have been blond once. She wears a flowery dress, which gives her a touch of elegance.

Nice to meet you, Michele Riondino.

– I'm the neighbour. I live in the flat below.

Have you been here long?

– A few years.

Did you know the person who lives here?

– No one has ever lived here.

And Mr Riondino?

– You are Mr Riondino. Are you not?

No, the other Mr Riondino. Juan Carlos. Reondino. Sorry, Rondino.

– Riondino, Reondino or Rondino, it's confusing.

Yes, you're right, I'm confused too. It doesn't matter. Do you know him?

– No one has ever lived here. Except ghosts. Ghosts do live in this flat. They walk. They move objects. Sometimes they play the piano. This time yesterday, for example. Yesterday I heard the piano being played.

It was me.

– Do you play the piano?

No . . . I meant: it was me, in the flat. But no one was playing the piano.

The woman stares at me. She then says: I don't know if *anyone* was playing the piano, but I know for a fact that the piano was playing.

I'm not lying to you.

– You are not Mr Riondino.

My name is Michele Riondino, I told you.

– Are you sure?

Yes.

– And why do the initials embroidered on your shirt say D.C. and not M.R.?

Michele coughs lightly, and it sounds fake.

It belongs to a friend of mine, I borrowed it from him – I answer instinctively. It's actually not true. Davide didn't lend me his shirt. I took it from him this morning, without telling him anything. When I was about to go out I noticed that mine had a small hole on the chest. Like a cigarette burn. I changed into the first clean shirt I found on the drying rack.

But the woman doesn't even listen to my answer. She's already gone back to her flat.

Michele takes a shirt from the drying rack and puts it on. It is a cream-coloured, high-necked cotton shirt. It has the initials M.R. sewn on.

My relationship with neighbours has never been idyllic. When I play the guitar, for example . . . sometimes I lose track of space and time. I look at the clock and realize it's late, that it's an inappropriate time to play. Sometimes I think the neighbours are envious, they hate me. It annoys me to think that people so close to me are actually hostile.

I lock up the flat and go out.

Only now do I realize that all this time I have been holding Schmit's music in my hand.

Schmit.

A Jewish musician, evidently. I think of this name, so implausible. Why was he in the middle of Misiti's scores, and not next to the other composers? Did he end up there by mistake? Misiti appears to be so tidy . . . What if he'd been placed there on purpose?

I hide the score under my jacket and, as if seized by a sense of guilt, I greet the officer in a different way. Only by raising my eyebrow.

He reciprocates with the same gesture. He smiles.

And he adds, in a low voice: See you tomorrow, Inspector.

6. Schmit

Tonight Davide's feeling a little better, even if he's very pale and looks like a ghost. He insists on staying up and talking, he's sorry he hasn't come to see the flat yet, he wants to know what it's like, if I've taken photos, video footage . . . The video camera, of course! I left it inside the flat . . . But I show him the score. He's a musician – I tell him. Misiti. A pianist. Davide flicks through the score. He's a writer, he can't read music. He yawns, closes his eyes, doesn't even notice that a newspaper clipping appears among the scores.

Michele shows a newspaper clipping.

He's tired. I let him go to sleep, I open a beer and sit on an armchair to read that newspaper, which seems so old.

Michele goes to the fridge, takes a beer, a Quilmes, and goes to sit on the armchair.

The clipping dates 6th October 1938, from the *Corriere della Sera*.

'The Instituto Nacional de Cine will present a new season dedicated to young Italian composers who have engaged in the creation of soundtracks for cinema and film documentaries. The season will be entitled *Portrait of the artist*. Among invited composers are Mario Castelnuovo, Luigi Dallapiccola, Ettore Feliciani, Giacinto Scelsi, Goffredo Petrassi.'

The article is accompanied by a handwritten note, probably by Misiti. The note says:

'Everything starts with a letter. At the end of November 1937, Schmit – I call him Schmit – received a letter of assignment from the Directorate General for Cinematography. An assignment that could have changed his life. A commission for a documentary soundtrack.

In February 1938 he gets invited to a meeting with the artistic director of the centre, who presents the project to him. A documentary dedicated to young composers who died during the First World War. The intention is to preserve their memory. Schmit seems interested in the project and he immediately gets to work. He writes a piece in ten fragments, which he calls *As a Dead Man*. The debut is scheduled for March 1939, but on that final evening, for the reasons we all know, the work of the Jewish composer will not be performed. The documentary will be presented without a soundtrack.

This is why I want to play *As a Dead Man* here, in Buenos Aires, in such a difficult moment in the country's history. I spoke about my project to the artistic director, but according to him this operation confronts us with a series of ethical questions. Would Schmit have wanted his music to sound like this, as we will play it? Do I, as a composer, lend my voice to the deceased musician, or do I simply replace his music with my own? Does performing his music in public mean preserving his memory, or stealing his life?'.

At the bottom there is a date: 10 June 1978.

It looks like a diary page. The brief engraved at the beginning of the note catches my attention: 'I call him Schmit'. Why would he say 'I call him'? Wasn't Schmit the composer's real name? Was it the pseudonym he had chosen for the project? That most implausible of names, which almost seems invented . . .? A Jewish stage name . . .? A political claim . . .?

I search the internet, but I can't find any work from the 1930s entitled *As a Dead Man*. Searching for 'Giacomo Schmit', however, I find a Wikipedia page of a Schmidt, with a 'd'.

Michele reads from the computer.

'Giacomo Aron Schmidt. Real name of Ettore Feliciani. Composer of Jewish origins born in Milan. He abandoned the Schmidt name to escape the barbarism of the Holocaust. He disappeared in 1941'.

Michele stands up, goes to the blackboard and writes: 'Schmidt', then 'Italy '41'.

What does 'disappeared' mean? 'Died'? 'Vanished'? 'Escaped'? Or simply 'disappeared from the music scene'? Wikipedia gives no other details. It doesn't even say whether Schmidt escaped the Holocaust.

I click on 'Holocaust'. Another page opens and this one, however, is full of details. At the end of the page an acronym catches my attention: N.N. *Nacht und Nebel*. Protocol applied in concentration camps for dissidents and political opponents, on whose detention no information was to be provided to families.

Nacht und Nebel, niemand gleich. It's a line from Wagner's *Rhinegold*.

Michele writes N.N. on the blackboard.

I turn off the computer and try to sleep. But I can't. I imagine the fascist police entering and taking away Feliciani, or Schmit, or Schmidt. I try to imagine the officer's words at the time of the break-in, but I can't find them. It is impossible to imagine them. It's easier to think that they entered in silence, took him in silence and left in silence. Maybe they burned his notes, his books, his scores, and what I have in my hands is the only original left. My thoughts get confused, I no longer know if I'm imagining or dreaming that they load him into a car and take him to the military station, where he is interrogated and tortured. When they take him out he's shaking, he can't stand on his own legs. They put him on a train. The only thing I'm not sure about is whether by then he already knew where that train was going to take him. I wonder if they kept the file of his detention in the concentration camp archives.

I once went to visit Dachau, where a cousin of my grandmother was imprisoned. I was surprised that the original barracks no longer exist. What visitors see is just a reconstruction. And the archives of the police, here, in Argentina . . .? Are those reconstructions too?

There's a knocking at the door.

A technician knocks on the door to the auditorium.

It's Davide.

He wants to come with me, he feels like going out, but he's shaking, can't stand on his own legs, and after 5 minutes I have to take him back to his room. I wonder if I shouldn't take him to the hospital to do some tests, and this thought occupies my mind all the way to the police station.

7. The kidnapping

The third day is the last in which I can visit the flat.

At the door, the officer hands me a file.

– It concerns a person who may be of interest to you, Inspector.

Who? – I ask instinctively.

– Misiti, who else? It arrived this morning. For the judge. Don't worry, it's legal. These documents are not classified, the archives are open to the public. I made a copy for you.

We don't talk on the way. I look out the window. I try to imagine Buenos Aires in the late seventies. I try to imagine the sounds, the languages, people's gestures, but I can't.

I find the caretaker at the front door of the flat. It's the first time we meet, but he greets me warmly, as if I'd always lived here. The first thing I ask him is what he knows about Misiti. The officer next to me looks away, while the caretaker leaves a moment of silence between my question and his answer, which I perceive as unnatural.

Michele coughs lightly.

– Very little. Forty-four years old, comfortable family, secondary education. Nothing that suggested a dissident or a political opponent.

So why?

He shrugs. – It could have been a mistake. Sometimes the police were given an address but then went from door to door. Maybe he wasn't the person they were looking for that evening. Maybe they were looking for the neighbour. Maybe it was the neighbour herself who reported him. A quarrel, some envy . . . Maybe Misiti played the piano at inappropriate hours of the night . . .

I shrug. He's a musician – and I no longer know if I say this or think it. Only a musician can understand another musician.

Then the same identical actions unfold like in the previous days: I go to the kitchen, drink a glass of water . . .

Michele opens a kitchen drawer, finds a bullet. He puts it in his pocket.

. . . look out the window and see the dark red Ford Falcon parked in front of the house. I sit down on the armchair and open the file. Photocopies of documents, a passport, the flat's land registry title. Photos. The same photos they sent me from the Ministry. A typed document. It's the kidnapping report.

Michele sits in an armchair and reads. Music: piece no. 10. The piano plays by itself.

'The break-in took place on 10 June 1978. To get in, we wait for 8pm, when the football match Italy vs Argentina is underway, a qualifier to access to the final phase of the World Cup. This way, no one would notice noises and shouts. In previous days we studied the layout of the space thanks to a series of photographs of the flat, which allowed us to build a model through which we prepared the operation down to the smallest detail. We monitor the subject's movements thanks to a voice recorder hidden under the desk; a spy camera positioned inside a volume on the bookshelves, connected to two monitors located at the military station; and a bug microphone attached to the body of an informer, who has free access to the entire building. Today is the third stakeout day. The same identical actions unfolded like in the previous days: the door opened, Misiti went into the flat, went to the kitchen, drank a glass of water, went to the window, looked at the street. He would sit at the piano, open a score and play. From the street we could hear the music. At the moment of the break-in, we cut off the electricity'.

The lights go off. Michele stops reading.

My vision blurs, I feel a pain in my chest, I can't continue. It's the fear. I try to imagine myself in this flat forty-four years ago. I try to imagine someone here, forty-four years from now, reading a file about me. How would I feel if someone reached into my clothes, read my notes, touched my things? How would I feel if I knew I was in front of a camera that was secretly filming me? There are no words, to talk about these kinds of things.

Michele remains in silence. He scrolls the text in front of the camera. The text scrolling is projected on screen.

'We get in with the keys given to us by the caretaker. The flat is on the third floor, left-hand door. We break in. Misiti is wearing a cream-colored cotton shirt with a high collar. That evening he's not alone. With him is a woman with long, blond hair, a flowered dress. Misiti is at the piano, the woman is smoking, on an armchair. I shoot, the shot passes between the two subjects, pierces the curtain and gets stuck on the wall to the left of the piano. The music stops abruptly'.

The music from the piano suddenly stops. Silence. During the silence, the projection ends.

I need a break.

Michele has a beer.

I close the file. I can't see any bullet marks on the wall. Of course, someone could have repainted the wall. Or the officer who filed the report may have lied. Things could have gone another way. Perhaps Misiti and the woman resisted. Maybe Misiti had a gun in his desk drawer. There could have been signs of a struggle, overturned furniture, scattered objects, papers on the floor. Perhaps the flat was turned upside down, and only later tidied up. To leave no traces.

I go to the piano, I notice a strange mark on the timber varnish, I knock on that spot, it sounds strange, I open the piano case and inside I find some books.

Michele opens a trap door under the floor and takes some books out. He then leaves them on the desk.

Left-wing writers. Marx, Engels, Gramsci . . . I'm looking to see if there's more, and yes, there's more. A gun. A loader. I take a bullet between the thumb and forefinger of my left hand.

Michele tidies up the carpet.

I open the door and behind the door I find the caretaker. Were you spying on me?

– I was just cleaning, tidying up.

I invite him to enter. He accepts. Instinctively he goes to the window.

– Do you know who he is? – he asks, pointing to the Ford Falcon.

A police officer. He has the keys to the flat.

– That one worked with the military.

Was it the military who took Misiti away?

Silence. A silence that I perceive as unnatural.

The caretaker is about to leave. But before he leaves, I ask him again, point blank: Do you know anything about Rondino?

Another moment of silence. But this time I don't perceive it as unnatural.

– Rondino who?

Juan Carlos Rondino, the guy who moved here after the kidnapping.

– I don't know any Rondinos and no one has ever moved into this building in the last forty-four years.

– And the neighbour, then? She told me she's only lived here for a few years.

He shrugs. – Often people need to lie in order to continue living. Especially those who still bear the scars of the consequences.

What does he mean by 'consequences'? Signs of torture? Was it her who spoke, who betrayed Misiti? Was she the woman who was with him that night? But I don't say any of these things, I only think about them. It's not easy to find the words to talk about certain kinds of things.

– Are you an Inspector?

Excuse me?

– Why are you asking me all these questions? What's this? Is it an investigation? Who are you?

Me? No, I . . . I'm just an actor.

Michele takes a few photos with his smartphone.

I take a last look at the home. And I think that in all this time I have forgotten Juan Carlos Rondino and have always dealt with Misiti. I identified with him, with his story. Perhaps because Misiti is a much more interesting character than Rondino. Everything about the latter, starting from his name, seems implausible.

Has Rondino ever lived here? When he bought the home, did he know that it had been expropriated from a *desaparecido*? Perhaps Rondino was one of the officers who took Misiti away? Or maybe he was a friend of Misiti, and he bought the apartment just to wait for him to come home? Maybe Misiti came back, maybe he continued to live here . . . Or maybe the person who lived here, and still lives here, is his ghost . . .?

Silence.

Too many questions and too complex for a documentary. But this is precisely the point: complex questions force you to seek complex answers, to question things and question yourself, to investigate . . . Isn't this our job?

I take some photos with my mobile phone, and send them to Davide. Then I light a cigarette and go downstairs.

I sit on the bonnet of the Ford Falcon. The officer also lights a cigarette. We smoke, in silence. For a moment I imagine this man forty-four years ago. A shiver runs down my spine. I put out the fag without thinking about it, on the hood of the car, ruined by time. Under the red paint, you can see the old enamel of the outer shell, of a dark green colour.

– In the car, Inspector.

I get in the car. The officer takes me away from the place that now feels a bit like my home, even if it isn't.

8. The pain of others

The technicians move the piano inside the flat. The wall with the blackboard is pushed open.

The next morning I find a note on the fridge. Davide has been taken to the Hospital Militar Central, the visiting hours are indicated below. I go to and visit him. I look up the address on Google Maps: the hospital is located near the Bosque de Palermo, not far from our Airbnb and the airport. I make my way there.

Davide is not in the room, but his ex-wife is there. She's more or less my age, with long blond hair, a flowery dress, which gives her a touch of elegance. In excellent Italian, she tells me that her grandfather was from Taranto. He was Jewish, and together with his brother he had been sent to Argentina during the Second World War.

She asks me what these days have been like, whether I found out what happened to Misiti.

I shrug.

She explains to me that the most common thing would have been for him to be taken from his home, loaded into a car and brought to the airport. The airport sheds were used as concentration camps, detention and torture centres: white, bare rooms in which the detainees were held, waiting, without being able to do anything. Then they were loaded onto a plane. The detainees were told that they would be taken to hospital for checks. The planes took off from the river bank, reached high altitude, made a half circle to the south. Then, when they got to the open sea, the convicts were dropped into the water.

Alive?

– Yes.

Conscious?

– Sometimes they knocked them off with sedative pills. At least that's what the autopsies say, which were carried out on the bodies that were found. Some corpses washed up on the beaches pushed by the waves, but most were eaten by fish. In any case, when a body appeared, it was not identified. An acronym was written on the register. *N.N. Nomen Nescio.* Unknown name.

And the files, the documents . . .?

– There was no documentation. Often false files were created, a false report was drawn up to reassure the families.

Silence. A silence that's difficult to bear.

Then a doctor advises us that we can see Davide. He struggles to speak, but he insists on discussing some important things before starting to work on the text.

We talk about the people I met, and that Davide was not able to get to know personally. Of the effort he will have to make to imagine. To imagine their gestures, their words. But above all we talk about the point of view from which the story of Misiti must be told. What right do we have to hypothesize about a past of which we know next to nothing? All of this confronts us with a series of ethical questions: would Misiti have wanted his music to sound the way we'll play it? Do I, as an actor, lend my body to the deceased musician, or do I simply replace his body with my own? Does my presence in front of the audience mean preserving his memory or appropriating it?

I have the impression that all these questions will not be answered.

Michele coughs lightly. Then goes to the blackboard. He recaps dates and events.

These seem to me a good starting point for our story. An Argentinian composer who disappears during the military dictatorship, while he works on the scores of an Italian Jewish composer who disappeared during the fascist dictatorship. In 1978 Misiti is forty-four years old. Let's assume that Schmit, in 1941, is also forty-four years old.

Davide thinks about it. – Too banal, he says.

What if . . . – says Davide, after a beat. What if instead Misiti wasn't working on the music of this deceased composer, but he had decided to appropriate it . . .? It's not a nice image, I know, but let's imagine that one day, during a trip to Italy, he discovers the scores of an opera entitled *As a Dead Man* in a flea market. He comes home, plays it, he likes it. He does some research but finds no news on that work, which evidently has never been performed in public. But he comes across an old article in the *Corriere della Sera* that can be useful to him. He invents the name Schmidt, but since he's Argentinian, he misspells a letter and omits the 'd'. Then he spreads the rumour that it's a Jewish composer who disappeared during Fascism, perhaps to make his story more plausible and attractive to the eyes of the director of the Instituto Nacional de Cine in Buenos Aires.

But there's a Wikipedia page on Schmidt.

– Anyone could have written that.

I don't say it, but I don't think so. I don't think Misiti made anything up, I think Misiti really wanted to save Schmit's music. This may all still be true.

Or perhaps I simply *choose* to believe that all of this is true.

Michele sits at the piano and plays Schmit's score. Music: piece no. 11. The piano is playing. But, for the first time, Michele really appears to be a musician.

The technicians and assistant director enter. They're now wearing jackets with a tag over their black t-shirts, similar to those of museum keepers. They place the crates that are on the stage in their allocated spot, turning them into pedestals for an exhibition, on which the following objects are displayed: a Quilmes beer bottle and a glass; an ashtray with a cigarette butt; a guitar.

A pedestal remains empty, waiting for the bullet to be placed there.

Some areas of the stage space are taped off, so the audience will not be able to access them.

When they're done, a technician takes some beers out of the fridge for everyone. The fridge remains empty.

The technicians and the assistant director attend the end of the concert.

9. The Trial

Michele reads the script.

'Good evening, everyone, and welcome. First of all I would like to thank you for being here. Thank you also on behalf of those who are not present, on behalf of those who unfortunately cannot be with us today. I'm going to take a few minutes to explain briefly why we're here and what's going to happen now. It's not easy to find the words. It's not easy for me, because normally my job is to bring before you a text that has already been written, while what I'm saying now, I'm saying spontaneously and informally. And also, the fact that I am here today in this hall so steeped in history binds me to an even greater responsibility as a judge. This hall which, as you may know, was once a military station, a place of detention and torture.

Please come closer. Don't be afraid. I know it's an unusual gesture, but I would like a relationship of trust to be created between us. For this reason, I ask you to get up from your seats and come here, where I am. I invite you to occupy this space. From now on, I would like you to use it for what it is: a public space; a space where you, the audience, can move freely.

Michele invites the audience to get up and join him inside the set. Among them is also Misiti who, at a given moment, as if by chance, goes to sit on the piano. Michele shows the script.

What you see here is the reconstruction of the flat that is the object of this judicial proceeding. I would like you to look closely. We have become so accustomed to hearing about the dictatorship and state violence, seeing certain kinds of photographs, certain kinds of videos, that we have become numb to words and images . . . But if we can enter a real place, to feel that real events happened there, then that's another thing. This should be the purpose of the opportunity like today's hearing.

I'll be brief, because we don't have much time left.

This court has ruled that the flat located in Buenos Aires, Avenida Luis María Campos 726, third floor, revert to the Misiti family for their private use. However, the family has informed the relevant authorities that their wish is for the flat to become open to the public, as a museum and place of historical memory'.

The reading of the sentence featured these words, which are so implausible in a similar context. I got the tribunal to give me a copy.

A technician joins Michele at the technicians' worktable.

Then the judge brings in a technician, who illustrates the plan of the house museum. A partial renovation of the flat will be carried out and some walls will be knocked down to improve visibility and circulation in the space. And on a large screen located in the upper part of the room, a fragment of a documentary will be projected, with original music by Misiti, in which the original kidnapping report will be made public for the first time. By the exit, a sound installation will be presented with Misiti's voice, recorded by the bug microphone on 10 June 1978.

The sentence doesn't surprise me. What surprises me is not seeing Misiti's family. But I get it. I can understand the pain of reopening wounds that one thought were healed. Although, probably, a wound of this kind never completely heals.

After the sentence is read, I go and shake the judge's hand.

He tells me that he is happy that a flat in such a touristy area as the Palermo district is open to the public as a museum and not as an Airbnb. Then he comments on the improvement of the situation over the past forty-four years, sure of the fact that certain errors of history will never repeat themselves.

Behind him, the officer greets me by raising an eyebrow. I withdraw my hand.

The airport looks different to me today. Hostile. At the security checkpoints they inspect my documents and my luggage. They ask me the reason for my visit.

A trial – I answer. A case related to the dictatorship.

They take me out of line and into a white, bare room. There an officer opens my suitcases, reaches into my clothes, reads my notes, touches my things. He takes my phone. He asks why I have a camera with me. I explain that I'm shooting a documentary for a show. They consult with each other for a time that seems interminable to me and I'm afraid of missing my flight. I'm there, like a prisoner, I feel I can't do anything. I can just wait. Finally they tell me that everything is fine and let me go. When I go out, a shiver runs down my spine, I realize I'm shaking, I can hardly stand on my own legs. I take the suitcases without looking at the officers in the eyes and I never turn back. I'm already at the gate, when I realize that my camera is not in the luggage. And neither is my computer. And that the photos on my phone have been deleted.

As you know, our original intention was to make a documentary theatre show about this story. But due to the confiscation of all the video material we shot, we had to give up. For this reason we asked a set designer, Charlotte Pistorius, to recreate Luca Misiti's flat here, based on the few photos I had already sent to Davide from my smartphone. Unfortunately, it was not possible to trace all the details from the photos. This is why the reconstruction was only partially possible.

I only managed to take one thing from the flat. And it's the only real object within this reconstruction.

Michele holds a bullet between his left hand thumb and forefinger. He places the bullet on the relevant display crate. Music plays on the radio: piece no. 12.

As my plane takes off, I watch the Río de la Plata join the Atlantic Ocean. The plane makes a half turn to the south and continues to go up. It goes up and up little by little, moving away from the water. I think about everything that has happened these days. I think of Schmit, Misiti, Rondino, of all these names . . . I think of my surname: Riondino . . . Río . . . Onde . . . Waves . . . I think of the quiet of this great blue expanse, of its beaches, of the tourists who dive in. And I imagine my body falling, descending fast, then faster and faster, until it hits the surface of the water. My body immersing itself and letting itself be carried away by the waves of that great river.

Blackout. Claps.

10. Epilogue. Portrait of the Artist as a Dead Man.

The lights come on. Virginia, the assistant director, enters with a microphone. She has long, blonde hair. She is wearing a floral dress, which confers a certain air of elegance.

Good evening. The artistic director of the Piccolo Teatro asked me to read this message.

'After Davide's passing, we have been wondering for a long time whether this show should be staged or not. However, everything had already been set in motion because of a co-production with the Théâtre de Liège, the Comédie de Caen and the Comédie de Reims. So, the director of this theatre, Claudio Longhi, asked Michele to finish what Davide was writing; and to me, Virginia Landi, as assistant director, to finish the show.

First we decided to change some of the details: for example, the Argentinian police officer's car was not a Ford Falcon; however, the dark green Falcon is a model that was widely used by the military police during the dictatorship. In reality, the car they drove around Buenos Aires was a modern Alfa Romeo. And Misiti's books were hidden in a trap door in the floor, and not in the piano, it's a detail we changed because we wanted the story to be more credible.

However, we kept most of the music. This is a show about narratives and language. On the possibility and resistance of language to discuss certain topics. We thought that music somehow offered us the opportunity to say what we couldn't put into words. Or that we were unable to say.

So for example, in the scene with the neighbour, we have replaced the moment when she shows us the signs of torture on her body with some music. We preferred not to include this part, because we felt that showing a real wound in the context of a fictional story would not have done justice to the fact.

This is also the reason why we decided, after a long discussion with the production manager, Alberto Benedetto, not to present this show at the Teatro Grassi, where it was originally planned. As you may know, between 1943 and 1945, a fascist military station named after Ettore Muti was established at number 10, via Rovello. It would not have been fair to build a fiction that deals with violence and dictatorship in this hall so steeped in history, which in the past had been a detention and torture centre.

The problem remained of how to end this story. Davide's proposed ending for the show was Luca Misiti playing his last concert on the piano, with Michele accompanying him on the guitar. A very poetic ending, but implausible. Thus, as a tribute to the dead author, we decided to end the show a note that Michele found in Davide's flat:

Michele moves within the set as if it were Davide's flat. On the desk there are notes, notebooks, some books, cigarettes, an ashtray, the usual pizza box, a packet of sedative pills. A script.

On the desk, notes, notebooks . . . some books on philosophy and politics – mostly left-wing authors . . . Marx, Engels, Gramsci . . . – a score, sedative pills. A script.

Michele opens the desk drawer. In the drawer there is a gun. Michele says nothing.

On the wall to the left, a blackboard full of dates and annotations, the kind that Davide often used when he was tidying up a story that was too complex. There I found this note, which says:

Virginia takes a note from the blackboard and gives it to Michele who reads it.

'The kidnapping of Misiti never took place. Misiti pretended to have been kidnapped in order to disappear and operate more freely as a clandestine man, so as not to create problems for his family and friends. The name Rondino, so implausible, is the alter-ego under which Luca Misiti hid. He spent the rest of his life pretending to be another person. An imaginary character.'

There is no date at the bottom of the page.

A reassuring finale.

Which for sure doesn't do justice to the real facts.

Although I'd like to think that Luca Misiti isn't dead.

That he's still alive.

And that he's here tonight.

Among us.

To play.

Michele coughs lightly, which sounds fake.

Unfortunately this is not the case.

All of this is probably just what Davide would have wished for.

All of this is probably just another invention of the author.

Sitting at the piano, a young man from the audience starts to play. Virginia sits on an armchair.

Michele takes his guitar from the display, connects it to the amplifier and accompanies Misiti in his last concert.

What happens next

As they exit the auditorium, the audience will find a display with a replica of the bullet that the actor showed the audience during the show.

The plaque on the display says:

'9 calibre bullet for semi-automatic Browning GP-35.

Manufacturing period: ~~*National Reorganization Process*~~ *Argentinian Military Dictatorship: 1976–1983.'*

At the exit, the theatre staff wear jackets with tags, similar to those of museum keepers.

They are, in effect, the keepers of a place of historical memory.

Gentleman Anne: Diary of a Seductress

Gentleman Anne: Diario di una seduttrice

By Magdalena Barile

Translated by Margherita Laera

First staged at the Teatro Filodrammatici, Lecite/visioni Festival, Milan, on 22 May 2021.

Characters

Today
Anna, 45-50 years old, Professor of English Literature.
Jo, 20-25, student.

1832
Anne Lister, 40 years old, an aristocratic woman.
Miss Ann Walker, 30 years old, an aristocratic woman.

I

Today. Not necessarily in England.

The living room of a large and imposing bourgeois house where renovations are underway. Some furniture is covered with fabric sheets. Some boxes full of books are scattered around.

A window overlooks the garden of the house.

Anna *contemplates the space around her. She sips a cup of tea.*

She starts putting a big pile of books in a trunk.

The doorbell rings.

Anna *leaves the room to go to the front door.*

Anna (VO) Who is it?

Jo (VO) It's me, Professor. I'm really sorry.

Anna (VO) You're early.

Jo (VO) I know, I know, I've just finished my shift in the workshop now and it's about to rain. I can come back later if you want . . .

Anna (VO) No, that's fine, it's just that I was expecting you in two hours, I was going to do some work . . . but come in, please . . .

Anna *enters the room followed by* **Jo**. **Jo** *is wearing a headband and a mechanic workwear overall.*

Anna Come in.

Jo I'm still all mucky, I'm sorry, but if I went home to change – I live fucking miles away, excuse my French, Professor – I would not have arrived in time.

Anna Would you like to go freshen up?

Jo (*she doesn't understand*) How do you mean?

Anna I just meant if you needed to use the bathroom . . .

Jo Ah no, that's very kind, not now, maybe later. Sorry for the invasion. I'll just steal five minutes of your time.

Anna If you don't mind, I'll finish putting these away.

Jo Need help?

Anna Thank you.

Jo *helps* **Anna** *put some books in a trunk.*

Jo (*she looks around*) There's a lot of stuff going on here. Are you refurbishing the house?

Anna Upstairs. We are expanding the library. The idea is to build a kind of Norman tower. Utter madness.

Jo Must be a lot of books. Your husband's the publisher, isn't he?

Anna *closes the trunk with a thud.*

Anna Would you like a cup of tea?

Jo Yes please.

Anna *goes out,* **Jo** *stays snooping around. She wipes her greasy hands on one of the furniture cover sheets.*

Anna (V.O.) Sugar?

Jo Four please.

Anna Four?! My goodness.

Anna *comes back with a cup of tea. She hands the cup to* **Jo**. *She sits down.*

Jo (*like a raging river*) Here you are, Professor, just like I picture you, stunning, in this smashing house surrounded by works of art, books and the rest of it. So full of inspiration. I'm sure that from this place it's easy for you to acknowledge an existence that goes beyond ourselves. From my garage it's more difficult, but I try. Because what would be the fucking point, Professor, if *this* was all? When I read the words that others have written before, especially women, I feel that my disasters – did you know my parents died in an accident when I was two? And it's not like there were grandparents, uncles, cousins, there wasn't a bloody soul, but I'm not here to feel sorry for myself, eh, I won't be the first or the last to start uphill – and this sense of sisterhood is the reason why I became a writer. If these authors had not written before me about their bloody miseries, the world would be a hostile and indifferent place. My love of literature is like an underground rock, deep and eternal, it is an inexhaustible diamond mine – it is my very being, so please don't tell me to flush my thesis down the toilet because it would be like telling me to cut off my own arm. Are you going to do that?

Anna The thesis is good. There are just a couple of things that are, how shall I put it, your own arguments, I know, but they are unfounded. They are inventions. I found them entertaining but . . .

Jo (*frowns*) Entertaining?

Anna In the sense of intellectually lively. If I said something that offended you /

Jo (*offended*) My arguments are well founded, Professor.

Anna On the fantasies of a passionate reader, of course, but you lack a sense of perspective. You cannot make certain comparisons and if the interested parties were still alive, you would have to deal with a lot of complaints.

Jo You are still alive. Do you want to sue me?

Anna (*ironically*) I have better things to do. But you can't publish what you wrote. You say you discovered the true literary genius of the 19th century: that money-obsessed cow! What's her name?

Jo Anne Lister!

Anna Anne Lister. Is this a joke!?

Jo Never been more serious.

Anna And then there's what you say about the Brontë sisters. Mine is a literature course, we don't invent writers' biographies, we just study their work.

Jo I have studied their work. And I also read your books, Professor. I've read them all. When will you write a new one?

Anna Who knows . . .

Jo The one I loved the most is the one on *Wuthering Heights*.

Anna *On the Moor*.

Jo That book changed my life.

Anna It's not what you wrote in your thesis. At one point you even accuse me of crafting stuffy romantic imagery.

Jo Nobody made me love nineteenth-century Romantic authors like you did. Fairies, spirits, immortal love that goes beyond time and space . . . I must have read it a hundred times.

Anna No less.

Jo I always carry it with me.

Jo *takes the book from her backpack.*

Anna The first edition. (*Sees the book.*) On the cover there's a collage of mine of the Brontë portrait that is at the National Portrait Gallery. (*Curious.*) Did you get it from the library?

Jo Three years ago, I never returned it. I should have, I know, but I couldn't do it. Inside it I found a treasure. I would never come here to criticize your book. I started from here to do my own research. It is you who encouraged us to think for ourselves.

Anna With your head and with reliable sources.

Jo I'm not inventing anything. (*Points to the book.*) You were the first to point out that in nineteenth-century England many women were fond of honey pots.

Anna Honey pots?!

Jo Fanny, pussy, enchanted bush . . .

Anna I know what you're referring to. But I don't think I wrote that.

Jo You wrote it between the lines.

Anna (*amused*) So I was the one who inspired your lesbian conspiracy theories? This is priceless.

Jo I went to the bottom of it as you'd awakened my imagination.

Anna One cannot write what one likes only to be original at all costs.

Jo There are documents that prove it.

Anna Not in a million years! I'm sorry, but the Brontë sisters were not '*all lesbians.*'

Jo That's just the title. Maybe it's a little bit too much, I can change it. In fact, out of five sisters, I'm only sure about Charlotte and Emily, who were one hundred percent lesbians. I'm not so sure about Anne. And two died too young to find out.

Anna What nonsense.

Jo Both *Wuthering Heights* and *Jane Eyre* were signed with male pseudonyms.

Anna To get published, like many other writers before and after them. It has nothing to do with their sexual orientation.

Jo Their father made them study like boys and fed their minds more than their vanity.

Anna They were poor, they lived isolated, their only wealth was a good education.

Jo It was not poverty, but their will not to submit to the male oppressor, that drove them closer to literature.

Anna Are you suggesting that at that time only lesbians were able to read and write? This is reverse discrimination.

Jo I didn't say that, but women who were less interested in having a family certainly had more time to study. You wrote that, at that time, deep female friendships often stemmed from the patriarchal prohibition of having a body under those absurd, huge dresses.

Anna I don't think I've ever used the phrase 'absurd huge dresses'. I was speaking of close and deep friendships, of long written correspondences, not of sex, which you go on a bit too much about in your thesis.

Jo Charlotte Brontë, in a letter to her friend Ellen, tells her that she would like to set up a household together and writes to her, exact words, *if I had been born a man you would be my wife.*

Anna So what?! Isn't it a game we all play, to imagine other lives? To live inside other bodies? Do these words unveil Charlotte Brontë as a lesbian or rather show that she had the freedom of a poet? Of course, as a woman of her time she couldn't have married whoever she wanted so she imagined herself as a man to do what she liked.

Jo Exactly! You're following me now! And I think I have a lot of elements to believe that Jane Austen was a trans woman and Lord Byron a crossdresser.

Anna Sure, right. And Virginia Woolf was a man.

Jo I've always thought she wrote like a man.

Anna Me too. But don't tell anyone, they might kick me out of the English Department.

Jo I made you laugh! You know you have a smile that lights up the whole room, has anyone ever told you?

Anna (*she still smiles*)

Beat.

Jo Want to know what part I love the most about *On the Moor*?

Anna Which one?

Jo *opens the book.*

Jo The dedication that you write on the first page.

(*Reads.*) To V., who has been me more than I have ever been myself.

That's beautiful. Who is V.?

Anna (*she hasn't heard, or pretends*) What?

Jo Who is V.?

Anna It's none of your business.

Jo It's not gossip, this is literature. You can tell me . . .

Anna An ex /

Jo / I knew it!

Anna . . . student. A former student. What did you know?

Jo No, I mean, you seem like a woman who has tried a bit of everything.

Anna Meaning?

Jo You know . . . A little bit of this, a little bit of that.

Anna She was a student of my first literature course.

Jo (*disappointed*) Only a student.

Anna Why would I lie? She'd helped me a lot with research.

Jo And so you dedicated your first passionate book, *On the Moor*, to one of your students?

Anna (*impatiently*) Mary-Joan, please, I don't have all day. I have to get back to work soon.

Jo Jo! I wrote it on the essay too. Jo! Nobody calls me that horrible name, only the fucking nuns. I hate it. My name is Jo.

Anna Jo.

Jo After Jo of *Little Women*. Who was your favourite little woman, Professor?

Anna Let's go back to your thesis.

Jo You've gone icy cold now. I'm sorry, don't hate me because I asked you about your friend. I wanted to find out if I'd ever have a chance.

Anna (*colloquial*) Gotcha.

Jo Ok. Ok. Last thing and then let's talk about the thesis. When I graduate, you'll have a drink with me, won't you?

Anna (*looks at her watch*) I don't think so.

Jo Not just with me. Someone else on the course too. Even men if you like them so much. You choose, I can't tell them apart, they all look the same to me.

Anna What nonsense.

Jo I do like nonsense, Professor. But if you're too busy between now and summer . . . with the publishing house and the Norman tower, I understand. You could change your mind at some point. Mind you, I would pick you up in my motorbike.

Anna (*ironically*) Is that a threat?

Jo I'm building one with my own hands, with the pieces I've found in the garage. Do you like motorbikes?

Anna Not my cup of tea.

Jo I actually think you'd have the time of your life.

***Sound of thunder.* Jo** *goes to the window.*

Jo I love storms. I would like to dedicate my thesis to all lost souls, those who can't find peace and run at breakneck speed through storms across the moor.

Anna Better get down to rewriting it before you think about the dedication.

Jo Oh, I forgot. I brought you some heather. Like in *On the Moor.* (*She takes some flowers out of her pocket.*) Sorry it's a bit squashed up.

Anna (*surprised*) Thank you.

Jo I made you laugh again. You're no longer mad at me. Thank you.

Anna *sniffs the flowers.*

Jo How I'd like to be that heather right now.

Anna *puts the flowers back on the table.*

Jo You're right, we will never know if Charlotte Brontë got laid with other women and we certainly have no proof. The only thing we know is that the Brontë sisters, with their stuffy soft lesbian romance, were wiped out by the hurricane Anne Lister.

Anne (*ironically*) Ah, here we are with your favourite topic again, the queen of lesbians: Anne Lister, a misunderstood genius. Don't go telling me that this bumpkin is the greatest writer of the 19th century!

Jo None of that pathetic symmetrical bewilderment the Brontës wrote about. With Lister, reality comes onstage and gets its hands dirty.

Anna And here, my dear, is where your thesis cracks and finally breaks. The only thing the Brontë sisters and Lister have in common is the Yorkshire region where they lived.

Jo Surely they would have met. Think about it, Professor. Charlotte taught at the school near Lister's estate. They knew each other, I swear. Someone like Lister certainly did not go unnoticed.

Anna Charlotte Brontë was a great writer, Anne Lister was not. You cannot compare the two.

Jo I don't compare them. I put Lister above all of them. Professor, Anne Lister is a true visionary. More than Brontë, more than Lord Byron. First of all, she wasn't a repressed lesbian. She always dressed in black, a true butch, and no woman ever rejected her. In a world where no one knew who Sappho was, she had more flings than Don Giovanni.

Anna A nineteenth-century lesbian who became famous because they found her saucy diaries. I recognize that it may be seen as a curious social phenomenon. Maybe a good topic for a course in Gender Studies, but to compare her to the immortal writers of my literature course . . .

If that butch is a writer, I may as well be Sir Charles Dickens.

II

DIARY OF ANNE LISTER

Anne Lister (VO)
1832, Yorkshire. Shibden Hall Estate.

My family took over Shibden Hall in the 15th century through marriage. The Listers' magnificent brick mansion stands on a rise in what is known as the backbone of England. The landed aristocracy is still the backbone of this country. May Heavens save us from plebeian rule. Our social system has changed in an unlikely manner. The working classes spend more time in radical meetings and breweries than at work. There's a deep feeling of hostility against traditional values of the past that is very difficult for me to accept. What was once sacred is no longer so, and by sacred I obviously mean the privileges of my class. With these unknowns, only a new marriage can secure the inheritance of my ancestors. The object of my desires has an income of at least three thousand pounds a year or so. She has the money and this can make up for her slightly lower rank. The lady in question still has no idea what I have in mind.

We'll see.

Anne Lister's *room.*

Anne Lister *and* **Miss Walker** *are in* **Anne**'s *room.* **Miss Walker** *is under a blanket.* **Anne Lister** *writes her diary.*

Anne (*aside*)   I truly and exclusively love women and women love me; my heart disdains any other love. Last night I looked at her queer and played with it gently. She appeared tolerably satisfied. She now seems very fond of me, during the day she is very reserved but at night she is sufficiently on the affectionate side.

Miss Walker (*calls her*)   Anne?

Anne   . . . and I'm truly confident I shall be satisfied with her very soon too.

Miss Walker (*calls her again*)   Anne?

Anne   . . . and I sincerely hope that we shall get on very well together.

Miss Walker   Oh, Anne! Come here! Come close, very close.

Anne   I can't today, Adny. My cousin's come for a visit.

Miss W   What a funny way to express yourself – your cousin!

Anne   My cousin arrives punctually every twenty-eight days. A very unfortunate inconvenience that I cannot oppose for all my good education . . . but God knows how gladly I would send her back and leave the burden of bleeding from below to others. In return, I would inflict myself a more honourable wound than that.

Miss W   If I could bleed for you in those days, I would. I would, do you believe me?

Anne   I will hold your offer in strong consideration, my dear, whenever the opportunity might arise. On those days it's best to eat ox liver.

Miss W   What is it you're constantly writing?

Anne   I write what I live and I live what I write.

Miss W   Sometimes I worry that you might write about other women.

Anne   What other women, Adny?

Miss W   Liar.

Anne (*aside*)   If I met someone I was really rather fond of, I think I would regret having committed myself. I like women, they've always liked me. No woman has ever turned me down.

Miss W   I have to confess something, Anne. Don't be angry at me. One day I found your diary, it was open, I didn't want to read it, but then . . . I wouldn't have looked at it if my attention hadn't been attracted by an incomprehensible language . . . is it possible, I said to myself, are you writing in Greek or Aramaic?

Anne   I should whip you for this indiscretion.

Miss W   I have not read anything and I have not understood what I read.

Anne It is a code of my own invention. An encrypted language.

Miss W A secret alphabet! To escape my understanding?

Anne I don't write for you, my dear. A diary is written for oneself, to put the mind in order. But what is written here could confuse the minds of curious onlookers, so I take precautions.

Miss W Whose mind should you confuse? You're boasting about your mistresses in there. You're lying.

Anne I'm not lying. I write about philosophy, anatomy and mineralogy. You know that I'm interested in these disciplines and my studies are also pioneering in the field of hydraulics.

Miss W What about Mariana?

Anne Your usual preconceptions. Mariana . . . What nonsense.

(*Aside*.) Mariana, my love, first thought in the morning and last before going to sleep. Let me be yours alone, at least as long as it makes you happy that I should be. But the moment you should no longer reciprocate, I shall disappear immediately and you shall never hear from me again. But I shall never belong to anyone else.

Miss W You were close friends with her growing up. Don't deny it.

Anne We were always legitimate friends, we only shared a bed once, in an inn out of necessity – I still remember her remarkable hesitancy.

(*Aside*.) Mariana and I went upstairs. We began love-making. I gave her a good kiss without pushing too hard, just pressing up and down – no blood came out. I'd done a better job than I'd anticipated and now she was no longer a virgin, which we were both pleased about. We are both delighted that I was the one to do the deed, as it shows that Charles does not hold much power and that she has always belonged to me. She will die as she lived, mine & mine alone.

Miss W Her husband Charles is a bit boring, don't you think? Maybe a little old for her.

Anne What nonsense, he's a very virile man. Respectable and solid. Everything I would have wished for dear Mariana.

(*Aside*.) I hate you, Mariana, for marrying that old ape, you shall suffer horribly when you know I'm about to settle down with . . . Miss Walker, here. You say she is not congenial to me and here you are wrong!

Miss W (*softly sighing*) My dear Mariana!

Miss Walker *stares into space.*

Anne (*aside*) I believe Miss Walker and I shall get along very well here. She's like a deer or a racehorse . . . she doesn't have a terribly sharp brain. But when it comes to body shape, hers is perfection. She could ride thirty miles a day on any road and I believe she loves me enough even though she needs to eat more frequently than I do, and she's prone to melancholy. Someone maliciously called her a lunatic – she doesn't come across as a lunatic to me. What are you staring at, my dear?

Miss W   Dust.

Anne   Dust? The rubble has come up to here! I'll send for Miss Poodle right away.

Miss W   Noooo! It's nice. I can see all the minuscule bits flying together.

Anne   What bits? (*Aside.*) Maybe they're not completely wrong. She's quite unhinged. But harmless and I love her quite a bit. The truth is, I wasn't born to live alone. I must have a companion. My happiness lies in loving and being loved.

Miss W (*approaching* **Anne** *and putting her finger on a line of her diary*)   What are you writing about here?

Anne   For dinner, lamb steak and partridge pie.

Miss W   And here?

Anne   About my plans to extend the house. The ceiling of the big living room will be demolished and on the west side I will have a Norman tower built to house my library. On the bedroom level, I've planned a water closet to avoid having to go out in the cold. My draughtsman says the house will look very impressive, worthy of my ancestors.

Miss W   Are your architectural projects so secret that they have to be written in code?

Anne   Do you want the whole county to build a Norman tower and a water closet before us? We shall be the first here in Shibden Hall. Of course, to claim our leadership you will be required to contribute a little something. Four thousand pounds to begin with.

Miss W   I don't know, Anne. I've just given you six thousand for the mining engineer and four thousand for the well.

Anne   The well is the well. What's up with you? Don't you like the project? You're still on about the dust? Why are you still staring into the void like that? Are you jealous of Mariana?

Miss W (*innocent*)   No . . . no, I know you love me. It's just that today when you were out talking to the tenants something happened. Some peasants came under the window and burned what appeared to be an effigy of us. Of you and me together.

Anne   Who do they think they're frightening, these bumpkins? Don't you worry about a thing, I'm here with you. They can say what they want, they can write articles in the newspapers, they can send ill-mannered fellas to ambush me, to scare me, but I shall not lose heart. We live life here in our own way. We are our own mistresses and no man can tell us how /

Miss W   / That's not it, Anne. They say we poisoned them. That the spring they drank from has become undrinkable. Do you know something about this?

Anne (*vague and guilty*)   Yes . . . I heard. Four workers poisoned the spring with a barrel of pitch.

Miss W   Good grief! Why in the name of God would they do that?

Anne   I ordered it. My lawyer advised me to do this. Darling, you can't let those villagers drink your water for free. The water comes from your property.

Miss W   But it's water. They can drink it, I don't care. Let's leave it to them.

Anne   Without making them pay?

Miss W   They are very poor, Anne.

Anne (*aside*)   She's not the sharpest tool in the box.

Miss W   Water must be public property. They'll take us to court if we deny this.

Anne   We haven't done anything. It was the four workers, I told you.

Miss W   Oh Anne, you did just tell me you ordered it! I don't like this water business. And all these real estate projects, I don't know. Plus, you also want to dig a mine now.

Anne   It's the investment of our lives. Coal is as precious as gold, my dear. You want everyone else to dig and not us. It will take a while to make the hole and dig deep but then we will send the whole village down to work and the bumpkins will thank us for giving them work, the women and children too, because they're smaller, their little hands are the right size to dig deeper.

Miss W   Oh, Anne. Do you want to send children to work in the mines?

Anne   They'll have fun. Look, we'll pay them, a little, but we will pay them.

Miss W (*thoughtful*)   Oh dear!

Miss W *looks into space.*

Anne   What are you looking at?

(*Aside.*) This is the right time for my big move.

Anne *takes a small pencil case out of her black jacket pocket. She opens it, she takes something that slips, unnoticed, into* **Miss W**'s *tea.*

Anne   I can pour some brandy in your tea. Would you like that? Think about how happy we will be. In our new big house.

Can I read you some Byron? You were so happy when we read Byron by the fireplace.

Miss W   This is not the right time for poetry, sorry, Anne. Too many thoughts . . . the farmers, my aunt who criticizes us openly . . . maybe I should take a trip to see my sister in Scotland to clear my mind.

Anne   Nooo, Scotland is a bad idea! The weather is awful and your brother-in-law is only interested in your money.

Miss W   True.

Anne *pours* **Miss W** *more brandy into the cup.* **Miss W** *takes a sip and nearly suffocates.*

Miss W (*coughs*)   Good God, I was about to choke. But what is this?! A ring!?

Anne   A promise.

Miss W   A black stone.

Anne   An onyx.

Miss W   Is that you, Anne?

Anne   Keep this stone with you all the time. It will protect you. Even from myself if necessary.

Miss W   Who else knows me like you do . . . who else loves me as deeply as you love me.

Anne   I hope no one. You've realised this. (*aside*) We don't need another rake from her past to come up with a promise to steal her inheritance.

Anne *kneels.*

Anne   Will you marry me?

Miss W   . . . I told you.

Anne   What? What did you tell me? Are there still any obstacles? Any man you feel any duty or obligation towards?

Miss W   No obligations. You know that with Mr Bell we've never gone as far as you and I have. I have told you everything.

Anne   That man took advantage of you, if I may say so. Can you think of any other obstacles?

Miss W   A small one . . . that appears and disappears.

Anne (*aside*)   Thank God my head isn't like hers.

Then your mind is unmade up about whether to marry me. What shall I do with you?

Miss W   Ah . . . I don't know what to say! I should write a note with a yes and one with a no and then draw lots.

Anne   Do you love me so much that you are prepared to leave everything to fate? One builds one's own fate, my dear. You adore me, why do you want to push me away? Your conscience still haunts you. Did you have that nightmare? Those two men who were jailed in town for doing bad things, does you mind dwell on them? Those two have nothing to do with us. Nothing! The things you and I do are perfectly natural, Adny.

Miss W   And you want me, Anne? Do you really love me? What if you get tired of me? Will you be faithful to me?

Anne You want me.

Anne *kisses* **Miss W** *and puts the ring on her.*

Anne Well then. It's decided. Where would you like to go for our honeymoon?

Miss W Paris.

Anne Where else? My Parisian friends will help us find a delightful accommodation, you'll see, it'll be a dream. (*Aside.*) When Marie the saucy dressmaker from Paris sees me with Miss W, she will be furious, I have never written to her since going on a getaway to Versailles with Virginie. (*To* **Miss W**.) That lovely little guesthouse on Rue de le Bruyère will do. Who knows, that old woman who rented rooms may still be around. She will be so glad to see me. She liked my ways so much.

Miss W I would like to go away immediately, Anne, away from these uncles, cousins, brothers-in-law and lawyers and notaries, this place is suffocating, everyone spying, gossiping, sullying. They don't know who I am, how can they know what's best for me? I'm so tired of this landscape, it's so monotonous, this wind-torn moor, only roots grow here, and this heather, I hate it! Pitiful little flowers. (*Throws the heather away.*) It drives me crazy!

Anne Calm down. You know I don't like drama.

Miss W I want to see other flowers, real flowers, all the flowers in the world, you've seen them, right Anne? Smell all the flowers until you go crazy. Will you take me to see all the flowers in the world?!

Anne They sell all kinds of flowers in Paris, my dear. I shall organize something. For your convenience, it would be sensible for you to let me manage everything and for you to give me that stipend . . . we've already discussed it /

Miss W / Oh no I'm feeling agitated again . . . I don't know anymore . . . I'm not sure I can make you happy. Maybe I should leave you to someone more stimulating than me. Someone who speaks better French and knows of archaeology and hydraulics.

Anne What?! If you left me, I couldn't survive. Look at what state I am in. My hands are shaking at the thought of losing you. With the works all in the air and the coal mine to be excavated. You have to make a decision and stick to it, my dear.

Miss W What is this light that filters from above?

Anne But if you left me now, mind you, it would be very foolish and all this just because you don't feel like signing your will. Focus your mind. You get too distracted, you follow the dust.

Miss W What hurry are we in now? All these oaths, these documents . . . Everything that's mine is yours already, you know that.

Anne I understand. Then your mind is unmade up about your love for me. Take some time to reflect. I warn you, separation between us will be immediate.

Miss W No! Why! You've just said I have time. I'll lose my mind. I'll write what you want me to, Anne, it's all the same for me, as long as it makes you happy. Let me sign.

Anne (*aside*) It's settled and she agreed. By virtue of her title as sole heir of the estate, she will not have to ask for permission and she will not be subjected to anyone's authority except mine.

Sign here, my love.

Miss W Is this my will?

Anne No, we need two witnesses for that, we'll go to the notary tomorrow. This is the document that establishes that we love each other.

III

Today.

Just after scene I.

In this second part the characters of **Anna** *and* **Jo** *retain signs of* **Anne Lister** *and* **Miss W** *and somehow overlap the two characters of the past in a similar dynamic of power.*

Anna She was an awful woman!

Jo She was so contemporary. Anne Lister's diaries are the Rosetta stone of lesbian language. Lister didn't let her passions overwhelm her like your Brontë did – she dominated them. From petty romanticism to the reality principle!

Anna I am surprised, Jo, that you are so attracted to her. Her sloppy and repetitive prose is like a diary of a country seductor. (*Imitates her.*) 'Women like me, they've always liked me, no one has ever rejected me.' She loved women, okay, but that doesn't make her a heroine! The only freedom that she was interested in was hers. And she poisoned the poor villagers' only water source, exploited child labour and insulted her wife. Nice piece of work.

Jo Very punk. *From the Moor to the Mine*. Do you like this title, Professor? *From the Moor to the Mine*! I think I will use it for my thesis instead of *They Were All Lesbians*. Do you like it?

Anna Yes, not bad.

Jo *indulges in a victorious dance.*

Anna (*romantically, looking out of the window*) So did they go to Paris?

Jo They travelled around the world. Those two really didn't want to live on that moor of yours.

Thunder.

Anna (*thoughtfully*)   The moor . . . there are those who run away, and those who yearn for it.

Jo   Are you thinking about your friend?

Time.

Anna   It's started raining. Quite a storm.

Did they live together all their lives?

Jo   Till death did them part. Theirs was the first lesbian wedding ever celebrated in England. Lister was a revolutionary woman!

Anna   She wasn't a revolutionary because she wasn't a woman. And you can tell from her way of lording it over other women, she did it like a man. Women don't love like that.

Jo   What do you know about how women love? Aren't you a straight married woman – or am I wrong? Am I wrong?

Anna   Gosh, not this again!

Jo   Woman, man, whatever she was, she was herself, Gentleman Jack. She may be a horrible human being and a bad writer, but her life was a work of art. Fortunately, not all works of art are beautiful to look at.

Kierkegaard invented existentialism but he was a slave owner, Voltaire the man of enlightenment, a male chauvinist, Anne Lister can be a shameless businessman and a beacon for women who love other women.

(*Teases her.*) There are many people, even today, who are still afraid to confess their love.

Anna (*does not react*)   There is a very elegant nineteenth-century expression, certainly more elegant than Gentleman Jack, to define a lesbian. Wintering in Rome. Literally spending the winter in Rome. You would have been one wintering in Rome in an English salon of the 1800s. Isn't that beautiful?

Jo   A little old-fashioned. I would prefer to spend the winter in Mikonos.

Sound of thunder.

Anna (*looking out the window*)   The perfect day for a run on the moor. The Romantic heroines you hate /

Jo (*protests*)   I don't hate them!

Anna . . . when they're upset they go out in a storm to take the spirits by the hand and get carried away by fury. After a few months they die of tuberculosis.

Jo   Would you like to take a walk in the garden, Professor? Come on, let's go down to the river through the park. We'll run in the rain. It'll be fun.

Anna (*amused*)   You're crazy.

Jo What are you afraid of? Nobody dies of tuberculosis anymore.

Anna It's freezing outside! I am not a heroine. I will die of something else.

Jo Come on! Let's go.

Anna Don't insist. No way, I'm not going.

Jo Then we can come back here, take off our clothes and light the fireplace.

Your husband isn't coming back tonight, is he?

Beat.

Jo Anna, can I call you by your name?

Why did you remove the dedication to your friend from later editions of your book? It's so beautiful.

Anna Things change.

Jo Where is your friend now?

Anna Somewhere in the heather hills.

Jo Meaning?

Anna She's dead.

Sound of thunder. Pouring rain.

Anna But she still comes to see me. When the wind is strong and nostalgia unbearable. She comes to the window, she calls me. Annaaaa! Come, Annaa . . .

Jo (*troubled*) Are you making fun of me?

Anna Was I speaking out loud?

Jo (*worried*) I was getting worried.

Anna Just a little bit of stuffy Gothic Romanticism. I thought you liked it.

Do you want to know what V. was like? She was beautiful and she was all on fire when she talked about poetry. She lived in the present in a devastating way. Your Anne Lister would have said she was unhinged. My book is dedicated to her because it is for her that I wrote it. She had written one dedicated to me.

Jo Has your friend's book not been published?

Anna The books had a similar focus and the publisher told us that they would only publish one.

Jo They've obviously published yours. The publisher is your husband.

Anna He became my husband later.

Jo Your friend must have been so pleased that you'd fallen in love with the publisher.

From here **Anna** *switches from formal to informal tone.*

Anna   How dare you say something like this?

Jo   I don't want to be too nosy, far from me. It is literature I'm concerned with, how it mixes up with the writer's identity. I'm a writer too and I know that the work cannot be separated from its author.

Anna   You don't know anything about me, just as you don't know anything about the Brontë sisters or about Lister. These are all fantasies, my dear, but at least now you have a lot of material for a novel.

Jo   I've already written one.

Anna   Of course you have.

(*Sarcastic.*) Everyone who comes to this house has a book draft in a drawer. Or have you already brought it with you?

Jo   I would love you to tell me what you think.

Anna   That's the reason for your visit and for all your flirting with me. The running in the rain bit too.

Jo   That I wanted to do for real.

If you had some time to read my work, your opinion would be so precious.

Anna   I don't have time, it's not my job.

Jo   Maybe you could talk to your husband about it.

Anna   Are you out of your mind!?

Jo   What? To ask for an audience at the tower? Don't you think I have the right to make my voice heard like everyone else? You know what it's like to have no one in the world who gives a shit about you. You know that I've been abused and harassed for years by those nuns, I was left cold and hungry in an orphanage.

Anna   I don't believe a word of what you say.

Jo   You don't believe my story?

Anna   This novel has already been written. I believe in the 19th century. And if your writing is as sloppy as the way you speak, reading it would be a waste of time.

Jo   Earlier you said my ideas were original. *From the Moor to the Mine.*

Anna   A handful of provocations is not enough to write a novel. Arrogance is the worst companion for a writer of your age. You'll have to work very hard to be able to write something readable.

Jo   At least I write my own books, I don't steal them from my lovers.

Thunder.

Anna (*ice*)   What did you say?

From here **Jo** *switches from formal to informal tone in addressing* **Anna**.

Jo   You didn't write *On the Moor*. You had it published in your name, but you stole it from your friend.

Anna   How dare you, little girl, come into my house and make all this stuff up.

Jo   I have evidence.

Anna   Get out now!

Jo *opens the book.*

Jo   People forget all kinds of documents in borrowed books.

In here I found a letter from V. to you. She says the book was hers. That she was robbed of everything. Of her words and her love.

Anna   A letter? And it would have been left in the book all this time?

Jo   It's clear that your book has not been consulted many times in the last few years.

Anne   I'd like to see this letter.

Jo *takes out a sheet.*

Jo   It is a dense handwriting that leaves no spaces between lines. Do you recognize it?

Anna *grabs the paper.*

Jo   It's a photocopy.

Anne *reads and rereads greedily then she tries to restore her tone.*

Anne   Didn't it occur to you that these accusations may be false? The delusions of an emotionally unstable woman whose feelings had been hurt?

Jo   Yes, I thought about that. I can't imagine the shock of coming home and seeing you with a man. The publisher you both wanted to meet. Your dreams of becoming writers. Maybe she heard when he asked you what kind of friend she was and you replied that she was just an ex-student.

V. found out and ran to the moor in distress and caught a cold in the rain.

Anne   V. suffered a lot because of me, but not for the reasons you think. She wanted me to be different, she wanted to be loved in a way that I . . . but that's not my nature. I like men. And she couldn't resign herself.

Jo   How good you are at staying in control. Not a single expression of fear. You're not at all troubled. Professor, you've nothing in common with your Romantic heroines. It's so obvious that you didn't write that book. You're like a perfect copy of Anne Lister, you've signed your luxury contracts and live here in your castle with a Norman tower.

Anne   It's so easy to judge people.

Jo No, I don't judge you. I'm like you. (*Corrects herself.*) I would love to be like you.

Anna Don't get near me, get out now or I'm calling the police.

Jo And what would you tell them, that I harassed you? It's your husband who's got that reputation, he gropes young women writers and you plagiarize them. Or maybe you grope them too?

Anna You came into my house to insult me and blackmail me. You should be ashamed.

Jo I'm just asking for a chance. Literature is my whole life.

Anna Do you really think that I would help you publish a line of what you wrote now, after all this?

Jo I will have this letter published. It will be a scandal.

Jo starts to leave.

Anna A scandal?! Then you're the Romantic one. No one is going to believe your word over mine. Rest assured that no one will ever publish anything against me, and that no one will ever publish anything of yours.

Jo You can't do that!

Anna / YOU CAN'T DO THAT!

You will no longer be able to come to my lectures. You will no longer be able to borrow a book. It was because of me that you'd been given a chance to breathe in this university. Now you're done.

Jo But that's not fair. I'm a great writer!

Anna You're an arrogant little brat, that's what you are!

Jo I worked my arse off to get here. I only ask you to read me, listen to me, look at me – if not with sympathy – pity will do, even contempt, but just look at me for a moment. Look at me! You know you like me!

Anna If you'd written anything good, if only you had a drop of the talent you boast I could still do something for you. I believe in literature, so I could overlook this unpleasant situation. But I don't think you have any chance of being of interest to anyone other than some ignorant diesel dyke like you. You haven't learnt anything in your life and what you've read you've clearly misunderstood. Go back to your motorcycle and your primary school prose. I've been hearing you talk for an hour now, you're such an ignorant basket case, you talk about reality as if it were the recipe for turning a girl's dreams into something that has finally acquired meaning. But it's quite the opposite, it's reality that confuses us, it escapes and annihilates us until we are no longer able to make sense of it.

What are you looking at? Where have you gone?

Jo (*annihilated*) Oh!

Anna It's the dust. It's everywhere because of the building works. It just goes everywhere.

Don't you want to blackmail me anymore? Don't you want to hit on me?

Are you regretting it now? What a pity.

Jo Anna. . .

Anna Don't call me that. Don't get any closer.

Jo Professor.

Anna Did you really think you would come here and uncover a secret?

The biggest secrets are already in the open for all to see.

Even those written in code are solved sooner or later. And when it happens, nobody cares anymore.

If you are too sure of what you are, you will never be a writer.

Jo (*pleading*) Teach me then, teach me. I would like to learn how to live my life. If only you knew . . . I've had so little from life. I've only learnt from books, but if I could find a human being who could teach me, who could guide me, a woman like you /

Anna You come here to destroy me and now you want me to be your mother or something?

Jo Couldn't you be charitable with me? Don't we all deserve a chance and redemption? I am ready to do anything for you. Anything. I can burn that letter and become your slave. Tell me what I should do and I'll do it. I want punishment for what I did to you.

Jo *takes off her clothes, she remains in men's boxers and vest.*

Anna What the hell are you doing?

Jo I'm going to get caught up in the storm and tomorrow I'll be ill and then maybe you'll love me a little.

Anna Don't be daft. I hate this kind of drama. Get back into your clothes. I don't want a crazy girl in boxers running in my garden.

Jo Look at me from the window. I'm doing it for you!

Anna If you think I'll do something for you, you're fooling yourself.

Jo *goes out.*

Anna *goes to the window to look at* **Jo**. *Sound of rain and thunder.*

Blackout.

Anna *remains in the dark. She feels a presence in the room.*

Anna Are you here?

Sometimes I can almost see you, but I can't make these moments last . . . I cling to them but they vanish.

Come back here, my love. Take the shape you want, I will recognize you. Haunt my nights.

She takes the copy of the letter she had crumpled up. She reads it. She kisses it. She then looks into the void.

Drive me insane with your curses. Whisper the words that illuminate the way.

You are the river that I drained only to remain without water.

Yet the only moments of absolute clarity in my life, I have lived with you. When everything was exactly as it should be and the world was new every day.

I've lived my whole life for those moments with you.

I'll never be anyone else's because you were me more than I am myself.

Jo *comes back in, she is wet. She looks like someone who has seen a ghost.*

Anna You're back already?

She collapses at Anna's feet.

Jo It's fucking freezing outside!

Anna (*softened, empathic*) What a silly idea to go out in this weather.

You're like a little girl, Jo!

Come here, take that underwear off. You have to warm up or you'll get a cold. You're shaking. Take this.

Anna *covers her with the 19th-century shawl.*

Jo Thank you.

Jo *takes off the underwear from under the shawl. She wraps herself in the shawl.*

Anna Can I?

Anna *rubs her back to warm her up.* **Jo** *lets it go.*

Anna Better?

Jo *nods but she remains curled up on herself. She looks like a little girl.*

Anna I have an idea. I'll make a couple of calls. I'll get rid of the rest of the day and we'll stay here, you and me. Let's light the fireplace, like you said. What do you say?

Jo *is silent.*

Anna My husband's coming back tomorrow evening. We're good.

Anna *looks at* **Jo** *half-naked in her living room.*

You're very beautiful. You have such fair skin.

Anna *starts to touch her shoulders then she pulls away.*

Bring me your novel to read if you want. I'll give it a chance.

That idea of Anne Lister sweeping the romance away with her crude list of orgasms is a good one. I really think so.

From the moor to the mine. It might inspire me too.

Who knows, it might even make me want to write again.

The shawl slides down **Jo**'s *shoulder and leaves it uncovered.* **Anna** *looks at her.*

Anna You are my muse on a motorbike.

When you walked in here . . . the way you looked at me. I'm not used to it anymore.

I bet you look at all women like that! I bet no one can say no to you.

My favourite character in *Little Women* is Jo. We're all crazy about Jo. Because she's free, more than anyone else. Just think if she'd also had a motorbike to run around . . . Do you still want to take me for a ride on your bike? When it's ready we can go to my beach house if you want. It's immersed in nature, no one will disturb us. It's less than two hours from here. Would you like that?

Have you warmed up a bit? Do you want some brandy?

They drink a drop of brandy. Their hands touch. **Anna** *strokes* **Jo**'s *hands and shoulders. Now it's* **Jo** *who pulls away.*

Anna What is it? Are you OK?

Jo (*like a confession of something that deeply shocked her*) When I went out she was there in your garden.

Anna (*alarmed*) Who?

Jo A girl was running in the storm. Then she stopped and started digging the earth with her own hands. As if something that was buried under there was still breathing. I didn't have the courage to look into her eyes but it was her, I know.

Jo *begins to get dressed quickly.*

Anna (*trying to simulate calm, incredulous*) It must have been your imagination. Don't worry. All those stories stuck to your mind, you're cold, you haven't eaten anything. Did you eat before coming here?

Jo It wasn't my imagination.

Anna I'll make you something. What do you like? Come here, where are you running away to?!

Jo (*dressing in a hurry*) I don't want to end up like V. I won't be the spirit under your window. I'd better stay away from the Norman towers and castle women. I made peace with who I am a long time ago, I'm not looking for more pain, thank you.

Anna I don't want you to be unhappy . . . I can help you do what you love. Your literature.

Jo No.

Anna *is in pain,* **Jo** *looks at her with tenderness.*

Jo If I liked you less than I do, I would stay the night, with your fireplace and your ghosts. Then, tomorrow morning *Bye, Prof. – See you later.* Take it as a sign of respect: I'm leaving now before anything happens.

Anna But it's already happened! Wait, please. Just a minute. We don't have to do anything. Don't leave me alone today. In this weather, in this state.

Jo Your husband is coming back tomorrow, he'll keep you company.

Anna Please.

Jo You know why Anne Lister gets on your nerves so much, you can't stand in others what you can't be yourself.

Anna A lesbian?

Jo Free.

Anna Oh, Jo. Do you feel sorry for me now?

Jo I had a big crush on you.

It will pass.

Anna What about your book? You don't want me to read it anymore? Bring it to me. I won't ask you for anything in return, I just want to help you.

Jo You're the one who needs help. I'll ask someone else to read the book.

As soon as I can, I'll send you the original letter: you have my word, I won't tell anyone about it.

Jo *starts to go.*

Jo And let her in, if you can, it's freezing outside.

Anna Wait, Jo, wait! Don't leave me alone.

Jo Bye.

Jo *goes out.* **Anna** *remains alone.*

Blackout.

The End

The Fattest Woman in the World
La donna più grassa del mondo

By Emanuele Aldrovandi

Translated by Marco Young

First staged at the Teatro Piccolo Orologio, Reggio Emilia, on 7 December 2018.

Characters

The Fattest Woman in the World
Husband
Downstairs Neighbour

Content warning: References to body shaming, fatphobia and depression

A One Act Play

The gigantic body of the **Fattest Woman in the World** *fills the entire stage, overflowing beyond it towards the audience. It doesn't have to be a realistic body. It could be made of foam, it could be inflatable, it could be made of paper or any other material. It doesn't even have to be physically represented, depending on what design choices are made. But if it is visible, it should be absolutely enormous.*

Scene 1

Downstairs Neighbour Morning.

Husband Morning.

Downstairs Neighbour I'm the downstairs neighbour. We moved in at the end of last year. It's nice to meet you.

Husband Nice to meet you.

Downstairs Neighbour I'm sorry to bother you.

Husband It's no bother.

Downstairs Neighbour I've come about the crack.

Husband What crack?

Downstairs Neighbour I thought you could see it from up here, too.

Husband No, I'm sorry, I haven't noticed any cracks.

Downstairs Neighbour It's in my son's bedroom. On the ceiling. We didn't notice it when we bought the flat because of the wallpaper. But we removed that on Sunday.

Husband Wallpaper on the ceiling?

Downstairs Neighbour It was the previous owners'. To hide the crack.

Husband That's a bit dodgy.

Downstairs Neighbour Well, it was our fault too. We should have checked. Anyway, I spoke with a friend of mine, an engineer. He said we most likely just need to install two iron beams to reinforce it.

Husband Good.

Downstairs Neighbour But first, he'd like to inspect your place, too. To assess the crack from above. It'll be five, ten minutes, tops. When do you think could work?

Husband Where did you say the crack was?

Downstairs Neighbour In my son's bedroom.

Husband   And where's your son's bedroom, in relation to our flat?

Downstairs Neighbour   Underneath.

Husband   Yes, but underneath what?

Downstairs Neighbour   It's the . . . second room on the right as you enter.

Husband   Oh, I see. I'm very sorry but it won't be possible to inspect that room.

Downstairs Neighbour   Why?

Husband   It's occupied.

Downstairs Neighbour   Oh. It's . . . what do you mean, occupied?

Husband   By my wife.

Downstairs Neighbour   Well, can't your wife – excuse me, but – can't she move?

Husband   No.

Downstairs Neighbour   May I ask why?

Husband   She weighs 460 kilograms.

Downstairs Neighbour   What?

Husband   My wife.

Downstairs Neighbour (*laughs, then becomes serious*)   You're joking. Right?

Husband   Why would I joke about something like that?

Downstairs Neighbour   I'm sorry.

Husband   Don't worry about it.

Downstairs Neighbour   I do apologize . . . .

Husband   About the crack?

Downstairs Neighbour   About your wife.

Husband   Why? She's perfectly happy.

Downstairs Neighbour   Right, sure, but she must have trouble moving . . .

Husband   My wife is a very sedentary person. She likes documentaries.

Downstairs Neighbour   I . . . see. So?

Husband   What?

Downstairs Neighbour   What can we do?

Husband   About my wife?

Downstairs Neighbour   About the crack.

Husband   Oh, I don't know. Like I said, I haven't noticed any cracks.

Downstairs Neighbour Just because you haven't noticed it doesn't mean it's not there.

Husband If you say so.

Downstairs Neighbour I say so because I've seen it.

Husband I wouldn't dream of questioning that.

Downstairs Neighbour Would you like to come take a look?

Husband No.

Downstairs Neighbour So what do we do?

Husband About what?

Downstairs Neighbour The crack!

Husband I don't know.

Downstairs Neighbour Look, it's a safety issue. I'm sorry to keep going on about it, but . . . surely it's concerning for you and your wife too? Do you have any children?

Husband No.

Downstairs Neighbour Well we do. One.

Husband Congratulations.

Downstairs Neighbour And we don't want him sleeping in a bedroom that could collapse on top of him.

Husband Move him into your bedroom.

Downstairs Neighbour Right, but the problem's not only with that one room . . .

Husband That's what you said.

Downstairs Neighbour I said the entire building is unstable!

Husband Don't get upset.

Downstairs Neighbour I'm not getting upset.

Husband It seems like you're getting upset.

Downstairs Neighbour I'm not.

Husband Anyway, I haven't noticed any signs of instability.

Downstairs Neighbour Are you taking the piss?

Husband Why would I be taking the piss?

Downstairs Neighbour Listen, I'm telling you, this building has structural problems. And if it collapses, we're all going to die.

Husband Well I hope not.

Downstairs Neighbour   Yeah, I obviously hope not, too!

Husband   Good, so we agree on that.

Downstairs Neighbour   Sure, but we can't just hope. We have to do something.

Husband   Like what?

Downstairs Neighbour   I just told you.

Husband   And I just told you that my wife cannot move.

Downstairs Neighbour   Yes, I understand that and I'm very sorry. But she'll have to move sooner or later, won't she? So it might as well be sooner. Living above that crack isn't safe for her either.

Husband   Why should she ever have to move at all?

Downstairs Neighbour   She'll have to when the construction workers get here.

Husband   I don't mean to be rude, but are we speaking the same language?

Downstairs Neighbour   It seems so.

Husband   So which part of 'my wife cannot move' do you not understand?

Downstairs Neighbour   Well I assumed it was a way of saying that it's very hard for her to move.

Husband   If it was very hard, I would have told you it was very hard. But I told you she cannot move.

Downstairs Neighbour   Alright, but . . .

Husband   You think it's possible to move a person who weighs 460 kilograms?

Downstairs Neighbour   Can't say I've ever thought about it.

Husband   Think about it.

Downstairs Neighbour   So your wife never gets out of bed?

Husband   Off the sofa.

Downstairs Neighbour   The sofa.

Husband   Exactly.

Downstairs Neighbour   Not even in special circumstances?

Husband   It's not about special circumstances, it's about physical impossibility.

Downstairs Neighbour   And couldn't we – forgive me, if I may – but . . . couldn't we move the sofa with your wife on it?

Husband   Wouldn't fit through the door.

Downstairs Neighbour   The sofa?

Husband   Neither of them. The sofa or my wife.

Downstairs Neighbour   So how did she get into the room?

Husband   She went in when she was thinner.

Downstairs Neighbour   So what do we do?

Husband   I don't know.

Downstairs Neighbour   And aren't you concerned about this? At all?

Husband   Once again: I haven't noticed any cracks.

Scene 2

The **Fattest Woman in the World** *is watching a documentary whilst eating a large sandwich with three sausages in it.*

When she finishes the sandwich, she pauses the documentary.

Fattest Woman in the World   Daaaaaaaaarling! Daaaaaaaaarling!

Husband   I'm coming. Sorry.

Fattest Woman in the World   Where were you?

Husband   The downstairs neighbour was here.

Fattest Woman in the World   Again? Does he come every day?

Husband   He's obsessed with this so-called crack.

Fattest Woman in the World   Don't open the door then.

Husband   I don't want to be rude.

Fattest Woman in the World   You'd rather neglect your wife than be rude to someone who's pestering you?

Husband   Neglect my wife? You're my queen.

Fattest Woman in the World   Something terrible happened while you were away.

Husband   What?

Fattest Woman in the World   My sandwich. It's gone.

Husband   Where'd it go?

Fattest Woman in the World   I don't know.

Husband   These sandwiches keep hiding away, don't they?

Fattest Woman in the World   They do.

Husband   Well what do we do now?

Fattest Woman in the World   I don't know. It's a very tricky situation.

Husband   Perhaps we need another sandwich.

Fattest Woman in the World Perhaps.

Husband Hmmm . . . well, I would make you one, except . . .

Fattest Woman in the World Except what?

Husband . . . I already have!

*The **Husband** pulls out another sandwich and hands it to her.*

Fattest Woman in the World Oh my goodness, I love it when you read my mind.

Husband So do you still think I neglect you?

Fattest Woman in the World No, you don't neglect me.

Husband That's right.

Fattest Woman in the World Wait a second. This sandwich . . .

Husband What is it?

Fattest Woman in the World There are only two sausages. Where's the third?

Husband It's . . . not there.

Fattest Woman in the World It's not there?

Husband No.

Fattest Woman in the World Where'd you hide it?

Husband No, love, it just isn't there.

Fattest Woman in the World Behind your back?

Husband No, really . . . I . . . .

Fattest Woman in the World In your trousers? Your pants? Your shirt?

Husband No, love, I'm sorry, I'm not joking. I didn't hide it anywhere.

Fattest Woman in the World So where is it?

Husband We're out.

Fattest Woman in the World We're out of sausages?

Husband Yes. (*A dramatic pause.*) I'm sorry, I didn't check. I'll go buy them later.

Fattest Woman in the World You don't love me anymore.

Husband Oh come on . . .

Fattest Woman in the World You never used to forget things like that.

Husband It just happened. Last time I checked we had lots of them and I didn't think . . .

Fattest Woman in the World . . . That's how it always starts. A missing sausage.

Then we start forgetting anniversaries, we stop talking to each other, we become strangers and eventually we leave each other.

Husband I would never leave you.

Fattest Woman in the World Then you must keep treating me like a queen. Forever.

Husband Forever.

Fattest Woman in the World What about the croquettes?

Husband They're in the fryer.

Fattest Woman in the World And the lasagne?

Husband It's in the oven.

Fattest Woman in the World And the smoothie?

Husband It's ready.

Fattest Woman in the World Come here. Give me a kiss. There's not enough mayonnaise.

Husband It's the usual amount.

Fattest Woman in the World Yes, but that's for a three-sausage sandwich. This one only has two. I don't like dry pieces of bread, you know that.

Husband I'll get you some more.

Fattest Woman in the World Wait. I might have some peanut butter left.

Husband Would . . . would that go well with the sausages?

Fattest Woman in the World Let's try it.

The **Fattest Woman in the World** *pulls a jar of peanut butter out from somewhere and starts spreading it on the sandwich.*

Husband I love how you spread that.

Fattest Woman in the World Will you take some photos of me today?

Husband Of course.

Fattest Woman in the World I've grown a bit, haven't I?

Husband I think so.

Fattest Woman in the World Shame we can't use the scales anymore.

Husband You can just tell.

Fattest Woman in the World Really?

Husband Yes.

Fattest Woman in the World You're not just saying that to please me?

Husband I'm saying it because it's true.

Fattest Woman in the World I love you.

Husband I love you too. You grow more beautiful every day.

Fattest Woman in the World No, wait. I want to finish my sandwich first.

Husband Alright.

Fattest Woman in the World Then I'm all yours.

Husband I don't know if I can wait.

Fattest Woman in the World It'll be worth it, you'll see.

Husband It's always worth it.

Fattest Woman in the World We could try something different today.

Husband Like what?

Fattest Woman in the World Like . . . not being careful.

Husband With what?

Fattest Woman in the World You know what.

Husband Seriously?

Fattest Woman in the World Yes.

Husband You want to . . .

Fattest Woman in the World Yes.

Husband Okay.

Fattest Woman in the World I thought you'd be happy.

Husband I am happy.

Fattest Woman in the World Happier.

Husband I'm happy if you're happy.

Fattest Woman in the World Right, but this is important. You have to be sure.

Husband I'm sure.

Fattest Woman in the World Doesn't seem like it.

Husband I just wasn't expecting it.

Fattest Woman in the World You usually enjoy it when I catch you off guard.

Husband I do, I am enjoying it.

Fattest Woman in the World But?

Husband   There's no but. If you want to, let's do it.

Fattest Woman in the World   But what do you think?

Husband   I think we'd still be happy if we didn't.

Fattest Woman in the World   Sure. But we'd also be happy if we did.

Husband   Yes.

Fattest Woman in the World   So?

Husband   Don't be pushy.

Fattest Woman in the World   Don't be evasive.

Husband   You know I love you. And not just because I'm physically attracted to you, but also because I admire you as a woman, for how you dismantled all societal expectations. You've become a symbol of freedom, of emancipation . . .

Fattest Woman in the World   Don't beat around the bush.

Husband   I'm not beating around the bush.

Fattest Woman in the World   I know you.

Husband   I was just going to say that perhaps this notion of becoming a mother is actually, in a way, conforming, it's something people do just because society . . .

Fattest Woman in the World   You think I give a shit about society?

Husband   No. Exactly.

Fattest Woman in the World   So what?

Husband   Don't get upset.

Fattest Woman in the World   I'm getting upset because you're not telling me the truth. Why don't you want a child?

Husband   I told you, I do.

Fattest Woman in the World   You told me you want one because I want one. But you didn't tell me why you're so unsure.

Husband   Perhaps because the doctor said it could be dangerous.

Fattest Woman in the World   Since when do you care what doctors think? You always say they only care about selling medicine.

Husband   Yes, true, but maybe in this case . . .

Fattest Woman in the World   Why this case in particular?

Husband   I don't know, I was just thinking out loud. I told you: if you want to, let's do it.

Fattest Woman in the World   Yes, but tell me what you think!

Silence.

Husband   I'm jealous. I'm scared our relationship will change.

Fattest Woman in the World   You're odd, you know that? You're not jealous of the millions of people who look at my videos and pictures . . .

Husband   . . . Well, that's different . . .

Fattest Woman in the World   . . . but you're jealous of something we would do together?

Husband   I just don't want us to stop being the most important thing to each other.

Fattest Woman in the World   Why would that stop?

Husband   I don't know. It's not something you decide. You make choices and you might not realise it, but in the long run . . .

Fattest Woman in the World   I like being the most important thing to you.

Husband   Am I the most important thing to you?

Fattest Woman in the World   Yes. (*Pause.*) The croquettes will be ready by now.

Husband   You're right. I'll get them for you right away.

Fattest Woman in the World   Take them out so they don't burn, but don't give them to me yet. I want the smoothie first. Do you know what free sugars do to me?

Husband   No, I don't.

Fattest Woman in the World   Yes, you do.

Husband   Tell me.

Fattest Woman in the World   You already know.

Husband   Yes, but tell me anyway.

Fattest Woman in the World   They turn me on.

The **Fattest Woman in the World** *leans back slightly and opens her mouth.*

The **Husband** *picks up a large clear plastic vat filled with a brown, lumpy substance. He picks up a funnel and puts it in his wife's mouth, ready to pour.*

Husband   Tell me when you want me to stop.

Fattest Woman in the World   You decide. I trust you. What did you put in it today?

Husband   Ice cream, crushed biscuits, sugar, butter, margarine, mascarpone and Nutella.

Fattest Woman in the World   Twenty more of these and I'll catch that Mexican bitch.

Husband My love, she has an advantage. She has a thyroid condition that helps her put on weight. You're better. You're doing it all on your own.

Fattest Woman in the World Not on my own. With you.

Husband With me.

Fattest Woman in the World I love you.

*The **Husband** pours the contents of the vat into the funnel. After a while, as the smoothie pours into the mouth of the **Fattest Woman in the World**, we hear a very loud sound. The sound of an earthquake. The stage starts to shake, the Earth starts to shake and the documentary on the TV also starts to shake. The **Husband** continues pouring the contents of the vat into the funnel.*

Scene 3

Downstairs Neighbour We really have to do something now. Immediately.

Husband You look exhausted.

Downstairs Neighbour I slept in my car all night. I didn't sleep a wink.

Husband Then you should say you 'were awake in your car all night.'

Downstairs Neighbour Now's not the time for jokes.

Husband I wasn't joking.

Downstairs Neighbour You stayed here?

Husband We're fatalists.

Downstairs Neighbour The crack has got bigger.

Husband Has it?

Downstairs Neighbour Yes. I called my friend, the engineer. He said it's best to stay away. Someone from the Council will be here soon.

Husband We can't leave. The Council already knows that.

Downstairs Neighbour What?

Husband Of course they do. Even when there was that flood three years ago, we stayed put. So even if the building were damaged . . .

Downstairs Neighbour . . . What do you mean if? It is damaged. That crack on the ceiling . . .

Husband . . . Don't get upset.

Downstairs Neighbour I'm not getting upset!

Husband I think you are.

Downstairs Neighbour I just don't want my son to have to sleep in the car.

Husband Then just stay inside too. You just have to tell the council that . . .

Downstairs Neighbour . . . I don't want to stay inside a building that could collapse any second!

Husband That's your choice. As I said, we're fatalists.

Downstairs Neighbour Can I speak with your wife?

Husband You want to see her, don't you.

Downstairs Neighbour No . . .

Husband You want to see if she's really as fat as she sounds.

Downstairs Neighbour I want to discuss the situation with her.

Husband You don't trust me?

Downstairs Neighbour Yes, I trust you, but . . .

Husband But what?

Downstairs Neighbour But I'd also like to speak with her. May I?

Husband She doesn't have time right now.

Downstairs Neighbour And what is she doing, may I ask?

Husband She's watching a documentary.

Downstairs Neighbour Can't she pause it?

Husband It's airing live.

Downstairs Neighbour Then I'll come back later, alright?

Husband It'll be dinner time.

Downstairs Neighbour Look, I'm trying to stay calm and discuss this in a civilised manner, but this situation is absurd.

Husband Why? I don't think it's absurd.

Downstairs Neighbour Oh, you think it isn't absurd that if we had started the renovation three months ago, the earthquake would not have made the crack worse and my son wouldn't be forced to sleep in the car? That's not absurd? I'm a teacher. My wife is a nurse. We don't make millions. We spent all our money and got a mortgage to buy a flat and now we can't even do any work on it just because . . .

Husband Just because what? Say it. Go ahead. 'Just because your wife is a fat piece of shit who can't move'? Say it. What, you think we're not used to being insulted?

Downstairs Neighbour No, no, look. I'm not insulting anyone.

Husband But that's what you're thinking. I can see it in your eyes. Always can.

Don't worry, we're used to it. We're well aware that our society is fat-phobic.

Downstairs Neighbour   Don't start playing the victim, please.

Husband   'Playing the victim?' I'm just stating facts. If an oppressed minority says they are being oppressed, are they 'playing the victim'?

Downstairs Neighbour   You're . . . you're changing the subject. That's not fair.

Husband   No, you've been doing that. Right from the off. 'Your wife can't move?' Would you have asked me a question like that if I told you she was disabled?

Downstairs Neighbour   If she was disabled she'd have a wheelchair.

Husband   See? You keep judging her.

Downstairs Neighbour   No, I'm just saying that I want to be able to live safely in my own home! Because I can't buy another one. This flat is the only place we can live, for God's sake.

Husband   Sell it.

Downstairs Neighbour   Who's going to buy it, with a crack like that?

Husband   Wallpaper?

Downstairs Neighbour   You are really testing my patience.

Husband   I'm sorry.

Downstairs Neighbour   No, if you really were sorry, you would do something.

Husband   And what could I do? Go on, you tell me: what can I do? What would you do if you were in my shoes? Go ahead. If it's so easy, you tell me.

Downstairs Neighbour   You could help your wife.

Husband   Help her do what? Roll out of the room? What should I do, push her out? So you can repair your crack?

Downstairs Neighbour   It's not my crack. It's both of our . . . cracks.

Husband   I still haven't seen it.

Downstairs Neighbour   Come look at it!

Husband   Can you even trust your own eyes? You know, people thought that the earth was flat for millennia because they trusted their own eyes.

Downstairs Neighbour   Alright, alright, calm down . . . you're trying to provoke me, but I . . .

Husband   I'm only trying to be helpful . . .

Downstairs Neighbour   Fine, I'll tell you what you should do. You should help her lose weight, OK? Lose weight!

Husband Congratulations. You're a genius. You think my wife and I never tried that?

Downstairs Neighbour You're using the past tense. That's not a good sign.

Husband I'm using the past tense because it didn't work.

Downstairs Neighbour When was this?

Husband A few years ago. We sat down and we worked out a detailed plan. To start with, we decided we would keep her average weight gain to less than 2 kilos a year. Ideally 1.5 kilos.

Downstairs Neighbour The average gain?

Husband At the same time, we decided to push for her body fat percentage to reach its peak as quickly as possible and kick start her metabolism, so she would then lose weight.

Downstairs Neighbour What's the point? Why not try to make her lose weight right away?

Husband Oh, no. She was in a rising phase. When something is in a rising phase, it's difficult to change its course. But once you reach the peak, your metabolism is under pressure, it kicks back in and that's the perfect time to start losing weight.

Downstairs Neighbour Who told you all this?

Husband And that's not all. We also decided to get together every five months to set increasingly ambitious goals.

Downstairs Neighbour Get together with who?

Husband My wife and I.

Downstairs Neighbour Every five months? Didn't you live together?

Husband Of course we lived together.

Downstairs Neighbour So you saw each other every day.

Husband But we didn't always talk about that. You think a fat person should spend their entire life talking about their fatness?

Downstairs Neighbour I'm speechless.

Husband Unfortunately, as I was telling you, this method didn't work. In spite of our best efforts. At that point we decided to give up on weight loss and aim for the opposite goal.

Downstairs Neighbour Gaining as much weight as possible?

Husband Exactly. What's wrong? You look shaken.

Downstairs Neighbour And in this genius plan . . . during all your meetings that sadly didn't yield any results . . . did you ever take into consideration the possibility of her eating less?

Husband No.

Downstairs Neighbour Why?

Husband Because my wife loves to eat. When she eats, she's happy. And I love seeing her happy.

Scene 4

The **Fattest Woman in the World** *is holding a plaque – or a celebratory sash, something like that – emblazoned with the words 'Guinness World Records – The Fattest Woman in the World'. She looks at it, holds it, then hangs it on display somewhere. Then she takes out her phone and starts recording a video.*

Fattest Woman in the World Hello boys and girls. Yesterday, we celebrated a milestone. Today, I want to talk about something a bit personal. I think many of you will relate. A few days ago, I told my husband I wanted to have a child. He said 'yes', but he wasn't enthusiastic. You know why? He felt possessive of our relationship. Sweet, right? Of course, I got upset, but then I thought it over and I got it. Can you hear me, love? I'm doing this live but I want you to hear this. I understand you. I think it's nice that you're possessive of our relationship. It's what I love most about you. You always put my happiness first. And I do the same for you. That's what love is, right? Making sure the person at your side is happy. And we're happy now. So why have a child? I'd have to split some of my love for you in half, and give some to the child. Which might ruin everything. That's what I was thinking, but then I told myself: no! I wouldn't have to split my love. I could give all of it to you, and all of it to our child. I just need to make more of it. Double it. Triple it. Grow as much as is needed. I can do that. Because I want to. Love is unlimited. And the fact that we're happy now doesn't mean we couldn't be even happier. Twice as happy. Three times as happy. However we want. As much as we want. Fuck, my battery's died. Can you hear me? Where are you, love? Can you hear me, my battery died! I have to finish my video, I can't leave it half done like that. Love! You've also got to make my burgers. How can I have breakfast without my burgers? Love? Are you in the kitchen? Come here, come on. You know I don't like it when you keep me waiting. Looooove! Can you hear me? Where are you? Is everything okay? Come on, answer me. Answer me! Looooooove! (*Silence.*) Heeeeelp! Heeeeeeeeeeeeeeeelp! (*Silence.*) Love! Where are you? Love! Heeeeeelp.

The **Downstairs Neighbour** *enters.*

Downstairs Neighbour What's happening?

Fattest Woman in the World Who are you? What are you doing here?

Downstairs Neighbour I'm your downstairs neighbour. I heard yelling and . . . .

Fattest Woman in the World Where's my husband?

Downstairs Neighbour I have no idea. I just got here.

Fattest Woman in the World Didn't you move out?

Downstairs Neighbour Yes, two months ago. We're sleeping in our car.

Fattest Woman in the World So what are you doing here?

Downstairs Neighbour I came in to make a coffee. I heard yelling and I came upstairs. The door was open. Is everything alright?

Fattest Woman in the World Can I ask you a favour?

Downstairs Neighbour Sure.

Fattest Woman in the World Can you check if my husband is in the kitchen?

Downstairs Neighbour Alright.

Fattest Woman in the World Or in the living room, the bathroom, anywhere else.

The **Downstairs Neighbour** *exits, or just looks around.*

Downstairs Neighbour I'm sorry, he's not here. Maybe he went out.

Fattest Woman in the World He usually tells me when he's going out. Sometimes he does the shopping while I'm asleep, but he should be back by now. For breakfast. Are you going to hurt me?

Downstairs Neighbour What? Me? Why?

Fattest Woman in the World Because of the thing with the crack. Did you hurt my husband?

Downstairs Neighbour I wanted to, let me tell you. But I'm not a violent person.

Fattest Woman in the World Can I ask you a favour?

Downstairs Neighbour Sure.

Fattest Woman in the World There should be a charger in the kitchen next to the computer. I never keep my mobile phone close to me when I sleep. Because of the radiation. Could you get it for me?

Downstairs Neighbour Yes, sure.

Fattest Woman in the World Thank you, that's kind of you. I'm sorry I was suspicious, but you know, my husband has disappeared and I . . .

Downstairs Neighbour Don't worry.

Fattest Woman in the World Oh, and . . . I'm sorry, I don't wish to take advantage of your kindness, but . . .

Downstairs Neighbour Go ahead, don't worry.

Fattest Woman in the World In the kitchen, in the cupboard next to the computer and the charger, there should be some packets of crisps. Could you bring me a couple?

Downstairs Neighbour A couple of crisps?

Fattest Woman in the World A couple of packets.

Downstairs Neighbour ... Alright.

Fattest Woman in the World Thank you.

The **Downstairs Neighbour** *starts to exit, then pauses.*

Downstairs Neighbour Excuse me, I know this isn't the time, but ... can I ask you something?

Fattest Woman in the World Sure, but first could you get me the charger and the crisps? If you don't mind.

Downstairs Neighbour Aren't you worried?

Fattest Woman in the World About what?

Downstairs Neighbour About your condition.

Fattest Woman in the World What condition?

Downstairs Neighbour Being ... overweight.

Fattest Woman in the World I'm not overweight. I'm curvy.

Downstairs Neighbour What?

Fattest Woman in the World Shapely.

Downstairs Neighbour Your husband told me you weigh over four hundred kilos.

Fattest Woman in the World Very shapely.

Downstairs Neighbour Sure, but ...

Fattest Woman in the World I bet you like thin women.

Downstairs Neighbour It's not about liking or disliking.

Fattest Woman in the World Don't be embarrassed, it's the dominant aesthetic. Thin and in shape. It's not a problem, I understand. But I'm no longer a slave to those stereotypes.

Downstairs Neighbour No, look, it's not about aesthetics ...

Fattest Woman in the World Everything is about aesthetics. Work. Friendships. Selling. Buying. Success. It's a whole dictatorship. But I've rebelled against it. It doesn't concern me anymore. Could you please get me the charger? I'm worried about my husband.

Downstairs Neighbour Yes, I'll go get it now, but ...

Fattest Woman in the World Please don't argue with me. I've been dealing with this for years, and I'm proud to be plus size.

Downstairs Neighbour Plus size.

Fattest Woman in the World Would you prefer another term? Chubby? Fat?

Downstairs Neighbour That's not what I said.

Fattest Woman in the World But it's what you thought.

Downstairs Neighbour You know, you and your husband are both very good at interrogating people on what they supposedly think.

Fattest Woman in the World It's not nice to feel interrogated, is it?

Downstairs Neighbour No, listen, I . . .

Fattest Woman in the World All it takes is a look. I'm used to it, don't worry. But please don't waste time trying to lecture me just because I want to eat a couple of crisps.

Downstairs Neighbour A couple of packets.

Fattest Woman in the World Yes, a couple of packets. So what?

Downstairs Neighbour Listen, even if I agreed with you about aesthetic appearance, there's something else you're not taking into consideration. Your health.

Fattest Woman in the World What do you know about my health?

Downstairs Neighbour Well, being unable to move can't be good for your circulation.

Fattest Woman in the World My uncle worked out every day, and died at forty from a heart attack.

Downstairs Neighbour What I'm saying is that eating this much . . .

Fattest Woman in the World How do you know how much I eat? We've just met.

Downstairs Neighbour Fine, eating unhealthily . . .

Fattest Woman in the World How do you know I eat unhealthily?

Downstairs Neighbour You just asked me to bring you two packets of crisps.

Fattest Woman in the World They're fried in olive oil. They're organic. Now, please, I want to phone my husband. I'm very worried. I'm scared that something has happened and I need to see if he picks up, so would you please be so kind as to . . .

Downstairs Neighbour No.

Fattest Woman in the World What?

Downstairs Neighbour I can bring you some apricots.

Fattest Woman in the World What?

Downstairs Neighbour If you're hungry. Instead of crisps.

Fattest Woman in the World We don't have any apricots.

Downstairs Neighbour I have some in the car.

Fattest Woman in the World I don't like them.

Downstairs Neighbour   What kind of fruit do you like?

Fattest Woman in the World   Listen, what do you think you're doing? That's enough. If you don't bring me the charger right this second, I'm going to sue you.

Downstairs Neighbour   Oh so you've gone from calling me kind to threatening me?

Fattest Woman in the World   You stopped being kind and started interrogating me because I'm fat. Yes, I'm fat. I'm enormous. I'm actually in the Guinness Book of World Records. You don't like me? Great. Plenty of other people do. There are people who find me attractive, sexy, there are companies that pay me to be their spokesperson. Does anybody pay you to be their spokesperson? Huh? But above all, the most important thing is that I like myself. Because I'm happy as I am. And nobody has the right to harass me. Understood?

The **Downstairs Neighbour** *exits.*

Fattest Woman in the World   Where are you going? Hey, where are you going?

What are you doing? You can't leave me here. Hey! Come back! Come back here right now!

The **Downstairs Neighbours** *re-enters with a bag of apricots.*

Downstairs Neighbour   They've been washed.

The **Fattest Woman in the World** *eats the apricots voraciously, and with disgust.*

Fattest Woman in the World   What do you think you're doing? You smoke, don't you? My husband told me. You smoke!

Downstairs Neighbour   Yes, I smoke.

Fattest Woman in the World   Smoking isn't good for your health either.

Downstairs Neighbour   Which is why I'm trying to quit.

Fattest Woman in the World   How's that going?

Downstairs Neighbour   It's not easy.

Fattest Woman in the World   Do you feel guilty?

Downstairs Neighbour   Sometimes.

Fattest Woman in the World   Well I don't. Not anymore. I used to feel guilty as a child, when all my classmates were skinny and in shape and I was the fat one. I'd go home, open the fridge, think 'don't eat the snacks, don't eat the snacks'. Then I'd eat them and while I was eating I'd feel sick thinking that I was never going to lose weight, that I was never going to be as beautiful as my classmates, that I was never going to have a boyfriend, that nobody was ever going to like me. I couldn't even enjoy the taste of food because I was so full of guilt that I felt sick, and the more I felt sick, the more I ate. The more I ate, the more I felt sick. Because I didn't accept myself. I didn't accept my own nature. But now I do. And ever since then, I've been happy.

Downstairs Neighbour Your happiness has consequences for other people's lives.

Fattest Woman in the World What?

Downstairs Neighbour My home is collapsing because of you.

Fattest Woman in the World See. There we go. My husband's been saying it for months. You think this crack is my fault.

Downstairs Neighbour No, I don't think it is. I know it is.

Fattest Woman in the World Oh, you know it is? Based on what?

Downstairs Neighbour Based on the fact that the ceiling was built to support 200 kilos per square meter, and when you add up the sofa, the wardrobe and your 460 kilos . . .

Fattest Woman in the World Are you talking about me as if I were an item of furniture?

Downstairs Neighbour I'm talking about weight, and you weight a lot more than the furniture.

Fattest Woman in the World You're insulting me.

Downstairs Neighbour No, I'm just telling you the truth.

Fattest Woman in the World Well, I don't believe it.

Downstairs Neighbour What?

Fattest Woman in the World I don't believe there's a crack.

Downstairs Neighbour Why would I make that up?

Fattest Woman in the World Propaganda.

Downstairs Neighbour Wow. Really? I would tell you to come see for yourself, if you could move.

Fattest Woman in the World Wouldn't make a difference. You could have drawn it on.

Downstairs Neighbour Oh, I get it. You think I'm a moron. Did your husband put you up to this? 'The guy downstairs is a moron, you can tell him whatever you want'. Drawn it on? There's a leak. Water is dripping down. Did I draw that too? And 'Propaganda'? To do what?

Fattest Woman in the World To ruin our way of life.

Downstairs Neighbour You think I give a shit about your way of life?

Fattest Woman in the World I don't know, you tell me. Maybe you're jealous?

Downstairs Neighbour Of how you do nothing all day.

Fattest Woman in the World Exactly. Of our serenity. Our wellbeing.

Downstairs Neighbour Your wellbeing? Your wellbeing means that my son has to sleep in our car, for fuck's sake! I'm a calm person, but this situation is making me lose my mind. Do you get that? I'm losing my mind.

Silence.

Fattest Woman in the World Listen. I'm sorry this tension has developed between us. You and I see things differently. Many things. But that's normal, isn't it? Everyone has a different opinion. We must respect them all, right? I respect yours and you respect mine. Even if we don't understand each other. You were very kind, bringing me those apricots. Now I'm asking you, please, could you at least bring me my charger? Please. I'm worried about my husband. I beg you.

Downstairs Neighbour Earlier you talked about aesthetics. You said 'I'm free from this dictatorship'. I think there's another dictatorship, a regime of opinions. People do the stupidest, most harmful things and then say 'well, that's just my opinion'. That's the real dictatorship. You know what? I do not respect your opinion. I'm sorry, I don't. We can say curvy instead of fat, plus size instead of obese, we can use all the politically correct terms you want, but eating so much that you cannot move, eating so much that you make the ceiling collapse . . . is wrong. It's not an opinion. It's a crime.

Fattest Woman in the World So you won't bring me my charger?

Downstairs Neighbour No. And I hope for your sake that your husband comes back soon, because you know what I'll do if he doesn't? I'll come back tomorrow and bring you some vegetables. Legumes. Grains. Healthy things.

Fattest Woman in the World How dare you? What right do you have? You can't leave me here, like this, with apricots and vegetables, cut off from the outside world. You can't deprive me of my freedom!

Downstairs Neighbour If freedom is what made you end up like this, you'd have been better off without it.

Scene 5

The documentary starts playing again, for three or four seconds, then pauses again.

Fattest Woman in the World No more spinach. I beg you. I can't take it anymore.

Downstairs Neighbour Courgettes?

Fattest Woman in the World No.

Downstairs Neighbour Carrots? Pumpkin?

Fattest Woman in the World At least give me some pasta. Some bread.

Downstairs Neighbour You ate carbs last week.

Fattest Woman in the World I beg you.

Downstairs Neighbour You'll get rice tomorrow.

Fattest Woman in the World With what?

Downstairs Neighbour Plain.

Fattest Woman in the World Plain rice doesn't taste of anything.

Downstairs Neighbour Alright. Then it'll be chickpea soup.

Fattest Woman in the World No, no, no chickpeas. I'll take the rice.

Downstairs Neighbour You shouldn't have complained.

Fattest Woman in the World Come on, please.

Downstairs Neighbour Keep this up and you won't get any chickpeas either.

Fattest Woman in the World You really are a piece of shit, you know that. A disgusting piece of shit. But this won't last. My husband will come back. Someone else will find me. I'm famous. People watch my videos, they buy pictures of me. Millions of people. When they realise I've disappeared, that I've stopped answering messages and emails, they'll come looking for me. They'll call the police and I'll turn you in, you bastard. I'll put you in jail, and I'll sue you for so many damages that your son will have to work his whole life to pay me off. You understand? I'll destroy you. I'll ruin your life, you piece of shit.

Downstairs Neighbour Whatever. Tomorrow is detox day.

Scene 6

The documentary starts playing again, for three or four seconds, then pauses again.

Fattest Woman in the World Can't we make an exception, just for today?

Downstairs Neighbour You've been making exceptions for too long. You've used them all up. I can give you an apple if you want.

Fattest Woman in the World Thank you.

Downstairs Neighbour Tomorrow, plain rice. OK?

Fattest Woman in the World Yes.

Downstairs Neighbour Even if it's tasteless?

Fattest Woman in the World Yes.

Downstairs Neighbour You've become so much more compliant, in only two months. You know, I put your phone on charge and then looked through it. It's true that some people write to you – 'post some new pictures!', 'why aren't you making more videos?'. Not that many people – not as many as you think, I reckon– but a few did write. So I got curious and took a look at your body of work. I've never seen such disgusting images. I think you misunderstand something. People don't adore you.

They follow you because you're revolting, and people are fascinated by revolting things. Deformities. The macabre. I can just picture all the teenagers, mocking one another: 'Ohhh is this your girlfriend?', 'No, no, she's yours', 'Gross, I wouldn't give her one even if I was dead', 'Oh, look at this photo, ewwww'. You're not a star. You're a charity case. And if you stop posting, people'll move on to someone else, like the world's shortest man, the hairiest woman, some guy with three nipples. Would you call the police because a guy with three nipples has stopped posting videos? Or would you think he went to get help?

Fattest Woman in the World   You're a piece of shit.

Downstairs Neighbour   Come on, now. I'm just being honest, and you insult me?

Fattest Woman in the World   I wish I could get up just so I could kill you.

Downstairs Neighbour   Well, that's a start. At least you want to get up.

Fattest Woman in the World   I'm not joking.

Downstairs Neighbour   Neither am I. And when you do get up, you'll discover a world of possibilities that you've missed out on by being stuck on the sofa. Like killing the guy who's trying to cure you, sure, but also things like going for drinks with your husband, strolling with him down the street, going on holiday with him . . . you still think something happened to him, don't you? He's probably just spending a normal day with a normal woman.

Fattest Woman in the World   Stop it!

Downstairs Neighbour   I know I should think you're stupid, but I actually find your naivety almost moving.

Fattest Woman in the World   I told you, stop it! Enough! Shut up!

Downstairs Neighbour   Alright. Tomorrow is detox day.

Fattest Woman in the World   No, no, no.

Downstairs Neighbour   You know, you really shouldn't raise your voice.

Scene 7

The documentary starts playing again for three or four seconds, then pauses again.

Downstairs Neighbour   Here's your herbal tea.

Fattest Woman in the World   Thank you.

Downstairs Neighbour   Are you still upset about what I said the other day? Perhaps I went too far. But things aren't going well for me, either. My wife went to stay at her mother's and I haven't seen them in two weeks. I got complaints at school because I was rude to some students. My colleagues say I stink and I can't even get to sleep in my car anymore. I'm falling apart.

Fattest Woman in the World Do you really think my husband has left me?

Downstairs Neighbour Well, it can't be easy to be with a woman like you. I wouldn't do it.

Fattest Woman in the World But I have beautiful bone structure.

Downstairs Neighbour Sure, but it's not the first thing one notices.

Fattest Woman in the World So why did he want to be with me?

Downstairs Neighbour How long were you together?

Fattest Woman in the World Seven years.

Downstairs Neighbour What did his family think?

Fattest Woman in the World He never introduced me to anyone.

Downstairs Neighbour No one? Not even any relatives, an uncle, a friend, a loved one?

Fattest Woman in the World He'd say 'I don't have any loved ones apart from you'. Do you think he did it for the money? You know, we did quite well with our videos. And since that Mexican woman died because of her thyroid, and I broke the Guinness World Record . . .

Downstairs Neighbour He shouldn't have led you on and then made you suffer like this.

Fattest Woman in the World I was thin once, you know? I was twenty. I weighed 200 kilos. I had an operation and within a few short months I was down to 80. Suddenly, boys looked at me differently. This old classmate of mine, a boy I'd always liked, who used to treat me like a friend and greet me by patting me on the back, well . . . I saw him one night at the pub and his eyes lit up. 'Oh, hi, I almost didn't recognise you, you look incredible'. And he asked me lots more questions than he ever had before, asked me how I was, what I was doing, where I was going . . . later he kissed me goodbye on the cheek. 'Let's stay in touch, let's hang out', he said. That was the first time I ever so much as brushed someone's cheek. I felt his beard prickle me and I got so excited. But then I started gaining weight again and the next time we saw each other his eyes didn't light up, he didn't ask me any questions and after talking to me for ten seconds he left and just patted me on the back. My husband was the first man to truly love me for who I was. He'd say he liked me just as I was. So I started liking myself, because he liked me. And then others started to like me. But it was all fake.

Scene 8

The documentary starts playing again for three or four seconds, then pauses again.

The Fattest Woman in the World *is crying.*

Downstairs Neighbour I bought some potatoes. I could roast them for you, if you fancy it.

Fattest Woman in the World Of course I fancy it.

Downstairs Neighbour Would you like some breadsticks, too?

Fattest Woman in the World You haven't let me eat carbs for seven months.

Downstairs Neighbour Yes, but lately you've been terrific. You deserve a cheat day, if you want one.

Fattest Woman in the World I don't.

Downstairs Neighbour You don't?

Fattest Woman in the World I've already cheated enough.

Scene 9

The documentary starts playing again for three or four seconds, then pauses again.

Downstairs Neighbour Today's the big day. Are you happy?

Fattest Woman in the World I can't wait.

Downstairs Neighbour Wait, don't push it. You need help. Your leg muscles are out of practice. You could fall.

Fattest Woman in the World Well help me, then.

Downstairs Neighbour I can't do it alone. (*A pause.* **The Fattest Woman in the World** *is upset.*) No, no. You've slimmed down so much. It's just that I have a bad back. Let's wait for my friend, the engineer. We'll help you get up, we'll take you down to the courtyard, we'll move the sofa, we'll finally take a look at the crack from above, and if everything is as my friend thinks it is, the contractor'll be here in an hour to do the job, and by this evening it'll all be done. What's wrong?

Fattest Woman in the World You're going to leave me waiting in the courtyard by myself?

Downstairs Neighbour Just for a few hours.

Silence.

Fattest Woman in the World I'm not sure I feel up to it. Maybe I need a few more days of dieting.

Downstairs Neighbour What? No. You're perfect.

Fattest Woman in the World Yeah, right. Perfect.

Downstairs Neighbour In a few years, you'll look back and think of this day as the day of your rebirth.

Fattest Woman in the World Will you still come and visit me, afterwards?

Downstairs Neighbour Of course. If you want me to.

Fattest Woman in the World I do.

Downstairs Neighbour You used to want to kill me.

Fattest Woman in the World Because you were hurting me. But you were just being honest.

We hear the sound of a door opening.

Downstairs Neighbour There he is, that'll be my friend. Come in here, come on in.

The **Downstairs Neighbour** *and the* **Fattest Woman in the World** *wait. The* **Husband** *enters, holding a plastic bag. They all look at one another.*

Husband What is he doing here?

Fattest Woman in the World Where have you been?

Husband In a coma.

Fattest Woman in the World Why didn't you tell me?

Husband Because I was in a coma. I ran here as soon as I woke up, I was worried. But I see you took the chance to strike up a new friendship.

Fattest Woman in the World I thought you left me because you were cheating on me.

Husband So you decided to cheat on me, too? As revenge?

Fattest Woman in the World Oh, no. I didn't cheat on you.

Husband So what is he doing here?

Downstairs Neighbour I've been taking care of your wife.

Husband I wasn't talking to you.

Fattest Woman in the World I would've starved to death. You said it yourself, you were worried. He took care of me.

Downstairs Neighbour See?

Husband He took care of you . . . as a friend?

Fattest Woman in the World Yes, as a friend.

Downstairs Neighbour As an acquaintance.

Silence.

Husband You've lost weight.

Downstairs Neighbour She's been eating healthy food.

Husband She doesn't like healthy food.

Downstairs Neighbour Well, sometimes we do things we don't like in order to feel better, don't we?

Husband Could you give me a moment alone with my wife?

Downstairs Neighbour Take all the time you need. But please, maybe do so in the courtyard.

Husband In the courtyard?

Downstairs Neighbour Yes, the construction company is coming today. To renovate the flat. Since your wife can stand up now. I was just waiting for my engineer friend to come help me move her, but if you want to, you and I can do it. Then I'll go to work and leave you two alone.

Husband Why are you renovating your flat?

Downstairs Neighbour Because of the crack.

Husband What crack?

Downstairs Neighbour The one we're standing on.

Husband I don't see any cracks.

Downstairs Neighbour Because it's underneath the sofa. If you help me move your wife, we can move the sofa too and you'll see the crack.

Husband She didn't even give me a kiss.

Fattest Woman in the World Because you're too far away. If you come over here, I will.

Downstairs Neighbour How about we all go downstairs, and you can kiss in the courtyard?

Husband Don't tell me when I can and cannot kiss my wife.

Fattest Woman in the World Why are you talking to him like that?

Husband And why are you defending him?

Fattest Woman in the World Look, if it wasn't for him . . . you disappeared out of the blue. Without telling me.

Husband I was in a fucking coma. How could I have told you?

Fattest Woman in the World I didn't know if you were dead, if you'd left . . .

Husband Didn't you think to call the hospital? The police?

Fattest Woman in the World My phone was dead.

Husband Until he got here. I bet he charged it for you, didn't he?

Fattest Woman in the World No.

Husband Why not?

Downstairs Neighbour It's a long story. I'm sure once you and your wife are alone in the courtyard . . .

Husband Why didn't you bring her phone?

Fattest Woman in the World In the end I stopped asking him.

Husband Because you didn't give a shit about me anymore.

Fattest Woman in the World I thought you'd left me for a thinner girl.

Husband A thinner girl? I don't like thin girls. Who put this thought in your head? The two of you are hiding something.

Downstairs Neighbour You're hiding something too. So don't you think it's best that we all go downstairs to the courtyard?

Husband And what would I be hiding?

Downstairs Neighbour You know full well.

Husband No, I don't. Go on. You tell me. What would I be hiding? Tell me.

Downstairs Neighbour If you really were in a coma, someone would have notified your wife, wouldn't they?

Husband We're not married.

Downstairs Neighbour What do you mean?

Husband Not legally.

Fattest Woman in the World We're not.

Husband Marriage is just a symbol, so we got married symbolically. So there, I'm not hiding anything. What about you two?

Downstairs Neighbour I had to be a little tough on her, at first.

Husband What? What for?

Downstairs Neighbour To help your wife lose weight.

Husband Did my wife want to lose weight? Did you want to lose weight?

Fattest Woman in the World At first, I didn't. But afterwards, I did.

Husband Afterwards? After he made you believe I'd run off with someone thinner? Did he guilt trip you, love? (*To the* **Downstairs Neighbour**.) Do you know how much we worked on guilt? It took us years to free her from her guilt. Perhaps you never thought of this because you have a one-track mind, 'The crack, the crack', but guilt is violence. It makes people feel bad just because they don't want to conform. 'You're wrong'. 'You must try harder'. Why? For what? To be the same as everyone else?

Downstairs Neighbour Look, I'm beyond trying to convince her. She can think whatever what she wants. And so can you, you can do whatever you want. As long as you just let me repair my flat.

Husband You see? He's just out for himself. He doesn't give a shit about you.

Downstairs Neighbour No. You're the one who doesn't give a shit, because you enable her weaknesses.

Husband How are they weaknesses, exactly?

Downstairs Neighbour Listen, I don't want to get into this with you. If you don't want to help me, I'll wait for my friend. Then we'll help her up . . .

Husband Nobody's coming into my home without my permission.

Downstairs Neighbour Fine, I'll do it alone. Who cares about my back.

Husband If you try to touch my wife, I'll call the police.

Downstairs Neighbour Aren't you going to say anything? That's it? Silent. Not a word to say.

Husband He can't talk to you like that. You let him talk to you like that? What happened, love? What happened to my queen? This hypocrite tried to brainwash you, to make you feel bad, just to fix some crack we're not even sure exists.

Downstairs Neighbour Oh no. That's too far.

Husband Oh, shut up. He doesn't care about you at all. You lost some weight, did you? But do you really want to spend your life eating . . . What did he feed you? Plain rice and vegetables? Just so you can be a little thinner? Would that make you happy? Tell me honestly: do you think you'd be happy?

Fattest Woman in the World But wouldn't you like to go on holiday with me? Wouldn't you like to do things with me?

Husband Well, of course I would.

Fattest Woman in the World We wanted a child, didn't we? I still do. Wouldn't you want me to be the type of mum who can go for a walk in the park with her child?

Husband Of course.

Downstairs Neighbour So what's the fucking problem?

Husband I just don't want that to make you feel anxious or unhappy. I don't want you to think that there's a right way to be and a wrong way to be. You're fine either way. I like you either way. You want to keep up the diet and lose weight? That's fine. I'll even help you to stand. I don't mind.

Downstairs Neighbour You're finally making sense.

Husband But if you want to eat a burger, you can eat a burger.

Fattest Woman in the World A burger?

Husband Here, look, I got you three.

Downstairs Neighbour No, come on. You're tempting her.

Fattest Woman in the World Well, you tempted me too.

Downstairs Neighbour Yes, but with a breadstick.

Husband I'm just showing her a burger.

Downstairs Neighbour Three.

Husband Three. So what?

Fattest Woman in the World Is there sauce?

Husband Yes.

Fattest Woman in the World And chips?

Husband Three portions.

Downstairs Neighbour I don't believe it. I don't believe it. You're seriously considering it? You genuinely want to go back to how you were?

Husband What was wrong with how she was? My wife has always been an extremely beautiful woman.

Downstairs Neighbour Your wife is an obese woman who until seven months ago was two obese women.

Husband She's curvy. And she has beautiful bone structure.

Downstairs Neighbour You couldn't even see her bone structure, for fuck's sake.

Husband Don't you dare treat her like that. Did he treat you like this? Tell me. If he treated you like this, I'll kill him.

Downstairs Neighbour I only did it to educate her.

Husband What makes you think my wife needed to be educated?

Downstairs Neighbour Something that you've been trying to deny since the first day we met: evidence.

Husband You seem to assume that what is evident to you is evident to everybody, but that's not the case.

Downstairs Neighbour You and I don't understand each other.

Husband We do not.

Downstairs Neighbour We never have.

Husband Leave my flat.

Downstairs Neighbour No.

Husband I'm telling you to leave.

Silence.

Downstairs Neighbour Fine. Do what you want. Destroy your life however you choose. Can I just ask you for one thing? Would you give me half a day? Just half a day to save my flat? Then you won't see me ever again. I beg you.

Husband If my wife is fine with it, so am I.

Fattest Woman in the World Yes, I'm fine with it.

Downstairs Neighbour Thank you.

Fattest Woman in the World Although . . . Are the burgers still hot?

Husband Lukewarm.

Fattest Woman in the World I don't like a cold burger.

Downstairs Neighbour You can reheat them in the oven later, can't you?

Fattest Woman in the World Ah, it's not the same.

Husband No, it isn't.

Fattest Woman in the World Give me a bite of one.

Downstairs Neighbour No, please.

Fattest Woman in the World Just one. And a couple of chips. Then we'll go.

Downstairs Neighbour No. Don't give it to her.

Husband Here you are, love.

The **Husband** *hands a burger to the* **Fattest Woman in the World**, *who starts to eat it.*

Downstairs Neighbour I beg you, couldn't you at least – as a compromise – walk while you eat?

Fattest Woman in the World I don't like doing things while I eat.

The **Husband** *hands another burger to the* **Fattest Woman in the World**, *who continues eating. The* **Downstairs Neighbour** *goes to say something, but hesitates. After a few bites, he knows there's nothing left to do.*

Downstairs Neighbour You two bring out the very worst in me. You know, I hope this kills you. So world can be rid of your presence.

The documentary starts playing again. Time passes.

Scene 10

Two years later.

The **Fattest Woman in the World** *and her Husband sit expectantly, both munching on a packet of crisps.*

There's a cot onstage, and the floor is littered with leftover food.

The **Fattest Woman in the World** *picks up her mobile phone and records a video.*

Fattest Woman in the World Hello, boys and girls. Thank you for all the messages you've sent me recently, asking how I was and why I wasn't posting any more videos. The thing is, from today . . .

She pauses, then starts again.

Fattest Woman in the World Two years ago I was ill, but this time it's different. I won't be able to post videos for a while, because . . .

She pauses, then starts again.

Fattest Woman in the World I wasn't ill two years ago. My neighbour kept me prisoner for seven months. I wanted to make a video about it to tell everyone, but I felt ashamed. Better to say I was really ill, right? A heart-breaking story. That's what you want, isn't it. Something thrilling. What do you care about the truth? What do you care about how people are really doing?

She pauses, then starts again.

Fattest Woman in the World Hello, boys and girls. Thank you for the messages. It's good to feel close to you all.

She pauses, then starts again.

Fattest Woman in the World Hello, boys and girls. It's been a while since my last video, but I'm not ill like I was two years ago. I just need a bit of . . . Thank you to those who wrote to me. It's good to feel close to you all.

She pauses, then starts again.

Fattest Woman in the World It's wonderful to have people take an interest in you, in what you do and what you say. But the truth is, when you're suffering, when you're startled awake in the middle of the night and your heart is beating out of your chest and your brain can't think of anything except how bad you feel, how much you feel like you're going crazy . . . you're all alone. None of those people are there with you. And it's not their fault, it's just that . . . the pain is yours, yours alone, you can't share it with anyone else, nobody can take a piece of it, carry it and ease your suffering. Nobody can. Only you can.

She pauses.

Fattest Woman in the World I can't do it.

Husband Can't you just say you're sorry that you didn't post any videos, you weren't feeling well, and you need to take a break? They'll understand. They've always stood by you.

Fattest Woman in the World They didn't stand by me. Nobody stood by me.

Husband I did.

Fattest Woman in the World No, you didn't.

Husband Why are you being like this?

Fattest Woman in the World I'm sorry, I just . . .

Husband Don't worry. Don't worry. I know. I know.

Fattest Woman in the World He's not coming, is he?

Husband I don't know, but we can't spend all our time waiting for . . .

Fattest Woman in the World It's been three days already.

Husband I told you. Calling him was a mistake.

Fattest Woman in the World We had no choice.

Husband Let's try it ourselves, one more time.

Fattest Woman in the World It's useless. You're an enabler.

Husband Because I love you.

Fattest Woman in the World If you loved me, you'd try harder. You're weak.

Husband I'm sorry.

Fattest Woman in the World See? Instead of actually reacting, you just apologise.

Husband It would've been better if I'd never woken from that coma.

Fattest Woman in the World No, don't say that.

Husband You're making me say it. You're making me feel like I'm the problem.

Fattest Woman in the World I'm sorry.

Husband If I wasn't here, everything would fall into place.

Fattest Woman in the World I said I'm sorry. It would be worse if you weren't here. It would be worse. But I'm not well.

Husband Neither am I.

The **Husband** *picks up a fried chicken drumstick from the cradle, and hands it to the* **Fattest Woman in the World**, *who starts eating it.*

We hear a door open.

The **Downstairs Neighbour** *enters.*

Husband Welcome. Have a seat. Please. Please. Thank you for coming. We're very grateful. You know, you weren't easy to find.

Downstairs Neighbour I moved.

Husband I'm happy for you. I actually tried leaving you a note under the door but . . .

Downstairs Neighbour I don't come here anymore.

Husband But you still own the flat, don't you?

Downstairs Neighbour What was I supposed to do, sell it for a fifth of the price?

Husband Turned out to be more structurally sound than you thought, didn't it? It's been two years and it's still standing.

Downstairs Neighbour   Have you made me come all the way here just to mock me some more?

Husband   No, no. Absolutely not. Actually, we wanted to apologise to you. And we wanted to tell you that we checked – well, I checked – I knelt down, looked under the sofa and I saw what is unequivocally . . . a crack.

Fattest Woman in the World   You were right.

Silence.

Husband   Aren't you going to say anything?

Downstairs Neighbour   Well, what do you want me to say?

Husband   Aren't you happy? After more than two years, we finally . . .

Downstairs Neighbour   No, I'm not happy.

Husband   I'm sorry. We were hoping . . .

Fattest Woman in the World   I want you to help me lose weight. I can't do it alone. And he doesn't know how to be strict with me.

Husband   It hurts me to see her upset. When she says she's hungry, I can't be strict.

Fattest Woman in the World   I've stopped gaining weight. But it's not enough.

Husband   That's why we need your help. And if you help us, my wife will be able to move, and you'll finally be able to fix your crack. Our crack.

Downstairs Neighbour   And why should I give a shit?

Husband   About the crack?

Downstairs Neighbour   About the crack. About you two.

Husband   If you renovate the flat, you can sell it. I'm sure some money would . . .

Downstairs Neighbour   Why should I give a shit about money?

Fattest Woman in the World   What's wrong with you? Are you drunk?

Downstairs Neighbour   No.

Fattest Woman in the World   You seem drunk.

Downstairs Neighbour   I'm tired.

Husband   I know there's been some tension between us. And we're mostly to blame for that. I'm mostly to blame. I admit it. But now, together, we could solve a situation that's becoming more and more concerning. You may not have noticed, since you haven't seen it in a while, but the crack is very large. I don't have any way to compare it to how it was before, but I'd say it must have definitely gotten worse.

Downstairs Neighbour   Shame it hasn't made the whole thing collapse already.

Husband   That's not very nice of you.

Downstairs Neighbour I don't care about being nice. You're telling me that I was right, but that's not true. Can't you see? The building is still standing. Everything is fine. I was the one who was wrong. I was stupid. I became obsessed with it, I listened to the Council, called an engineer, slept in my car. I should have behaved like you. 'We're fatalists'. That would have been better. We're still here, aren't we? We'd all still be here. I'd still have my wife and child. I'd still have a job. I'd still be a normal person, with peace of mind, wellbeing. I wouldn't stink. Wouldn't drink. Wouldn't wander around like a nutter. I should've just acted like it was nothing. Looked the other way. You want me to help you? No. I'm going to look the other way. I've been stupid enough already. Goodbye.

The **Downstairs Neighbour** *goes to exit.*

Fattest Woman in the World Wait.

Downstairs Neighbour What.

Fattest Woman in the World Why did you come?

Downstairs Neighbour I don't know. Maybe it was a mistake.

Fattest Woman in the World Listen. It's not just about the crack. We called you because . . .

Husband No, love.

Fattest Woman in the World We called you because we're desperate. We tried to have a child. The doctor said it was dangerous, but we did some research and we read online that some not thin women manage to have children.

Downstairs Neighbour 'Not thin'.

Fattest Woman in the World We tried anyway. But we lost it. (*Silence*) Then a year later, we tried again. I got ill. I almost died. We lost it again.

Husband It's okay, my love, it's okay.

Fattest Woman in the World The doctor said it was because of my excess weight.

Downstairs Neighbour I can only imagine your surprise at such an unexpected diagnosis.

Husband How dare you? How can you not be sensitive to . . .

Downstairs Neighbour Listen, in case I wasn't clear, I have no intention of being sensitive.

Husband You see? Calling him was a mistake.

Downstairs Neighbour Yes it was.

The **Downstairs Neighbour** *starts to exit.*

Fattest Woman in the World I beg you. I'm not well. I can't sleep at night, I feel like I'm going insane. I can't think of anything else. I feel guilty. I feel . . . like I caused the deaths of two children.

Husband You didn't cause them.

Fattest Woman in the World Yes, I did. It was me. No point pretending otherwise. I can still feel their blood on my hands. You were right. About my health. About making sacrifices. About everything. You were right about everything. I'm begging you, help me. Please. I know you think it's too late. But it isn't. Not for me. Not for you. Not for the building. Let's repair this crack. Together. Like we should have done two years ago. Let's save ourselves, and then start our lives all over again.

A long pause.

Downstairs Neighbour There isn't just one crack.

Husband What?

Downstairs Neighbour There are two.

Husband No, look . . .

Downstairs Neighbour I said, there are two.

Husband No. I knelt under the sofa. I saw it. I can assure you that . . .

Downstairs Neighbour If you want my help, you have to admit that there are two.

Husband What?

Downstairs Neighbour Now there are three.

Husband Alright, what next?!

Downstairs Neighbour Four.

Husband What's the point of this?

Downstairs Neighbour Five.

Husband Why? You know there's only one. Why are you . . .

Downstairs Neighbour Because you're the ones who called. You're the ones begging me. You want my help? You have to admit that there are five cracks. Six. Seven. As many as I want. Do you understand? As many as I want! How many? Answer me! How many are there?

Fattest Woman in the World How many do you want there to be?

Downstairs Neighbour Seven.

Fattest Woman in the World There are seven.

Downstairs Neighbour How many?

Husband According to you? Or for real?

Downstairs Neighbour For real? Since when do you give a shit about what's real?

Husband Since now.

Downstairs Neighbour Why? Why start now?

Husband Didn't you hear what my wife said? I did everything wrong. I always believed it was important to be open, to deny that anything was objective. Look where that got us. Look where that got us. I don't want to live like this anymore. I don't want to see my wife like this. I want to be happy.

Silence. The **Downstairs Neighbour** *starts laughing.*

Downstairs Neighbour Happy. You two want to be happy. And you think a child will make you happy?

Husband Yes.

Downstairs Neighbour That's why you want one? To be happy?

Fattest Woman in the World Yes.

Downstairs Neighbour Still?

Husband What do you mean, still?

Downstairs Neighbour Do you want to eat it?

Husband What on earth are you saying?

Downstairs Neighbour Yes, you want to eat it, don't you! That's your idea of happiness. Eating. Eating everything. Everything there is. No limits. No boundaries. Without ever getting full. You want to eat me, too? Why yes, of course. You called me because you wanted to eat me. You tell me I was right, that you've changed, so I can help you be 'happy'. But it's not true. It's all bullshit. You haven't changed. Your way of thinking is still the same. You've simply changed the menu. 'I don't feel like Guinness World Records anymore, I feel like a child'. And once you've eaten the child, you'll change again. And again. And again. Until you'll have eaten everything. Until your teeth and your tongue will have destroyed and chewed up every corner of the world, until you'll have stuffed yourselves so full that you won't be able to breathe. But even then . . . even then . . . you won't be happy. You will never be happy. Never. Do you understand? Never. Never. Never. Never.

We hear an extremely loud sound. The sound of an earthquake, like the previous one, but much louder.

Fattest Woman in the World What's happening?

The stage starts to shake. The Earth starts to shake. The earthquake is powerful and lasts for a long time. The **Fattest Woman in the World**, *the* **Downstairs Neighbour** *and the* **Husband** *raise their arms to the sky, as if to protect themselves. The building collapses, and with it, everything else that mankind has built. Only ruins are left on the stage.*

Scene 11

A **Dinosaur Guide** *enters, followed by two Dinosaurs.*

Dinosaur Guide And here we come to the most mysterious section of our museum, which houses the human bipeds, a very peculiar species that inhabited our planet approximately two hundred million years ago. In this room, we can see the findings of one of the most significant archaeological discoveries of the last few centuries. This is a vertical lair across two floors. We were able to reconstruct it using largely original materials. We also reassembled the skeletons of three human bipeds. Just think: nearly all the bones in their bodies had been fractured.

Female Dinosaur Poor creatures.

Male Dinosaur Why were their bones fractured?

Dinosaur Guide We hypothesize that their vertical lair suffered a structural failure and that this caused their death.

Female Dinosaur Poor creatures.

Male Dinosaur Well, they should have noticed their lair wasn't stable and fixed it, shouldn't they?

Female Dinosaur Why do you say that? Maybe they didn't have the tools. They weren't as evolved as we are.

Dinosaur Guide Actually, madam, it appears that the human bipeds had incredibly advanced scientific instruments at their disposal.

Male Dinosaur See?

Female Dinosaur So why didn't they do anything?

Male Dinosaur Because they were stupid.

Female Dinosaur Their hands are facing up. Poor creatures, they were trying to protect themselves.

Dinosaur Guide Actually, madam, we've pondered the meaning of this position at some length, but only recently came to a unanimous conclusion. These three specimens were praying to avert the collapse.

Female Dinosaur What?

Dinosaur Guide They had invited a priest for this very purpose. Look, the individual in the centre is larger. He must have been the priest of their cult. He's larger than the others because his physical shape evoked the cult of fertility.

Dinosaur So, instead of repairing their lair, they called a priest to pray to their God that it wouldn't collapse?

Dinosaur Guide Exactly. It appears that the human bipeds were very religious, especially in the later phase of their evolution. This is evidenced by the enormous number of sacred objects that were found inside the vertical lair. For instance, look at this sacred image.

The **Dinosaur Guide** *indicates a plastic bag that once contained crisps.*

Female Dinosaur What a strange object. What is it made of?

Dinosaur Guide A chemical compound derived from petroleum. Apparently, the human bipeds used to call it 'plastik'. All of their sacred objects were built with this material.

Female Dinosaur Why?

Dinosaur Guide Because it's very durable. Just think, two hundred million years later it still hasn't decomposed. The human bipeds thought, in their naivety, that by filling their vertical lair with as many sacred objects as possible, they would be demonstrating their devotion to God, and as such, God would protect them.

Male Dinosaur How absurd.

Female Dinosaur Alright, they were primitive creatures, bless them. But you can't judge a primitive species with the consciousness of today, it's not . . .

Male Dinosaur I'm not judging them. I'm just saying it's absurd. It's a good thing they went extinct.

Female Dinosaur Don't say that. How would you like it if someone said that about us, in two hundred thousand years, when we'll have gone extinct because of some meteor.

Male Dinosaur When they'll find our relics, they'll say we were a marvellous species.

Dinosaur Guide Well actually, madam, according to the latest expert research, it appears that the human bipeds did not in fact suffer extinction because of the impact of a meteor, as had always been believed.

Female Dinosaur They didn't?

Dinosaur Guide No. It appears that – for some reason that scholars have yet to understand – the conditions on Earth actually became incompatible with life.

Female Dinosaur Poor creatures. And they didn't realise it.

Dinosaur Guide Actually, it appears that they were fully aware of it.

Female Dinosaur Oh.

Dinosaur Guide We believe it was a conscious decision: to ignore the problem and devote themselves entirely to mass suicide, as part of a deliberate ritual sacrifice. (*Silence.*) As I said, they were very religious. Right, follow me, we'll now move on to the mating section.

The three dinosaurs exit.

Blackout.

Antigone Power

**By Ubah Cristina Ali Farah
after Sophocles**

Translated by Atri Banerjee

First staged at the Cantieri della Zisa, Palermo, on 26 July 2018.

Characters

Antigone
Creon
Ismene
Tiresias
Haemon
Eurydice
Chorus
Soldier 1
Soldier 2
Soldier 3

Content warning: racist language, bereavement and suicide.

Scene 1

Chorus Thebes awakens, saved from shipwreck. The city floats, like a huge sea creature, on a cloud of heat and dust. Not a breath of wind; the oily water bubbling red, brown, and white. The invaders are on the run, they have abandoned their weapons. Only Polynices and Eteocles remained on the field until the last: two brothers, sons of the same mother and the same father, their rivalry like a river in spate, a river that overflows and can no longer be contained. Polynices, full of arrogance, sided with the vagrants from the sea, while Eteocles defended our borders. They killed each other and now they lie on the beach, entwined in death.

Tiresias, *the soothsayer, enters, and turns to the* **Chorus**.

Tiresias Thebans, beware. Yours is a heavy city, overwhelmed by filth. In war, children are not born, they die; vultures and stray dogs feast on the flesh of the young. You will find no refuge in the world of the living, they fill your mess kits with food and you think yourselves safe. The inconstant chatter of charlatans clouds your minds, peace is the most precious thing – oh Thebans, what has become of you?

Chorus Don't get your head in a spin, Tiresias, don't get confused. The country had to be defended from invaders, or were we meant to have let them seize our possessions? It would have been our turn, then, to go elsewhere, as refugees, begging every day for a prescribed ration.

Tiresias You are naked already and have lost your dignity, in war children are not born, they die. One day you too will be exiles in a hostile and arid land, because you believed the lies of your politicians. With parched throats and swollen lips, it will be useless then to weep or even to pray.

Chorus Shut up, Tiresias, you are mad. All we wish for is to see the rain fall; all we wish for is our green earth; all we wish for is milk in abundance.

Tiresias Is it right to fight in the name of belonging? Is it right to fight a civil war? Is it right to bury our youth? To those who don't listen to reason, death will appear with a fierce look: it will have yellow hair and pink skin, a nightmare and a terror that will freeze the blood. Don't you hear the incessant lament for the dead? Oh, citizens, hear me: let justice be your pillar, he who is blinded by ambition is always bound to perish, preach peace and stop this war.

Chorus Our heroes departed in the afternoon, they departed in the afternoon. Gods, let them escape death, let them escape death. Have our children departed? They lingered in the afternoon, they lingered.

Tiresias *exits.*

Scene 2

Creon *enters.*

Chorus Here, at last is Creon, come to proclaim the return of the fighters. Now, let us forget war, let us forget death, let us celebrate all night and toast Victory. The people are singing.

Creon Citizens, disaster is averted, the harsh riptide. We are back on course! Spread the word, tell everyone: the foreigners, the terrorists, have gone back to where they came from!

Chorus Lord, you describe a great victory to us, but it would please the city even more were you to parade chariots through the streets, carrying our men, laden with mimes and dancing girls.

Creon I will, but have patience. There are still risks. Did you perhaps see me lay down my weapons? Our borders are still threatened by loathsome vermin attacking our happiness and prosperity. So far we've fared well. But there are still insurgents hidden among us, rats that threaten our citizens' well-being. I have summoned you all here because I appreciate your loyalty, to Oedipus, to our party. His sons have bestowed death upon each other. All power passes automatically into my hands. Now listen carefully. First of all, I don't trust any man who puts the interests of foreigners ahead of his neighbours'. Any man who scorns his homeland, I do not want him by my side. By these rulings I will make Thebes rich! I hope you approve.

Chorus A righteous ruler shall never want for friends. The State signifies safe harbour; we people on board, sailing straight ahead, feel strongly that we belong.

Creon I am at your service, I advocate for the interests of all. How does one measure the greatness of a State? By the splendour of a palace, built for its princes? By the magnificence of the temples erected to its gods? No! That counts for nothing compared to the happiness and prosperity of its people. But have you ever wondered who is responsible for maintaining this happiness, and this prosperity? Naturally, it is I, your servant! And furthermore, have you considered the measures to which a lord must resort in order to protect the welfare of his people? The answer is simple. The law! And what does the law do? The law is nothing less than a shield that I, a humble servant, bear, to defend you, my dear citizens.

But on to today. I've proclaimed an edict regarding the sons of Oedipus. Eteocles is a soldier, he fought for his people: let him be honoured with funeral rites.

The other, Polynices – the traitor, the dissident, the friend of terrorists, who returned from exile to set fire to his land, to drink the blood of his countrymen – I forbid his burial. I order his corpse to remain untombed, his naked flesh left as carrion for dogs and gulls. This is the law. I will never confound virtue with crime. Only he who gives everything for his country, dead or alive, will I always recognise with honour. I have spoken.

Chorus Bravo, Creon. You are the master of the law. It is up to you to decide the fate of those slain in battle, as well as the fate of us, the living.

Creon See to it that my order is carried out.

Chorus You should entrust this task to the army.

Creon That's not what I mean; soldiers already guard the corpse.

Chorus Then what are we to do?

Creon Some will not like my decision. You must hold fast against those who oppose me.

Chorus No one is foolish enough to risk death.

Creon Openly, no. But hidden among us are many dissident illegals; we must root them out and cleanse the city. Whoever violates my order will be punished by death.

Scene 3

Antigone *hears the edict proclaimed on the street: she sees it posted on the wall, she tears it down and runs breathlessly to* **Ismene**.

Antigone Ismene, my sister, I've called you out here, in the open, so that no one can overhear us. Did you see? Did you hear this decree cried out in the marketplace?

Ismene I have not slept all night. Our brothers dead on the same day, a hopeless pair, criss-crossed with blows. The invading migrants, rebuffed, wander aimlessly through these dark hours. I went out before dawn and the posters were already hung up. Creon orders that Eteocles should have the funeral he deserves, whereas it is forbidden to bury Polynices. Sacrilege, a new woe.

Antigone They leave him to the birds. Whoever breaks the law will be stoned by the people.

Ismene However I see, in your hands, that you've torn the order down. What do you plan to do? You have a fiery look in your eyes.

Antigone I have come to ask for your help. We must bury our brother. We cannot abandon him to the beasts.

Ismene I thought that's what you had in mind.

Antigone So, are you with me?

Ismene Oh sister, your heroics. You left me alone when our mother died, do you remember? Oh how much I hated you! I sought out your warmth, but you were no longer with me. Sleep was interrupted: I held out my hand but I could never touch you. You had dissolved into a fine, shining dust. After that, even my dreams deserted me.

Antigone I had to leave without warning. I couldn't leave our father, blind and alone, do you understand? Who would have taken care of him? And, as for you, I wanted to spare you that miserable life of wandering, the madness of always being lost. But the deepest affections are made of a lasting, unbreakable fibre.

Ismene But, leaving me here alone like that, amidst the rival brothers, Creon, the palace plots, schemes, secrets, courtiers? Did it suit me? Oh, how I would have loved to have woken up with you in the woods in the morning, kissed by the sun's rays, singing and begging at the crossroads, living on the bare essentials. Yes, then I would have been free. As free as you are to tear down the law, to carry out high and holy deeds.

Antigone If you are against this, I will not pressure you. If you were to help me you'd be doing so against your will. Do as you see fit. I will go now and bury him.

Ismene Antigone, I know you, you follow our father's example; but his hopes, his dreams, they're the wrong kind of heroism for me. You know it's not in my nature to die for the sake of ideals.

Antigone You are younger than me, you have seen fewer horrors. It is not enough to forget the past merely because it is past.

Ismene Wait. Listen to me. You know that among the people there are many who oppose the sacrilege Creon is about to commit. Only they dare not oppose his will. Let's summon them to an assembly, let's make it clear the citizens are on our side.

Antigone There is no time for politics. When I was on the road, I didn't know where to go, I was following Oedipus, who inhabited the whole past and absorbed the future. All that was left was the present, and it's in the present that I've always lived. Being present means not having time to plan ahead.

Ismene And so you'd abandon me again? You hate me, you think me soft, spoiled by the privileges of a princess? But I have lived a hard life, a web of negotiations. Ah, you are blind? Don't you see my body changing, don't you see the future drawing near, the nephew who will be born to you; and Haemon, what will become of Haemon? Don't you dream of our children playing together on the beach?

Antigone Oh sister, on this sad day you make me tremble with joy. Haemon will be by my side. Now I know my task is even more necessary. I will carry it out for you too, for your children, for the future you make incarnate.

Ismene Leave me, in despair, you have no pity. Why chase after the wind?

Antigone Polynices' body lies unburied on the beach, under the scorching sun, decomposing already. If I want to honour his death I have to do so now. If later I die, I will not care. I'll die by his side, a devoted outlaw.

Ismene Go, then, and attempt the impossible. My fate will still be that of those who are left behind.

Scene 4

Three soldiers are guarding the corpse of Polynices nearby.

Soldier 1 (*opening a bottle*) Cheers, friends!

Soldier 2 (*holding his nose*) Give me a swig! I can't take any more of this stink!

Soldier 1 We've survived war, we've survived bullets, and it's this stench that'll make us drop dead! Give me back my bottle! (*He pours water to wash his face with a disgusted expression.*)

Soldier 2 Boss, can't we go higher up the hill? We'd have a perfect view and . . .

Soldier 3 Quiet! Private, watch your mouth. Is that how you talk to a superior officer? Just because the war is over, eh? I'm the only one giving orders here! Since when did you start having a sensitive nose?

Soldier 1 (*chuckles*) . . . your nose is always blocked up with allergies! They could chuck you in a pigsty and you'd smile as if you were breathing in *eau de cologne*.

Soldier 3 You, you shut up too! Come on, we'll march to the hill.

Soldiers 1, 2 Sir, yes, sir!

They move on. **Soldier 3** *settles down a little further off.*

Soldier 2 (*in a low voice*) This heat is making me sleepy!

Soldier 1 Keep your eyes open! Wouldn't want the boss to catch you like that time in town, with your mouth hanging open in your sleep and your fly undone!

Soldier 2 Listen.

Soldier 1 What is it now?

Soldier 2 Why did Creon refuse to bury Polynices?

Soldier 1 What's it to you? I chose to join the army to earn a soldier's wage. When the boss tells you that you must not bury the dead, well, I obey without a word. Orders are orders.

Soldier 2 I agree, pay's important. I enrolled as a volunteer, I did.
 But this man's body, left to the beasts, to the birds. The birds will peck out his eyes.

Soldier 1 If I had carried on being a baker like my father, would I have heard the end of it from my wife? You are young and single, but if you decide to settle down, you'll see the difference. A soldier married with two kids, for example, earns as much as a superior officer. It's a question of benefits: child welfare, health insurance, housing . . .

Soldier 2 They could have buried him in a mass grave with the others.

Soldier 1 I was meant to go from private to corporal this year, but I haven't been promoted yet. Maybe I'll be promoted in September. After eighteen years of service, it's about time!

Soldier 2 I mean, he won't be able to rest even a bit. And I heard he was a good solider.

Soldier 3 (*approaching*) Hey, you two! What are you talking about?

Soldier 2 Nothing, boss, just passing the time.

Soldier 3 Stay alert, keep your eyes wide open. Watch the body! If anything gets past us we'll be in big trouble!

Soldier 2 Oh yes! There'll be no point then in accusing each other, beating each other up, insulting each other. And it'll do no good to say, 'I don't know who did it, it's not my fault'! They've stolen the body; someone, who's escaped, has buried the dead.

Soldier 3 They've evaporated! You know very well that there are traitors in this city who whisper against Creon, who rebel in secret.

Soldier 1 Traitors? Rebels?

Soldier 3 Yes, yes, immoral people who sell themselves for money, mercenaries funded by Polynices' friends, communists, priests and terrorists. Don't you know the banks of Thebes are full of their money?

Soldier 1 But Polynices has lost the war.

Soldier 3 If anything gets past us, it will be useless to plead with Creon, to appeal to his sense of justice. He will accuse all of us of having sold out for self-interest!

Soldier 1 We get it, boss. Don't worry. I'm meticulous, me. And I have a wife and kids waiting for me at home, I care about my skin.

Chorus Sitting high on the hill, the three soldiers do everything they can not to fall asleep. In the boiling heat, suddenly, a whirlwind of dust is stirred up, covering the valley, ripping the branches of the trees and forcing everyone's eyes shut. At midday, the smell rises and the air shudders like jelly.

A soldier gets up to ask his comrade for a smoke and he spots Antigone standing next to the corpse. She screams with all her might, a piercing cry, like a bird in front of its empty nest. She fills the amphora and lifts it, scattering as much sand on the body as she can, a delicate shroud to cover her brother.

Antigone Oh Polynices, if only the water could wash your blood and make it flow again! If only the earth might soak it up and swallow it in a stream. Blood is not made to scab as hard as stone. Oh my brother, could the two of you not love each other without destroying yourselves, killing each other for power, could you not forgive each other for spreading so much death? But rest now, may your wandering spirit find peace.

Chorus Behold, the soldiers run towards her, but Antigone carries on, she does not stop, nor does she try to escape! They seize her and she does not look dismayed, standing there with her sweet, suffering expression.

Antigone Wait, wait, I haven't finished yet.

Soldier 1 You've got some nerve! (*Grabbing her arm*.)

Antigone (*turning to* **Soldier 3**) Tell him to let me go, not to touch me with his filthy hands!

Soldier 3 You can talk, handling corpses on the ground?

Antigone I know I'll die, I know the punishment, I'm not afraid. I will come quietly and admit my guilt. I am Antigone, the daughter of Oedipus.

Soldier 2 Yeah right, the girls we pick up at night also tell us to watch out, because they're the nieces of the kings of Morocco. (*They burst out laughing*.)

Soldier 3 Come on, move it! And you two, stay here on guard.

Scene 5

Chorus Man is indefatigable. He crosses the sea by night and sails in winter. He ploughs the earth, ensnares the birds, and with cunning captures the wild animals lurking and roaming in the woods. He tames the horse, harnesses the bull. He knows how to protect himself from wet winds, malarial marshes, lashing rain. He thinks. He speaks. He sets down codes, he heats and shelters his home. Only from death he has no escape. He who knows no enemy is an enemy to himself. In moving forward he mercilessly crushes his fellow man. Man does good and man does evil. He is a good man if he listens to the laws of heaven and earth; he ceases to be one when he stops listening. The State rejects those who are full of arrogance; it cannot stand those who dare too much.

Soldier 3 *enters, dragging* **Antigone**.

Soldier 3 Caught in the act. We found her digging and pouring out sand. But where's Creon?

Chorus There he is, he's coming right now!

Creon What's going on? Why are you dragging the girl? Let her go immediately!

Soldier 3 Sir, I'm in charge of the watch. Interrogate this young woman. She's the guilty one. Put her on trial and make her confess.

Creon Idiots! Where did they arrest you?

Soldier 3 She was burying the body, sir, I caught her red-handed.

Creon You are sure of what you're saying, right?

Soldier 3 Yes I swear, she was burying the dead man, the one that was banned.

Creon And you, with your eyes fixed to the ground? What do you have to say for yourself? Didn't you know I forbade anyone from going near your brother's corpse?

Antigone Yes, I knew it. The order is public, posted all over the city. I am responsible, I confess.

Creon (*addressing* **Soldier 3**) Get out, you're dismissed. Leave me alone with her.

Soldier 3 *exits.*

Creon (*turning to* **Antigone**) You knew my command yet you had the audacity to ignore it. Why did you attempt to bury your brother?

Antigone I had to. Those who remain unburied wander eternally without ever finding rest. Polynices is dead, his body was nothing more than an empty shell on the beach. He could no longer do harm nor do good to anyone. You are but a man, Creon. Even if your guards watch over those who break your law. I will never be guilty before the gods, not for any man. Your threats, your ban, they mean nothing to me. I am faithful to the laws not of an hour, not of a day, but to laws that are mysterious and eternal. I will die young, all the better. But, in leaving my brother's body to the vultures, I would never have had peace. Do you understand?

Creon You are my niece, you are my son's betrothed and you thought, because of this, you could defy the law? If you had been a servant, you would have stayed at home and mourned your brother. You knew I would never dare send you to your death.

Antigone That's not true, I would have done the same thing. And you're wrong, I knew I didn't stand a chance.

Chorus Behold, Oedipus' daughter. She is proud; human misery is not enough for her. She battles against fate, she fights death hand to hand. She does not resign herself to doom.

Creon You challenge me outright, Antigone, you mock me and boast of it. I am tired of heroics. Thebes deserves a fresh start, I have more important things to deal with than pathetic, personal matters. Mine is a hard job, a job like any other. Put you to death? I cannot. Apologise in front of everyone, save yourself, can't you say you're sorry and avoid such a severe punishment?

Antigone *does not reply*.

Creon Tell me, why are you so stubborn?

Antigone Do not feel sorry for me. Do you want more than my death? Do what you must. But do it in haste. Why drag this out, why waste your time? You have your reasons, I have mine. All these citizens would applaud me, were it not for the fear paralysing their tongues. The lords are deaf, they say and hear only what they want.

Creon Listen carefully. Don't try your luck little girl, you see me only as a tyrant, but if I really were a tyrant I would have ripped your tongue out by now. Don't you see that I want to save you? No one thinks ill of me in Thebes, no one sees it like you do.

Antigone Do you think they'd tell you if they did? In your presence they are silent, they are mute and wag their tails. Not out of fear, no. They lap up your proclamations, your corrupt speeches. The tyrant presents his devious arguments and the people applaud him dumbly.

Creon God knows how much I have to do today. Yet here I am with you, patiently. You can't die in a matter of politics. You are worth more than that. Because your dear Polynices, his body decomposing on the beach, is just a matter of politics. Don't you think I'm also troubled by the thought of his rotting corpse?

Antigone So why, then? You won't persuade me. The truth is I frighten you. You'd rather have little Antigone alive and silent in the palace; you know you'll have to send me to my death. Why do you honour Eteocles and not Polynices? Were they not brothers?

Creon You know I couldn't treat them equally. Polynices waged war against me.

Antigone Polynices opposed you. It wasn't enough for you to reign over my brothers in your city, you had to drag them far away, in order to control them better. You made one of them into the scourge of a peaceful country, whereas you exhibit the other one, rotting, like a scarecrow for your enemies.

Creon (*addressing the* **Chorus**) Do not encourage her, she is insane, insane with heroism. Don't encourage her, if you value your life.

Antigone Instead, I implore you: help me. Because he who thirsts for power is like an alcoholic – he can't stop, and he keeps on drinking.

(*As the* **Chorus** *falls silent.*)

So you submit, you do not rebel!

Creon Oh my God, you little fool, stop it. I have tried to understand your reasons, but someone has to steer the ship. There's water everywhere! Ragtag enemies are attacking us by sea. The crew is about to mutiny, plunder the hold, the officers are thinking about building a raft just to save themselves. And the wind whistles, the mast creaks, and we'll all die unless someone takes the helm. Do you think I have time to be judicious? All that's left is the ship and the storm, don't you understand?

Antigone You invoke unity and yet you live in discord. Know that violence begets violence: in using it on others you cannot spare your own kind. Must you always kill each other? Do you believe that if you don't kill, you're not a man? Enemies, homelands . . . justifications are never lacking. A lord is not a lord unless he keeps killing. Can't you love anything without breaking it, for the sake of wanting to take it all?

Creon And, say, if in the chaos Thebes ended up in the hands of enemies, would you not care?

Antigone Oh, this is what you lords are always threatening, that the city will fall, torn to pieces by the hands of foreigners, so we bow our heads leaving you free to commit evil deeds. The city disintegrates and because we are bowed we don't see what we're heading towards. We only see the earth crumbling beneath our feet.

Creon Wretched girl, you insult your land, you oppose me, like Polynices who attacked his homeland while the other one defended it. Subversives and patriots cannot be treated like for like.

Antigone Death demands one law for all. Your borders have no meaning for the dead.

Creon A dead enemy will never become my friend.

Antigone I live for love, not hate.

Creon Life is not what you think it is. It's like water, that you young people let drain away without realising. Clasp your hands together, clasp your hands, quickly. You too will learn that life is about finding joy in the little things.

Antigone I don't care, I'm revolted by your little joys. I wish to be certain of everything; to live, or die at once, for my principles. I'll shout them out to every citizen.

Chorus Here is poor Ismene in tears. Mist on her eyelids washes her face, burning with pain.

Ismene Antigone! Here I am with you.

Antigone Do not despair; by now my fate is sealed.

Ismene Recant, sister, I beg you. You've carried out the ceremony, you have done what needed to be done. How can I live without you? Fate has deprived us of our parents and our siblings. Your crime is my crime.

Antigone You shall live, Ismene. Do it for me. Live for what is denied me. Be a bride, be a happy mother. Grow old gracefully. Die only when your time comes. My destiny is to die.

Ismene If you die I don't want to live, don't leave me alone again. I don't want to be without you.

Antigone Stop your lamenting now. You must think of the future, of your child. The tears you shed for me later will be a blessing – they will wash you clean. I was caught in the rain so many times whilst walking with our father and we had nowhere to shelter and that rain was good. It was good even when it was hard-going outside. It was thanks to exile that I discovered the meaning of home.

Ismene I never went anywhere, I neither went out nor in, there were so few that saw me. They didn't even see me when I was right in front of their eyes! But you, sister, you always saw me. Your words of light and shade. When I was a child I stayed and listened to you and the hours flew by and I became like a butterfly on a green leaf, weightless, by the water.

Antigone Do you hear it? Heart of flesh fluttering like a butterfly. Save her before it's too late and send me to my death! I hate you, I hate your little joys and your political motives! What are you waiting for, call your guards!

Ismene Oh, Creon, I beg you, spare my sister! Can't you see she's not making sense?

Creon Crazy, you're both crazy. Dissenting voice that runs wild and hears no reason. Enough, I've had enough of your ravings. I have no choice. Guards! Take her away!

The guards drag **Antigone** *away, while* **Ismene** *follows them in despair.* **Creon** *exits.*

Scene 6

Enter **Tiresias**.

Tiresias Travellers from the sea are gathering at the borders, although many of them already live peacefully among you without your knowing. You're all too busy defending a past that never was; you don't notice the decay plaguing Thebes, you betray your own principles, tricked, as you are, by false reports.

Chorus These illegal immigrants will infiltrate our borders and invade our homes, seize our wives and slit our children's throats; the sky streaked, the sun behind a grate.

Tiresias Do you no longer remember your own ancestors, prisoners of the calm sea, aboard a carcass of a ship on the unmoving water? When the breeze ceased and the sails fell down, flimsy as cobwebs? How they perished in great numbers, their lungs swollen with water and their dreams dashed?

Chorus Not a breath of wind, the sea floor stinking, and water, water, everywhere, but not a drop to drink. They exchanged looks with burnt throats and glassy eyes, the stars faint in the foggy night. Of the helmsman, they could only glimpse the pallor of his face by the lantern's light. In the sky an iridescent moon. But they were going to work; these come to pillage.

Tiresias Travellers from the sea will arrive in the thousands, on rafts, fleeing colonial ports. They'll bring their wives and children with them, dates and unleavened bread; in their pockets, holy scripture, to ward off ill fortune. They'll disembark in Thebes, dressed in T-shirts made in China and rubber sandals and they'll ask to be seen for what they are: old brothers with their sons and dates instead of figs.

Humble stowaways, always weak, always victims, always blamed, always subordinate, who, like you, just want to live and dream and lie out in the sun, their skin fresh with dew. And if you don't adapt yourselves to their law, if you keep driving them out like lepers, then an avalanche of crimes will overwhelm Thebes, war and plague and never peace again.

Tiresias *exits*.

Scene 7

Chorus But here is Haemon, the youngest of the sons, distraught that his betrothed is about to die.

Creon My son, is it because you've heard your fiancée's sentence that you hasten here? If you're coming to me not as your lord, but as your father, then know that you come in vain. Forget her, Haemon, forget her!

Haemon Father, I belong to you. You guide me, you are a beacon to me. Is it not you who lifted me on your shoulders when I was a child? That giant, whom I loved and admired? Who saved me from monsters and shadows?

Creon I swear to you, I tried everything. I wanted to save her. But she opted for her foolish heroics and death. She spoke in front of everyone. The whole city knows what she has done.

Haemon I implore you, father, don't let them take her away. You are wise, your name is feared by the people. Your presence strikes dumb the man on the street. I, on the other hand, hear voices in the wings that would displease you. Kinship has this advantage, it can reveal truths to you that are otherwise concealed. The city is on Antigone's side, even though it doesn't approve of Polynices' treachery. 'What? She is condemned to death for having buried her brother?' This is what the people say. As for me, I respect your rule above all else.

Creon I am bound to put her to death. This is what it is to be a man, my son. If they're turning against me in my own home, what can I expect from the rest of my citizens? Tough on all or tough on none. There is no greater plague than anarchy. It destroys cities, sets families ablaze. And if the anarchist is a woman, then the danger is even greater. I'd rather succumb to the hands of a man than for people to say I surrender to women. They should be keepers of the hearth, not sowers of discord. Do you think the people should tell me how to lead? Should others be leading the country?

Haemon Father, no city belongs to one man. Calm yourself, show that you can change your mind. I am young, but I know I pursue a cause most just.

Creon Must we then bow down to terrorists, to invaders?

Haemon I am not asking this of you.

Creon Please, forget her. Let it not be said of my son, 'the boy is the woman's ally'. My heart, my heart, don't be led astray by love. Every word you speak is to protect her. You beg for her!

Haemon Were you not my father, I would say you were losing your mind! You are mad!

Creon Resign yourself, child. Take courage. For each one of us there comes a day when we must finally accept that we are men. For you, that day has come today. Look at yourself: with these tears, and a broken heart.

Haemon Do you think I can live without her? Ah, I implore you. I will be too alone and the world will be too empty if I don't have you to look up to, and Antigone to love.

Creon We are alone in the world, Haemon. Becoming a man means accepting one's loneliness; it means learning to make hard choices.

Haemon You talk non-stop and don't listen to anything. If that's what becoming a man means to you, I shall never become one! You're the sort who, in order to be on top, must cast others down as far as possible. Even all the way underground, where they revolt. This is the last time you'll see me. Farewell!

Chorus Oh, Lord, Haemon has left and is running like a maniac. And here is his mother Eurydice, arriving dishevelled. She has heard the voice of her son.

Eurydice What is going on? Your shouting was so loud it shook me in the quiet of my room. Where's Haemon?

Creon Your poor son: he is in love.

Eurydice Creon, you are my husband, I have always obeyed your will. But today, I tell you: if you condemn your son you will lose me too, forever. Do not continue, my lord, do not think you alone are in the right. Look: by the banks of the stream, the tree that bends in the current holds on to its branches. The one that becomes rigid, instead, collapses, with its roots in the air. The captain who rashly holds the sail straight capsizes, and is shipwrecked.

Creon Leave me, woman, with your weeping. Your tears, your affectations are the cause of his softness. It is not I who has condemned him, but rather Antigone. She shall be led out of the city, among the stones, she shall await death, buried alive. These are my orders, lest Thebes fall into disgrace.

Eurydice You are blind, don't you see this condemns our son too!

Eurydice *collapses at* **Creon**'s *feet, grabbing hold of his legs in supplication.*

Chorus Love that inflames hearts, that makes the poor rich and the rich poor, love that crosses the stormy sea. I too can see, at this very moment, Antigone walking towards her tomb, and I weep.

Scene 8

Enter **Antigone**, *surrounded by guards.*

Antigone Citizens, look at me! I go now on my final journey. Imprisoned between the rocks, a virgin among the stones, because nothing will be born of me in death. Condemned to a lonely death. I will have no wedding, no children to cradle. I am a wreck.

Chorus You are not dying of sickness, you are not dying of wounds. It is great solace for you to be dying as mightily as the heroes.

Antigone Ah, you mock me! Oh my fellow citizens, you push me, laughing, into an unmarked grave.

Chorus This is what you asked for! You have violated justice. It is because of your pride that you are lost: burial is sacred, yes, but you must not disobey power. Bow to your destiny.

Antigone Do not speak of destiny, but speak rather of those who condemn me, an innocent. You have followed Creon in his war of invasion, you who were pretending to export democracy are only interested in guarding your wealth, and in plundering oil and gas; you will see the holds of your ships will not return full, but empty. Oh Thebes, my city. My heart grows so tight at the fate that awaits you. Thebans, say to those who ask after me: we have seen her entering the tomb.

Antigone, *led by a guard, descends into the cave.*

Chorus Antigone turns and enters her tomb. She feels her way in, as if she were entering its bowels, until she arrives at the point where the mouth of death opens, to slide in, sucked in by the earth.

Antigone Every dawn I went towards the rising sun, the pure light of the morning. Oh, this light that steals in and seeks me out will be my worst torture. I will not rebel against my grave, no. It will be my cradle, my nest. I have always longed to hear the voices of these stones, white as the break of day. Guard, have mercy and leave these torches alight so I don't die in the dark. My death will be quicker then, starved of air, but illuminated.

The guard lights torches around her.

Antigone   Here is the stone shutting over me forever. Here is my grave. The earth is hard for one who has just been born, expelled from its womb. Because I have not renounced life, but love. Where is my love? I shall no longer see the light of the sun. I shall no longer see Haemon. Where are you Haemon? May you live in happiness and forget my dreadful lot. Yet, I hear a groan. A shadow.

Haemon   Antigone, it's me.

Antigone   You, in this tomb?

Haemon   Upon hearing your sentence, I crept secretly into the tomb that was opening for you. Here, out of sight, I wished to die with you, to die this inevitable death.

Antigone   Of all men, you are the only one to die for me, for my principles. The others have gone to their deaths for their own affairs, private affairs, political affairs. A dream is destroyed if one does not tend to it, life is lit up by dreams as bright as torches. No city is born like a tree, all are founded by someone coming from afar. Yet the exiles and castaways are no longer taken in, having been thrown onto the beach by the storm, like wreckage or treasure.

Haemon   I think only of you, Antigone, you are the woman I love. In this crumbling world I cannot live without you. I come to you as a bridegroom does, totally whole.

They lie on the rocks.

Haemon   The angel of death comes shining down upon us. The sky unfurls, the gasping ceases. The ecstasy of immortal love begins. We bid farewell to Earth.

Antigone   It is true. Farewell, Earth. Farewell, wars. We have chosen the path of justice. May our wandering souls soar towards the light.

Scene 9

Creon *and the people celebrate the victory over Argos and the end of the war.* **Tiresias** *enters, led by a little boy.*

Tiresias   Slow down, little one, don't get caught up in the dance. In this city of madmen they celebrate victory. Thebans, here I am. Two of us have come with the sight of one. This boy guides me so that I may be your guide.

Creon   What now, Tiresias? What are your grim mutterings about war?

Tiresias   I say to you that you dance like madmen ahead of Victory.

Creon   You don't like parties and therefore you judge us with a forked tongue.

Tiresias   I cannot see, but my mind is clear; that's why I've come to you, citizens. Hark what fate has in store for Thebes, drunk with victory, deafened by song and dance. I've heard horrifying, ominous noises in the air; an unnatural motion of birds, a flurry of wings. The altars and hearths reject the offerings because they have been desecrated by dogs and birds that have gorged themselves on the remains of Polynices. Only smoke rises, greasy, and the flesh of the victims sizzles and froths. And it's you, Creon, who are the cause of this mayhem. Listen to me, child. To err is human, but to persist in error is for fools. Do not rage against the dead; erect a burial mound where Antigone has carried out the ceremony.

Creon   Old woman, you're like many archers, all aiming their arrows at me. Alright then, get rich. Make your deals. Pocket your coins, but know I will never bury the traitor. I regret nothing.

Tiresias   But there's more.

Chorus   Sir, let her speak, let's listen to the seer.

Creon   Speak, then. But don't barter. You sorceresses are always thirsty for money!

Tiresias   And you dictators for metal and taxes! Has it come to this? Know, then, that war will leave you nothing. Stop this premature celebration of victory!

Creon   You two-tongued villain! The war is over!

Tiresias   Not only is the war not over, but it has spread, seeping into your very home. War expands and escalates, from plunder comes always plunder, and hardness demands hardness. The death of your son and your wife will punish the crime of burying Antigone alive. Your palace will remain empty, overgrown with weeds. You are alone, Creon, just you against yourself. (*Turning to her guide.*) Let's go home, little one. May this man learn to control his tongue and vent his anger on those that are younger than me.

Tiresias *exits.*

Chorus   Her prophecies are never mistaken, my lord!

Creon   I know. I am in pieces. To fold would be folly, but it is folly also to stay obstinate. It is awful to surrender, but so too is it to be stubborn, to tempt disaster. What's your advice?

Chorus   Save the girl. But make haste, the gods' vengeance trots almost like a galloping horse.

Creon   If I must. But how much effort it costs me!

Chorus   Go, go yourself. Don't entrust any others.

Creon   I fly; you here and others I cannot see, follow me, bring axes and picks, quickly. I have anguish within me, a foreboding. Men, make haste.

Creon *runs towards* **Antigone**'s *tomb followed by the* **Chorus**.

Scene 10

Chorus   Behold Creon, our lord gloriously alone at the helm; he was an idol, winner of war, fruitful with offspring. Now everything evades him. Wealth and power, what are they worth without joy? We hurry, we throw ourselves on the piled-up stones. The lord sweats, his hands bleed, with blows of the pickaxe we open up the rock. A crack appears in the stones. Creon enters the chasm. He gropes in the dark. We light our torches. And there, where the cave ends, we find them. It is over. Knotted together in death. They had no chance; they lie as if asleep on a nuptial bed, with sheets made of stone.

But here comes Eurydice. What is she doing? She doesn't say a word. Silence frightens more than desperate cries.

Still in silence, **Eurydice** *moves away.*

Eurydice (*speaking to herself*)   Now, it is too late. I have been blind, withdrawn in my room, blind, beside a murderer. Murderer of children, of brothers, of nephews, murderer of wives and sisters. I will hang from this tree by the cords of my girdle. They will clutch my throat like a necklace made of coral. Unhappy and devoted I will go to my death, I, an ignorant mother and wife.

The **Chorus** *gathers around* **Creon** *to announce the death of* **Eurydice**.

Creon   Oh my son, my wife, I have killed you, I am a murderer. Ah, insane folly. Kill me! Is no one here ready to cleave my breast? I cannot wipe away my guilt. I no longer wish to see the light of day. They should sweep away this useless man, son, I who killed you unwittingly. With my own hands I have turned the whole world upside down.

The city slowly transforms into a huge cemetery. **Creon** *remains alone in a dead world. He wanders around the graves without finding peace.*

Bidibibodibiboo

By Francesco Alberici

Translated by Flora Pitrolo

First staged at Il Dialma Cantiere Creativo, La Spezia, on 25 January 2024.

Characters

first actor
Real Daniele and **Pietro**

second actor
Daniele

third actor
The Lawyer

first actress
Manager and **The Mother**

fourth actor (or actress)
Stage Hand

fifth actor
Real Pietro

a young music student
(him/herself)

*For those who wake up
and think about music
(and especially for you)*

*Without music to decorate it,
time is just a bunch of boring production
deadlines or dates by which bills must be paid.*

Frank Zappa, *The Real Frank Zappa Book,* Touchstone Books

*Quello che non ho è un treno arrugginito
che mi riporti indietro, da dove son partito*

*['What I do not have is a rusty train
to take me back, back from where I came']*

Fabrizio De André, *Quello che non ho,* Dischi Ricordi

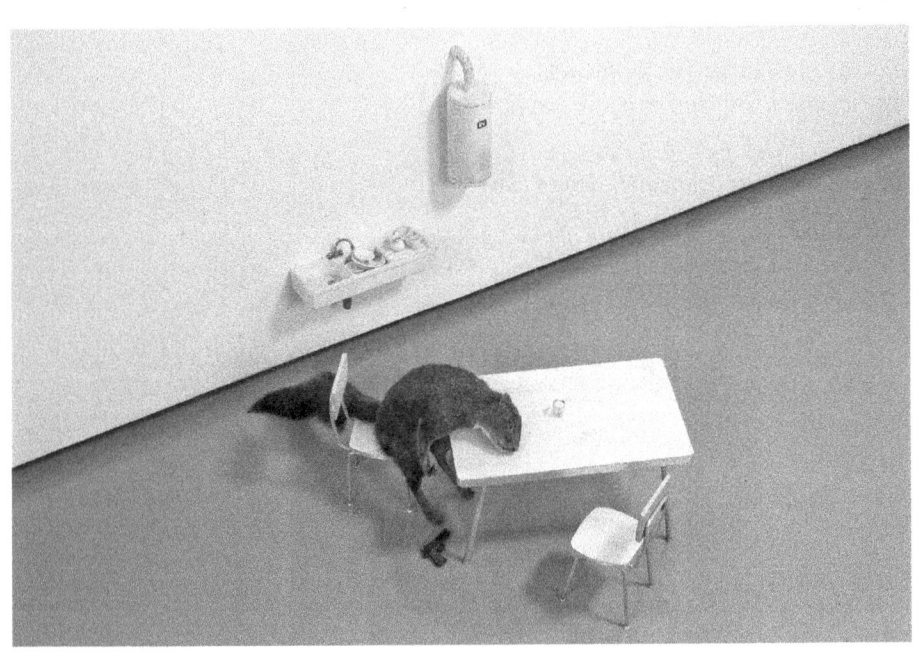

1 Maurizio Cattelan, 'Bidibidobidiboo', 1996.
Taxidermied squirrel, ceramic, Formica, wood, paint and steel.
45 cm. × 60 cm. × 48 cm.
Installation view: *Italics. Arte italiana fra tradizione e rivoluzione 1968-2008*, September 26, 2008 to March 22, 2009, Palazzo Grassi, Venice, Italy.
Fondazione Sandretto Re Rebaudengo, Turin.
Photo: Zeno Zotti.
Courtesy: Maurizio Cattelan's Archive.

Prologue

Subject: important question
On Tuesday 24 November 2020 at 22.34, Daniele danirucc@gmail.com wrote:

Hi Pietro,
How are you and Alice doing locked up in the house? I hope all is well.
I seem to have lost track of time somewhat. Mum keeps calling me compulsively on skype, I think she's feeling a bit lonely. I'm sure she does it with you too.

I know it's weird for me to be writing you an email, but I feel I can make better sense of my thoughts in writing. I have something important to ask you.

Let me start at the beginning: looking for ideas for the new play I have to write, I read a book called *Pressed for Time* by Judy Wajcman (it's brilliant, read it!). In the preface she describes a life experience she had as a young woman in a fishing village in Papua New Guinea. This is what she writes:

I recall one day, as it was nearing Christmas, spending an entire day making coconut milk. Young and ignorant as I was, I suggested that if we altered the method by which the coconut flesh was squeezed in the cloth, we could make the milk much faster and increase productivity. The young people I was doing this with looked quizzical and told me that the making of the milk always took a whole day. They were not in a hurry. They were not interested in speeding up the process – it always had and always would take a whole day to make. Now, forty years later, as I write this book on time pressure, I wonder why I so insisted that saving time should be our overriding orientation, an unquestioned good. I have since learned that the important things in life can't be quantified, timed, measured or accelerated.

It makes you think, right? I thought it was quite exciting.
You know when someone says something so well you feel like you've thought it yourself?
Although when I bought the book I didn't go for a relaxing browse in a bookshop, I got it delivered because I wanted to read it straight away. Delivered in a box!

That's when I thought of you! That's when I realised what I wanted the play to be about: I want to tell the story of your job at ███████, the whole story from start to finish.

I know the whole experience was terrible. I remember.
So this is the important question: **what do you think?**
If it's in any way painful or if it's something you don't want discussed in public, I'll let it go.
Honestly it wouldn't be a problem.
Let's talk about it on the phone if you want (since we can't meet in person).
Don't worry, I won't do anything without your consent.

hugs,
Dani

Subject: RE: important question
Tuesday 24 November 2020 at 11.17, Pietro pieboita@hotmail.com **wrote:**

Hello Dani all good, we're a bit pissed off by now but hey.
I see mum every night on skype in prime time, right after the news.

So let me answer in order:
- Brilliant idea to talk about the ▮▮▮▮ *affair*.
- Personally speaking: it doesn't bother me at all, in fact on some level it actually makes me happy.
- Technically speaking: my lawyer at the time explained there's a whole set of things I can't talk about to stay on the safe side legally. Maybe you could ring him so he can explain?

Other than that, you really should write about what happened to me, because they're a bunch of pricks.

P.S. you know, as I was reading your email I thought: yes, I got fired from ▮▮▮▮. I can say it out loud now, and I have no shame.

Pietro

Subject: RE: RE: important question
Wednesday 25 November 2020 at 00.12, Daniele danirucc@gmail.com wrote:

I've been thinking more about it. If you like the idea, then I'll do it.
That's all that matters to me. I don't give a shit what the ▓▓▓ legal department thinks.

I'll change some details here and there, won't name any names etc., so the specifics of the story won't be recognisable. We won't mention ▓▓▓ directly, we'll speak of a large company.

It's theatre anyway, not investigative journalism: I can say things that feel true but aren't. In the unlikely event that one of these sharks comes to see the show, and somehow realises what I'm talking about, we'll say we made the whole thing up.
Besides I wasn't quite thinking realism.
I can do whatever I want.
Even a musical!

The only thing I'm sure about right now is that I want to play you.
Not sure why but that feels important.

P.S. you know what really pisses me off? Every time I type the word ▓▓▓ in these emails my spellcheck flags it, not because it doesn't recognise the word but because I write it lower case.

When we come out of lockdown we can discuss in person.

Thank you,
love you,
Dani

Subject: RE: RE: RE: important question
Wednesday 25 November 2020 at 00.17, Pietro preipa@hotmail.com wrote:

love you too
If you decide to do a musical can I do the music lol.
You know I've started playing the piano properly again?

Oh and by the way, I loved the coconut milk story! It does make you think, totally.

I was thinking though optimising production in a fishing village in New Guinea is actually kind of counterproductive: what do you do the rest of the time? : D

(That said, I'm pretty sure the CEO of ▮▮▮▮▮ would use the rest of the time to build an empire)

Pie

Part One

The set is a large-scale reproduction of the work Bidibibodibiboo, *by Maurizio Cattelan (image 1).*

With some variations: there is no squirrel and no gun, and on the table there's a parcel; there's a piano stage right; downstage, a row of coffee machines like the ones you find in office buildings.

Real Daniele Good evening, welcome.

I am the author and the director of this play, and this play is about my brother.

It was actually supposed to be a show about other things.
I wrote it during the pandemic.
I couldn't work, because theatres were shut,
and I found myself with a ridiculous amount of time on my hands
yet I kept feeling like I didn't have any,
like everything was slipping away from me.
I felt like I couldn't make the most of the long days,
like I was always stressed, always late,
like I was always desperately chasing after something.
I realised that if I don't work I can't enjoy time,
because free time turns into wasted time.

So yes, the play should have been about that, but then I dropped it
because it all felt a bit navel-gazing,
like it wouldn't have been useful to anyone else but me.
After all, even during the pandemic, most people,
real, normal people, they kept working.
As did my brother.

Before we begin, I just want to say
that my brother's story I'm telling tonight
is a figment of my imagination,
even if it is based on facts.

I wrote his lines of dialogue.
Some of them are things he really said.
Others are based on memories of when we were kids
and we lived together in the same house,
you'll know this if you have a sibling: there's a part of life that's almost symbiotic.
Others still are purely fictional,
words I imagined he could have said,
or words I would have liked him to say,
or words I wanted to say on his behalf.

While I was writing, I often got mixed-up.
I didn't know if I was talking about my brother or about myself,
about his problems or about my fears.

I couldn't tell if I was describing my frustration or his anger,
in short, whether it was his story or mine.

I'll be playing my brother tonight.
First of all because I look like him
– the way he talks, the way he laughs – we grew up together.
Secondly because I know him better than any other actor could.
Before I become him though,
I'll just say one last thing about myself.
I have a degree in economics from a prestigious university,
and people often ask me why in spite of this I decided to make theatre.
I always answer the same way:
after I graduated, I had my first interview
with a bank
and when they told me I got the job,
in that exact moment,
I felt a kind of burning feeling,
something like an urge to be sick,
and I realised that I didn't want to lead that life.
An office, a house, a salary,
certainties, stability.
So I made up an excuse, declined,
and walked away.

I basically always got away with this little anecdote
which highlights my brave dismissal of a life of certainties
in order to risk a career as an artist.

Thing is, this little story is actually a lie.

The truth is that I graduated two years late,
my parents wasted loads of money on my education,
and I missed out on any chance of getting those decent well-paid jobs
which my coursemates – who had actually graduated on time – were already doing.
My first interview wasn't for a bank,
it was for an insurance company.
They offered me a job selling insurance policies door to door,
with a very low base salary
and a small bonus for each policy I would sell.
Declining their offer didn't cost me anything.
It's true: I did decide I really wanted to make theatre in that exact moment.
But only because the alternative was awful,
there was nothing fascinating about it,
and it didn't even grant me any real stability.
Walking away from that job offer wasn't really a choice –
it was just the inevitable consequence of my own string of failures.

While he speaks the words above, **Real Daniele** *changes into a new costume, until he eventually becomes* **Pietro**.

Daniele *enters the scene dressed in the same clothes* **Real Daniele** *was wearing before changing.*

Daniele   Have you spoken to the lawyer?

Pietro   Yeah, he said to be careful
and to send him the final version
so he can have a look and tell you if something's out of order.

Daniele   Perfect. We're not naming any names anyway.
Did he say whether we can use *large company in the –*

Pietro   We can't.

Daniele   We can't?

Pietro   No. *Large company* is fine.

Daniele   Just . . . just *large company*?

Pietro   Or large *entreprise*?

Daniele   Generic?

Pietro   Generic.

Daniele   We can't specify the field of–

Pietro   No.

Daniele   How about we gesture towards–

Pietro   *Large company* will do fine.

Daniele   Ok then. And did he say something about the idea of making it into a play?

Pietro   Who?

Daniele   The lawyer.

Pietro   He said *nice.*

Daniele   Is that all?

Pietro   Dani, I don't really care what he thinks about it, it's not like I asked him outright.

Daniele   Okay.
Good evening everybody, and welcome.
My name is Daniele and this is a show about my brother Pietro.
Welcome, Pietro.

Pietro   Thanks.

Daniele   Are you nervous?

Pietro   A bit.

Daniele Fair enough. Is this your first time on stage?

Pietro No.
I've done a lot of piano recitals,
and a few gigs with my band later on.
But it's the first time in this capacity.

Daniele How old were you when you started playing the piano?

Pietro Six or seven.

Daniele And how long did you study for?

Pietro I'd say about ten years or so with a teacher.
But then you never really stop learning with an instrument.
I don't actually think there is an arrival point, you kind of study it forever.

Daniele I know this is a family get-together kind of question,
but would you play us something?

Pietro Of course I would.
I could play you one of the first things I learned, the Chopin Waltz in C-sharp minor.

He walks over to the piano and plays it.

Daniele Thank you.

Pietro You're welcome.

Daniele So you didn't go to music school.

Pietro No.
I sat two exams and then I dropped out.

Daniele Why?

Pietro I don't know.
I'd just finished high school
and I was preparing my third exam,
I was supposed to play Debussy's *Clair de Lune*.
But it was that moment in life when you're figuring out what you're actually going to do,
and I chickened out.
I tried to be logical,
to find a compromise between my passions and reality.
And in the end I never sat the exam.

Daniele You did statistics.

Pietro Indeed, statistics studies.

Daniele Do you ever question this choice?

Pietro Sometimes.
But I also think if that's what happened,
that's what had to happen.

Daniele What was your first job interview like?

Pietro So after I graduated I applied in a few places,
but I decided to only do the interview for the one that seemed better than the others.
I can't name it though.

Daniele How do you mean *better*?

Pietro It's an important company,
but it was all quite low-key.
When they invited me for the interview they said informal dress code,
and when I went everyone was wearing normal clothes, no suits and ties.
The people I saw round the offices seemed quite happy in their environment.
My recruitment agent was in a t-shirt . . .
and he had this witty attitude,
this sharp way of speaking

Daniele What's a recruitment agent?

Pietro Just the recruiter basically, the person who interviewed me.
He said: we don't really give a shit when you get here or when you leave,
your working hours are up to you
our business philosophy is based on work-life balance,
if you're fulfilled in your private life you'll be fulfilled in the workplace,
and this will make you even more fulfilled in your private life,
it's what we call a virtuous circle.
Their word for it is actually life-work *consonance*, but you get the gist.

Daniele And did they offer you the job?

Pietro Yeah they offered me an internship.
To be honest I was over the moon.

Daniele Can I ask you a slightly touchy question?

Pietro Definitely.

Daniele Can you remember how much you weighed at the time?

Pietro Seventy-four or seventy-five kilos.

Daniele Ok, thank you.
So you said earlier we can't name this company you're talking about.

Pietro That's right.

Daniele Do you think anyone here this evening might know it?

Pietro I think everyone here this evening knows it. And uses it.

Daniele Great, can we say the area this company works in?

Pietro No.

Daniele Can we say what your exact job was?

Pietro Not my *exact* job,
better off not.

Daniele Right. So tonight what we're going to say is that Pietro's job in such company was 'selling flowers'.

Pietro . . . yes, perhaps we can say on the phone.

Daniele Of course, so then: Pietro's job was 'selling flowers' on the phone.
For a multinational.
Moving on.
What was the internship like?

Pietro Not quite what I expected.
You could choose your own hours,
but really nobody ever left their desk before 8 PM,
they could have
but they didn't.
And the workload was designed like you were working all the time,
even at the weekends.
I remember this colleague who lived quite far from the office,
he'd explained to his manager
that he couldn't make the deadlines because they were too tight.
They put him in remote working for the week,
so he could use the time he'd spend commuting on finishing his work.
Maybe I could tell you about a specific episode?

Daniele Of course, go ahead.

Pietro Just to give you a sense. While I was doing the internship
I took part in an event this company runs every year,
I can't say what it's called.
It's basically a whole day just spent trying to sell flowers.
It's supposed to feel like a game.
At the end of the day they rank everyone who took part,
based on the number of calls.
Whoever wins gets a 50 euro voucher.
I came 57th, so I was in the bottom half.
The next day my manager asks me
why I didn't classify in the top half.
He goes: they noticed this higher up, you know.
You better play your cards better next time and inflate the number of calls,
it's just a game but you better start taking it seriously.

Daniele How long was the internship?

Pietro Four months.

Daniele And after that?

Pietro And after that I applied for an actual position.

Daniele You applied?

Pietro Yeah.

Daniele But you said you didn't like it.

Pietro Selling flowers?
No I didn't like it.

Daniele So why did you apply?

Pietro A few weeks ago I found this note in my journal from the time:
I'll do the interview because I can't not, it's a permanent contract, it'd be stupid not to, but I really hope I don't get it.

Daniele And?

Pietro I got the job.

Daniele Do you mind if I ask you how much you weighed at this point?

Pietro Eighty kilos, give or take. And I had psoriasis.

Daniele Psoriasis?

Pietro Yeah, here, on my elbows and on my forearms. And behind my ears as well.

Daniele You started playing the piano three years after I did.
I remember you coming back from school angry one day,
you threw your backpack to the floor, sat at the piano,
and started improvising.
You'd been playing for under two years and you were improvising.
I'd been playing for five and had no idea how you were doing it.

Pietro I don't remember that.

Daniele I do, because that's when I decided to stop playing.

Pietro But I actually think I only started because of you.

Daniele How were you improvising after two years?

Pietro I don't know, it just came to me.

Daniele It certainly didn't come to me.

Pietro I think you were too scared of getting things wrong, you know?
If you want to play well, if you want to improvise, you kind of need to care a bit less about making mistakes, even if it means you're a bit reckless.

Daniele I think you were just more talented than me.
Do you ever think you could have been a musician?

Pietro Sometimes. But I don't think I really tried. I'm afraid I never really tried.
I could have maybe, but I chose not to. When I could have, I made other choices,
maybe I was thinking more about financial stability,

the idea of building a career in a big company, that kind of thing.
Although what I really care about in life is music, I've actually always known that.

Daniele Why didn't you just change paths there and then?

Pietro Cause it's tough though when you've got a permanent contract,
you don't really want to leave unless they kick you out.
I still have colleagues in there who tell me how shit everything is,
I say why don't you look for another job but they don't.

Daniele When would you say your issues began?

Pietro When my new boss came,
Roughly three years later or thereabouts.
They told me I was having some performance issues,
so they were putting me
under observation, let's say.

Daniele What does performance mean?

Pietro It's basically a calculation,
it's the results you deliver against the target they set,
and it's the number they used to evaluate me.
In theory it's an objective evaluation of your labour,
because it's based on hard facts,
but the truth is so many other indicators come into it,
many of which are qualitative – how you share your results with your managers,
how much of a team player you are –
so in the end it's really a subjective view, it's discretionary.

Daniele What do you mean discretionary?

Pietro I mean the parameters are actually very broad.
It's more like an essay than a maths test.
In a maths test
either you do the exercise right and you get the right result or you don't,
that's all the teacher can really judge.
Whereas with an essay, unless there are actual typos or grammar mistakes,
everything depends on the teacher's sensibility.
And if your teacher doesn't like you, it can be an issue.

Daniele And who didn't like you?

Pietro My new boss. I think so anyway.
Things started going downhill when he arrived.
Nothing major, we just didn't get on.
Say like – he'd always tell jokes in the canteen area,
everyone would laugh – probably just to gain his favour – and I didn't.

Daniele And did he tell you this was an issue?

Pietro No. But I do think he noticed.

It wasn't . . . I wasn't trying to cross him in any way, you know?
I just . . . you know when you just don't like someone?

Daniele So you said they put you 'under observation' meaning . . .?

Pietro I was basically monitored non-stop, in terms of performance objectives.
I was producing periodic reports and evaluations
analysing my strengths and my weaknesses,
and then my managers would give me periodic feedback sessions,
and so would my colleagues.
Really it's just an increase in pressure. Everybody is constantly judging you.
It's quite demotivating.

Daniele How so?

Pietro Because it's like sitting in the naughty chair.
I was constantly checked on. Like you can't keep up,
so they need to watch you all the time.

Daniele So you can get help.

Pietro More than help though it's like they want to provoke a reaction.
They expect you to rise to the challenge
out of some kind of pride
or they want to get you to push back,
to show you don't deserve that kind of treatment.
You're supposed to go: I'm better than this
and I'm going prove it.

Daniele It's a power struggle.

Pietro Basically.

Daniele Do you mind if I ask you how much you weighed at this point?

Pietro Eighty-six kilos.

Daniele And had your psoriasis gone?

Pietro No. It was still there and
apart from my elbows, my forearms, and behind my ears,
I now had it on my scalp and even on my face.
And I had dermatitis on my back.

Daniele Can I ask you another sensitive question.

Pietro Go for it.

Daniele Up until this point of the story,
you hadn't spoken about this to anyone,
right?

Pietro I'd spoken to Alice, my girlfriend.

Daniele But not to me.

Pietro No.

Daniele Nor to mum.

Pietro No, I hadn't.

Daniele You started telling us about the whole situation roughly a year later.

Pietro Yeah.

Daniele When things were much worse.

Pietro Yeah.

Daniele Why?

Pietro Hmm.
Why?

Daniele Why didn't you tell us?

Pietro I don't know,
because I wanted to protect you,
maybe.

Daniele What from?

Pietro Not sure.

Daniele Didn't you want to protect Alice?

Pietro Of course I did.

Daniele Why didn't you tell your brother?
Why didn't you tell me.

Pietro (*switching back to* **Real Daniele**)   Don't overdo that line.
You're asking him honestly,
you're not laying into him.
You're not mad at him, you're mad at yourself,
for not realising how ill he was,
that something was deeply wrong.
You're mad because you didn't help him
and he didn't let you.

Daniele Okay.

Pietro (*switching back to* **Real Daniele**)   When he finally did tell you about the whole thing, after a year almost,
you felt like you were light years away from him,
you suddenly realised you were two adults –
not two kids who sleep in the same bed and pull each other's hair
but adults – and all you have in common are your memories.

Daniele Okay.

Why didn't you just say at the time?
We would have helped.
We would have found a way.

Pietro Honestly I don't know.

Daniele We could have helped you, or given you advice.
Me, mum,
we know the job market
we'd been through it.
We had the tools to
We could have

Pietro Sorry.

Daniele I'm your brother, you could have talked to me.
Why keep it all to yourself?

The parcel on the table explodes.
A loud bang, a lot of smoke, debris.

Part Two

Pietro *with a plastic bag, out of which he takes some food and starts arranging it on the table, he takes his jacket off and places his phone on the table as well.*

Lawyer *and* **Manager** *are evoked through the dialogue between the two brothers, so their appearances will be sudden and unexplained.*

Pietro I got supermarket
roast chicken with potatoes

Daniele Can you please tell me
how the fuck
you never said anything
for this whole time
Why?

Pietro Dani.

Daniele Why the fuck would you do that?
It's
it's
just

Pietro Honestly I don't know.

Daniele I'm

Pietro Do you want some?

Daniele No

my stomach is
what on
what on earth

Pietro Look,
let's eat now shall we.
Also because

Daniele I can't eat.
You know what?
These fucking
unbelievable
pieces of shit
fuckers
honestly

Pietro Mayonnaise?

Daniele No
Mayonnaise doesn't–

Pietro It's quite nice.

Daniele Honestly
tomorrow I'm going into that shithole of an office
and I'll shit in their
seriously
We should go look this fucker in the eye

(*Notification: the phone on the table vibrates*)

read it.

Pietro Alright.

Daniele Who is it?

Pietro A colleague.

Daniele And what are they saying?

Pietro Oh come on.

Daniele Read it to me, please.

Pietro *Hi Pietro I heard*
I'm so sorry
I don't know who's right or wrong
and I don't feel I should comment on the whole thing
but I hope you reach a good outcome quickly
lots of love

Daniele How do they know?

Pietro I don't know

I suppose word gets around.

Daniele Who else knows?

Pietro I don't know.

Daniele Write back *fuck off and die.*

Pietro Why would I do that?!

Daniele *I don't know who's right or wrong?*
What the actual fuck

Pietro Can you just chill out?
You're not actually helping

Daniele I'm not helping?

Pietro No you're not.

Daniele You want me to chill out?

Pietro I do.

Daniele Are *you* chilled?

Pietro No.

Daniele So?

Pietro You're not me though
this is happening to me,
not to you.

Daniele Okay fair enough.
But *I don't know who's right or wrong*
seriously?

Pietro At least he texted.

Daniele He's covering his arse.

Pietro Yeah but he's saying he's sorry to hear.

Daniele And he's covering his arse.

Pietro Amongst other things.

Daniele You don't cover your arse
by saying, *I'm so sorry*
By saying, *this is unfair.*

Pietro He's showing solidarity,
in his own way.
Without putting himself in the crossfire.

Daniele What kind of a friend is he if he doesn't

Pietro He's not a friend
he's a colleague.
And he's texted me
other haven't, so.

Daniele So everyone knows.

Pietro I don't know.

Daniele You can tell me you know

Pietro Dani, please

Daniele *Dani please*
sorry but what the fuck should I do then?
What
What do you want me to say?
Oh okay never mind fine.
Fuck's sake!
You show up you go
oh I've been mobbed for a year
my manager spoke to me today
it looks like I'll get fired
and what the fuck should I say?
That it's fine?
That the whole thing isn't absolutely disgusting?

Pietro Nobody's mobbing me.

Daniele I totally think they are actually.
You can't see it because you're in it,
but I can.

Pietro Oh you see everything, don't you?

Daniele No
Pietro
But what the fuck

Pietro All
I'm saying
is please
don't get mad.

Daniele Alright then.

Pietro You can't be angrier than me.

Daniele So you *are* angry.

Pietro Of course I am.
But what do I do?
Start shouting my head off

punch the wall and break my hand
and?
I've actually got to go back there tomorrow
I need to go there
sort out some stuff
look people in the eye
which
isn't easy
I can't go in there like I want to
like I want to kill everybody
see what I mean?
Calm down, please.
Let's have some food

Daniele Okay.

Pietro It's not bad.

Daniele No it's alright actually.

Pietro They always say not to buy it at the supermarket
because the stuff at the deli counter sits there all day
but, it's nice.

Daniele So why did you have to add the mayonnaise?

Pietro Dani.

Daniele Sorry just saying

Pietro Well don't.

(*Phone call: the phone vibrates*)

Daniele Why don't you answer?

Pietro Because I don't feel like it.

Daniele You haven't told her have you?
You're not answering
because you haven't told her.

Pietro No.

Daniele No you haven't told her
or no, you're not answering but *not* because you haven't told her?

Pietro I'm embarrassed.

Daniele You're embarrassed so you haven't told her?

Pietro I feel like when you fail in school
and you pretend it doesn't happen,
because it's humiliating.

Daniele So you haven't told her.

Pietro No no no no fuck no
I haven't told her
It's fucking hard to tell her for god's sake.

Daniele Fuck.

Pietro I feel like you're
trying to control me.

Daniele I'm just asking.

Pietro You're not *just* asking
you're
you're harassing me
and it's pointless.
I'm exhausted
I've been thinking about the whole thing
since this morning
even if I don't talk about it
I keep thinking about it
non-stop
and I can't find

(*the phone stops vibrating*)

Daniele I didn't want to harass you.
I'm just worried.
You look tired.

Pietro I am.

Daniele I know you feel like you're drowning in shit.
I know you feel there's no way out. But

Pietro But?

Daniele I don't know.
I'm not sure.
I think you should speak to a lawyer.

Pietro To a lawyer?

Daniele Yeah.
Just to figure out whether
maybe
I don't know
maybe a lawyer
could help you
see things more clearly.

Pietro And what am I going to tell a lawyer?

Lawyer Just simply
what happened
tell me the story.

Pietro Starting where?

Lawyer Wherever you wish.
Are you working right now?

Pietro Yes.

Lawyer Who do you work for?

Pietro For a large company (*he looks at his brother as if asking for help*) . . . that sells flowers.

Lawyer Flowers?

Daniele (*visibly irritated*) Flowers . . .

Pietro Let's say flowers.

Daniele No names.

Pietro I'm not naming it because . . .

Lawyer Don't worry.

Pietro I've been working there for four years, almost.

Lawyer Okay.

Pietro I have a permanent contract.

Lawyer Of course.

Pietro They've
hmm

Daniele Tell him they've been mobbing you.

Pietro It's not mobbing though
here's the thing.
A year or so ago I started having some issues

Lawyer What kind of issues?

Pietro Performance issues.
I
We get evaluated on our performance
about a year ago
they started monitoring my performance
because my results weren't up to standard.

Lawyer Up to what standard?

Pietro The

I don't know
the required standard.

Daniele Don't say I don't know.

Pietro Up to the required standard.
This situation went on for six months or so.

Lawyer And then?

Pietro And then that was it,
in the sense that
my performance results went back up again.

Daniele Get to the point.

Lawyer What is the point?

Pietro The point is
that this morning
my manager asked me
she asked
if
if we could have breakfast.

Lawyer Outside of normal working hours?

Pietro Yes
before clocking in
by the coffee machines.

Daniele By the fucking coffee machines.

Pietro She hmm
she said:
things aren't going well
we've been getting requests for feedback on you
and we're not able to give any positive feedback.

Lawyer Who were the requests from?

Pietro From my boss.

Lawyer Who isn't the same as your manager.

Pietro No, my manager is
there's like an interface between me and my boss
she's the person I speak to.

Lawyer Okay.

Pietro So she goes: do you understand what's going on?
Your performance is getting a negative evaluation.
You're young
you can take a year's salary and look for another job

something you like better
there's a lot of work out there
you don't have to work here.

Lawyer   Did she tell you you were about to get fired?

Daniele   Say yes.

Pietro   No
I'm not about to get fired.

Lawyer   Did she seem to imply so?

Pietro   No
I mean
not yet.

Lawyer   What were her actual words?

Manager   Would you like a coffee?

Pietro   Yes please.

Manager   Drop of coconut milk?

Pietro   Thanks but
I'm lactose-intollerant

Manager   So am I.
That's why I use coconut milk
the texture is similar to cow's milk,
but
it's lactose-free.

Pietro   Oh I didn't realise.

Manager   A lot of people don't!
Coconut milk is designed
precisely for people who are lactose-intolerant
so they can still drink milk.

Pietro   Amazing.

Manager   The joys of progress!

Pietro   Okay then I'll have a drop.

Lawyer   Don't get bogged down in the details.

Pietro   Sorry.

Manager   Look, let me be really clear with you:
we're not making you redundant, alright?
What we're doing here is supplying you
with an exit strategy
or two, actually.

Lawyer Which are?

Manager You have two options:
A, you leave now with a golden handshake,
a non-negotiable cash package
or B, you go into another evaluation period.

Lawyer Would that be . . . performance evaluation?

Pietro Exactly.

Lawyer You said your performance has already been evaluated.

Pietro Yes, a few months ago.
But this time it'd be different
shorter
two months.

Manager Sixty days
with a detailed plan of action
which *is* a little taxing I have to say.

Daniele Taxing?

Manager Let's say it's a last-ditch effort
after which it's make or break:
if you stick to your deliverables
the period ends and and everything's fine
otherwise you can still leave,
but with a different package of course.

Lawyer Otherwise you *can* leave or you *have to*?

Pietro I don't know. I suppose if I don't deliver the plan then I *have* to.
I'm not sure.

Daniele So it's not a proposition, it's blackmail.

Pietro It's not blackmail because I have two options.
Would you like a coffee?

Lawyer No thanks.

Pietro Coffee?

Daniele I don't want anything.

Lawyer And what is this exit?
You get made redundant.

Pietro No I don't get made redundant
I get to sign a form

Manager It's just to confirm you've read the terms.
Your signature just means: I've read this,

and I understand the proposition the company is making,
it's basically like showing up at registration.
What happens next is up to you.

Lawyer Did your manager deliver this news to you over coffee?

Manager I shouldn't be telling you this
you know
because of my own contractual obligations
that's why I'm speaking to you
here.

Pietro I see.

Manager Off the record.

Pietro Of course.

Manager I'm ever so sorry you find yourself in this position Pietro
honestly for me it's like a personal failure.
I just want to be really clear with you
because I know you're applying for a mortgage with your fiancée,
and I'm trying to spare you any financial duress.

Daniele *Duress*?

Pietro I know
I suppose she was trying to say:
this thing is going to happen
whether you like it or not
so you better be ready when it comes.
In a way she was being helpful.

Daniele She was fucking you over.
You don't say something like this over coffee
Before you even clock in
you say
you send an email a letter a document
something official

Pietro Thanks for the coffee
oh and for the advice on coconut milk.

Manager Chin up.
You need to see the silver lining in this situation.

Manager *exits.*

Pietro Alright.

Lawyer Do not sign that form.

Pietro What do you mean don't sign?

Lawyer Don't sign
they can't make you.

Pietro But then how

Lawrer You're being misled.
You don't have two options,
you actually have three.
You can go for voluntary termination,
or you can opt into another performance evaluation period – which would lead to voluntary termination in any case should the process be deemed unsuccessful –
or you can also not sign anything.
If they're asking you to sign something like this
I can assure you
it's because they don't have valid reasons for your dismissal.
However if you choose to sign now
you opt out of option three
and you're left with one and two.
So don't sign it.

Pietro I hadn't even thought about that.

Lawyer Which is perfectly normal
don't worry
it's my job to think about these things.

Daniele Fuck, I hadn't either

Lawyer Now you stop talking to anyone
colleagues, bosses, managers
not a word from now on.
And when they ask you to sign this form
don't sign.
Just say you've informed your lawyer
and ask for a contact I can speak to.
From now on,
with your permission,
I'm going to speak on your behalf.

Pietro You have my permission.
Do I need to sign anything?

Lawyer Let's leave the red tape for later
shall we?
Just relax.

Pietro Thank you.

Pietro, *exhausted, moves across to the piano stool.*
He collapses onto the keyboard, producing a loud noise.

Part Three

Daniele *and* **Lawyer** *still sitting at the table.*

Daniele Are you sure you don't want a coffee?

Lawyer No, I'm alright.
Thank you.

Daniele Not at all.
After everything you've

Lawyer It's my job.

Daniele Of course.

Lawyer Duty.

Daniele Do you like it?

Lawyer You mean my job?

Daniele Yeah.

Lawyer Very much so.

Daniele Is it what you wanted to be as a kid?

Lawyer Honestly?
I can't remember.

Daniele I wanted to be a film director.

Lawyer So you came quite close.

Daniele Sometimes I feel
I didn't even try.

Lawyer So why don't you?
You definitely still have time.

Daniele I don't know about that.

Lawyer Trust me, you do.

Daniele No, of course, I hope so anyway.
But I think even in the time I have I won't try.
You know when you want something so much,
that it's actually kind of better if it doesn't happen,
if it stays in this suspended wish-space,
like a dream.
I mean if you don't really try at least you don't really fail.

Lawyer You're not a big fan of reality are you.

Daniele It's just so much harder than I thought.
After all it's not so bad, saying: I never tried,

but I'm sure that if I had . . .

Lawyer Maybe,
as a kid,
sometimes I wanted to be George Harrison.

Daniele George Harrison?

Lawyer Don't tell me you don't like the Beatles.

Daniele No of course I do.
It's just that George Harrison
isn't exactly a job.

Lawyer Well what can I say.

Daniele It's actually wonderful,
I'm sorry I didn't mean to sound dismissive.

Lawyer I've written a book about the Beatles you know? About their solo careers.

Daniele I didn't know that.

Lawyer On the Seventies and Eighties, after they split.
Did your brother not tell you?

Daniele No.

Lawyer You know how old George Harrison was when they split up?

Daniele Twenty-eight.

Lawyer Twenty-seven. He was twenty-seven years old when the Beatles ended. Makes you think doesn't it?

Daniele Hmm.

Lawyer I gave your brother a copy of the book.

Daniele He didn't mention it.

Lawyer He doesn't have to tell you everything.

Daniele Of course not,
it's just that sometimes . . .
you know.
There's two years between us,
I'm the eldest.
Is it really obvious?

Lawyer I'd say so.

Daniele You try to get over these things
but it's like they're ingrained.

Lawyer I understand that.

Daniele When we were kids he was always a fan
of all the bands I was a fan of.

Lawyer That's typical of younger brothers:
the eldest becomes a kind of hero.

Daniele And you know what I did?
I didn't want him to touch my records
I'd put them on the top shelf
so he couldn't get to them.
What a dick.

Lawyer Hmm yes, sadly, I have to agree.

Daniele I didn't know you were into music.

Lawyer It's the main thing your brother and I talk about
apart from the issues we're dealing with of course.

Daniele Do you play anything?

Lawyer Drums.

Daniele Me too I used to play, you know?

Lawyer Oh, you used to? And then?

Daniele I wasn't talented enough.

Lawyer You play for pleasure,
you play because it's something you enjoy doing,
not because you're talented.

Daniele Maybe.
I can't really see it like that.

Lawyer Well you're missing out.

Daniele Thank you
for choosing to represent my brother.

Lawyer Don't mention it.

Daniele I've been trying to do so too.
Sometimes I feel like everyone knows him better than me,
like all I have is this hazy idea of him,
all wrapped up in childhood memories.

Lawyer You're doing your best to represent him.

Daniele Have you read the script?

Lawyer Your brother showed it to me
to check it was alright
legally speaking.

Daniele And what do you think?

Lawyer Hm.
It's really crucial that nothing is recognisable
that none of the characters are.

Daniele Of course.
But, I mean, beyond that
what do you think?

Lawyer To be honest,
I think it's a bit naive.

Daniele Naive?
Why naive?

Lawyer You see, your brother's predicament,
unfortunately,
it's not as rare as you think.
Especially with these big *floral* corporations,
these kinds of thing happen quite a lot.
From my point of view, paradoxically, it's a good thing:
the more cases there are
the more precedents there are for me to base my work on.
These companies have the perfect environment to act like this.
There are hardly any common laws across countries.
Every country has its own regulations,
but there's always some kind of loophole.
Take your brother, his is a dispute over performance,
correct?
But this concept of performance doesn't exist in our legislation.

Daniele Really?

Lawyer Really.
So let me ask you this:
is it fair to evaluate an employee
and to ask them to resign
over a concept that in legal terms doesn't exist?

Daniele I guess not.

Lawyer The thing is: what is your objective here?
Is that what you're trying to say?
Do you want your audience to become aware of
the injustice, the exploitation, the total lack of regulation,
or of unions, of workers' rights, in this kind of corporation?
Do you want them to see the horrific working conditions
of the globalised workplace?

Daniele Maybe.

Lawyer Perhaps by having a minor character deliver
a long monologue explaining the whole affair,
making them say everything you've been thinking, reading about, researching.

Daniele Maybe.
I just want to raise awareness,
I know I can't change things,
but at least I can leave the audience with a question.

Lawyer Right, and I think that's naive.

Daniele Why?

Lawyer Because it probably won't have any impact whatsoever.

Daniele You're saying this because it's theatre, aren't you?
Because the theatre is elitist. I get it, you do have a point.
Hardly anyone goes to the theatre, we all know that.
And anyone who does is already on the same page,
they're progressive, informed, aware.
I mean, in theory at least.

Lawyer It's not about the theatre,
I'd say the same thing
if this were a novel or a film.

Daniele Or a musical?

Lawyer Sure.
What I'm saying is that public opinion isn't paying attention,
and at the same time it's completely over-stimulated.
You can light your great fire of indignation if you want, but it'll just sizzle out.

Daniele So I shouldn't talk about it?

Lawyer I didn't say that.

Daniele But you're saying it's naive to do so.

Lawyer I'm just saying you should do it indirectly,
you should make people curious instead of lecturing them.
But of course that's your call.
May I ask you something.

Daniele Go ahead.

Lawyer What do you want to achieve with this play?

Daniele I'm not sure.
I'm trying to figure it out.

You see, my brother was put into a corner,
I was there, I
I remember.

Psychologically, they demolished him.
Taxing plans of action,
sets of *challenges*,
just to
to provoke
a reaction,
pushback,
so that he'd start delivering,
all this horrific language
all of it drenched in
in competition,
like everything is a race,
a
like you should somehow earn your right to work
like it's a concession or something
and if you don't deserve it then,
then they punish you, they harass you, they exhaust you
and then, once you're down, once you're tender prey,
that's when you get offered the *option* of getting fired
and then they go chin up, see the silver lining.
Oh and all of this because the employee is responsible of their own actions,
it's because you're the master of your own destiny,
it's completely misleading,
it's a perverse, inhuman idea of what labour is,
you know what they call it?
Corporate Darwinism.
Like, actually: in books, websites, business manuals.
It's disgusting.

I want to avenge my brother,
I know it's a fantasy, I know it's not worth anything,
but at least in the realm of fiction I want to avenge him.

You know, my brother and I,
we had similar trajectories
up to a point,
we were almost running parallel to each other.
Then,
I don't know,
we both had a,
an *artistic sensibility* when we were younger.
Him especially, perhaps.
I acted, he played the piano.
But then when we had to go to university,
I studied economics and he went off to do engineering.
You must be asking yourself why,
how come we

Lawyer No
I mean,
it's quite common really.

Daniele This is what we chose to do,
what can I say?
Both of us.
It's –
I don't want to start saying things
but our family definitely had something to do with it.
Our mother,
in particular
she
I mean she definitely

The Mother (*played by the same actress as* **Manager**, *wearing the same costume*) Don't say it.

Daniele Mum?

The Mother I know what you're about to say,
and I'm asking you
please don't say it.
Please.

Daniele Why not?
Because it's not true?

The Mother Why is it that you always, always come back to this?
Every single time.
It's very hurtful, I've told you before.
And now you put it in your script,
so that everyone
can hear you say it.

Daniele Because it's what happened,
it's true.

The Mother I (*she wells up*)

Daniele Don't start crying now.

The Mother I'm not crying,
I don't want to cry.
I'm just trying to explain.

Lawyer I might just leave you to it.

Daniele No, wait!

The Mother The truth is only your version of events isn't it.
The joys of selective memory.

Daniele My memory is the memory of a seventeen-year-old boy,
who gets told, day in day out, that if he wants to study philosophy, or theatre,
he'll end up being a bus driver, like that's the only possible outcome.
You *were* quite manipulative mum.

The Mother Manipulative????????
Daniele, how can you–
I
I hope you have kids one day
and that you see how it feels,
your son telling you this.
Aren't you ashamed of yourself?

Daniele Don't bring shame into it.

The Mother All those years of therapy
and you're still so angry at me.
You're an adult,
you're not a child who can make
these wild accusations
wild
without taking any responsibility for them.
You're an adult, you're not a child.
You can't just hurl these things at me.

Daniele I'm not making wild accusations
but for god's sake
all I'm asking you to admit is that you did have an influence on us
on the choices we made,
that's all.

I'm not saying you're evil,
you did it to protect us.

The Mother I'm not having this conversation.
This thing
just
do you know I think about it every night?

I'm your mother
how can you think I

I love you both with every inch of my being,
every inch.

I lie there and I think
where did I go wrong?
It keeps me awake.

Everybody makes mistakes you know.

I never forced anyone,

you did what you wanted to do.
I swear.

Daniele   That's just not true mum.

Lawyer   I'm sorry but really, I'll just
leave you two to it.

Daniele   Just a minute.

Lawyer *exits.*

The Mother   Was I supposed to not give you advice?
Was I supposed to just watch you do your thing?
My parents never helped me make decisions,
because they weren't equipped to,
they hadn't studied.
It was hard you know,
making mistakes, life doesn't always forgive you.
I thought it was
right to help you out
a little bit
to let you do what you wanted
but why put you through what I had gone through,
that leap in the void?
No.

Daniele   You're you're
okay listen, I'm sorry alright?
But please don't cry now.
Let's not get sentimental,
it's not helpful.

The Mother   I'm not crying
I'm trying to get through to you, to make you see my point.
You're my son.

Daniele   Sorry I'm not up for this right now.

Daniele *exits.*

Part Four

The Mother *who's also* **Manager** *is on stage;* **Pietro** *has fallen asleep on the piano.*

The Mother/Manager (*weeping and under her breath, so as to not wake* **Pietro**)

Pietro

Pie

Pie

Sorry, please, tell me you don't feel the same as him
I didn't want to
I hope you don't think it's my fault

my responsibility

I'm so sorry about this whole situation

Pietro (*rousing from sleep*)   Mum?

The Mother/Manager   I just wanted to help you

help you choose

you weren't ready to choose by yourself
between these two options we gave you

I know it's hard
even though you never said anything
a mother knows these things.

Pietro   It is quite hard.
For sure I've had easier moments.

The Mother/Manager   Honestly I promise, it wasn't my choice
this is just how it works,
it's the company's policies.
It's not my job to defend or attack them,
all I do is deliver them.
But honestly, it's not my responsibility,
I promise.

I just wanted you to make the best choice after high school,
I wanted you to be happy,
to be fulfilled,
that's all.

Pietro   That's okay mum, it's just a moment,
it'll pass.

The Mother/Manager   You see, the issue is that every year
we need to cut ten percent of our staff,
it's just the policy,
in order to hire new staff,
to keep things moving,
to get new energies flowing.

I never wanted it to happen to you,
my son,
never.

Pietro   I know,
I know mum,

honestly don't worry.
I know.

The Mother/Manager   I really wanted to stand up for you,
but I couldn't.
I have to follow the rules too you know,
even though as a mother I find them unacceptable sometimes.

Pietro   Mum, is it you?
I can't quite tell what –
I had drifted off.

The Mother/Manager   Why did you have to bring a lawyer into it?
You do know it complicates things,
don't you.

Pietro   It was Dani's idea
I took his advice

The Mother/Manager   Your brother has it in for me
I cannot for the life of me
I gave you both all the love I was capable of, all of it.
And now? Now he has to defy me,
defy the company,
or actually no,
he has to get *you* to defy –
why?

Pietro   I don't
I don't know.
He thinks what you're doing to me is wrong,
I suppose.

The Mother/Manager   You shouldn't have listened.
A lawyer. Why?
It just wasn't the right way to handle this Pietro.
You know how it's going to end up.

We'll just find a random reason to fire you,
we'll start a disciplinary procedure,
we'll put a low grade on your report,
and we'll use it to get rid of you.

Pietro   I didn't mean to be bad,
I always tried to do my best.
It's not fair
you're getting rid of me.

The Mother/Manager   We'll do it anyway Pietro.
This is how things go that's all.

Why can't you just accept it,
it would do you the world of good.

What's your plan?
Do you want to go to court?
Against your mother?

You know you'd lose.

Pietro I don't want to go to court against you mum,
what are you talking about?

The Mother/Manager You're my son,
don't play the hero, it doesn't make sense.
It's your brother who wants you to play the hero,
because it's not him we're talking about,
we're talking about you.

Don't do it Pietro.
You'll end up a martyr, not a hero.
We'll spend a ton of money on lawyers,
get the best in the country,
and you'll burn all of your bridges,
you won't get any more work,
nobody will go near you once we're finished with you.

Pietro I don't want to mum,
all I want to do is leave, I can't deal with this anymore.

The Mother / Manager It was me who bought you that piano, you know.
We knew you had talent,
I cared.

It was me who insisted we put it here,
it the office,
so you could play it whenever you wanted,
take a break off work,
let off some steam.

It's crucial to achieve a sense of harmony between your private life
and your work.
We're sensitive to these issues,
everyone needs a breakout area.

Pietro I haven't played it for a while,
I don't have the time to mum.
I know you put it here because you care,
but it's actually a bit annoying,
it reminds me of what I didn't do,
of what I could have done mum.

The Mother / Manager When you were still in my belly,
I used to make you listen to classical music,
both your brother and you.
Babies understand music, even when they're in the womb.
I wonder if you remember.

Thinking about it now brings tears to my eyes,
you're grown ups now,
I'm so scared of the mistakes I might have made.

Pietro Mum it's okay
please
you're stressing me out.
Things are bad enough as they are.

(*Phone call: the phone on the table vibrates*)

It's mine.

The Mother/Manager Do you want me to make you a coffee?

Pietro No thanks mum, it's fine, really.

The Mother/Manager I can put some coconut milk in it,
it's lactose-free,
I know you're allergic.
A mother knows these things.

Pietro I'm not allergic, I'm lactose-intolerant.
Sorry
I must take this, it's Alice.
I really
I really need to talk to her.

The Mother/Manager Remember that everything we ever did,
we did it for your own good.
Bye Pietro.

Pietro I will.
Bye mum.

The Mother/Manager *disappears as she appeared: slightly mysteriously, behind the coffee machines.*

Pietro (*on the phone, almost in tears*) Hello my love.
How are you? I miss you so much.
They sent me a letter,
it's a disciplinary.
I so wish you were here.
They sent it to me directly, they bypassed the lawyer.
They made up loads of stuff,

they say I failed to attend meetings I never knew anything about,
meetings they didn't tell me about,
they accuse me of things I didn't do.
The lawyer says they're going to fire me,
he says the warning is the prelude to dismissal,
it's an excuse to fire me basically,
it's fake,
and they know it,
but they don't care because they know I won't take them to court,
and anyway even if I do they'll destroy me.
I'm
I'm drowning in shit, my love.
I feel
I'm so ashamed of myself
I feel filthy
but I didn't do anything wrong.
I wish you were here, my love.
I just
I just wanted to
Alice, my love,
do you want to marry me?

Just for a moment, this is a musical.
Slow fade to black.

Part Five

A group of stage technicians are sanitising the stage, they're all wearing face masks.

Amongst them we recognise the actors who played **The Mother** *and* **Daniele**, *also dressed as technicians.*

A technician addresses the audience, without looking at them directly; he talks as he keeps on working.

Technician When I swim I don't think about anything.
I count the number of lengths, either one at a time or in sets.
Sets of four, sets of six, sets of eight.
Front crawl, backstroke, backstroke, front crawl.
Or front crawl, breast stroke, back stroke, back stroke, breast stroke, front crawl.
One, two, three, four, five, six, seven, eight.
Or one of one, two of one, three of one, four of one,
one of two, two of two, three of two, four of two.

I also count the strokes. In sets of three or five.
One, two, three-breath, one, two, three-breath.
Or one, two, three, four, five-breath,
one, two, three, four, five-breath.

Always odd numbers so I breathe once to the right, once to the left.

If I count, the numbers are all I think of,
I empty my head and I don't feel tired,
so I don't need to stop.

No distractions, no digressions, no sudden or useless thoughts,
no flashes from my imagination,
no repressed desires and no feeling hot or cold,
just numbers.

If someone else is in my lane the race is on.
Not openly – they don't know it – but it becomes a competition.
If they're crap I win.
If they're good everything gets much more tiring.
When the person overtakes me I feel like pulling them down by the legs and beating them up.
I don't obviously, I don't even look at their faces.

Even when I'm by myself in my lane the competition kicks in.
I race against the person in the next lane.
And if I'm alone in the pool,
I imagine my opponent. I make them up.

The same technician sits down at the piano to check it's in tune. He plays a few notes.

Then he starts playing Chopin's Waltz in C-sharp minor. **Real Pietro** *enters from backstage and walks on. He's not wearing a mask; we sense that he's confused and very embarrassed.*

The technician stops playing.

Technician You're not allowed here.

Real Pietro I'm sorry
I'm
I'm terribly sorry
I don't

Technician It's just authorised staff on stage please.

Real Pietro Honestly I'm sorry I
I didn't mean to interrupt

Technician Who are you?

Real Pietro I'm – I'm

Technician Mask.

Real Pietro Oh yes of course!
I did do a lateral flow on my way in.

Technician Mask.

Real Pietro Sure (*puts on his mask*)
I didn't mean to interrupt the play I'm mortified
I didn't think I'd end up on stage

Technician Who are you?

Real Pietro I am the brother of
he was behind me and he told me to
I lost him, I was waiting to

Technician You're not allowed to be here.
It's just authorised staff on stage please.

Real Pietro Yes yes I'm leaving
okay so it hasn't started yet.
I thought you were an actor

Technician I'm a technician, let me show you the way.

Real Pietro You play really well, I must say

As they exit, they come across **Real Daniele** *who is entering.*

Real Daniele Pietro!!

Real Pietro Hey.

Real Daniele Where are you going?

The **Technician** *exits.*

Real Pietro That guy was telling me not

Real Daniele Take your mask off.

Real Pietro Aren't we supposed to wear masks?

Real Daniele It's just rules and regs, don't worry about it.

Real Pietro The technician was saying you can't be on stage without it
they're all wearing masks.

Real Daniele Take it off, don't worry
did you tell him you're my brother?

Real Pietro And that I was waiting for you, yes of course I did. (*takes off his mask*)
He played really well, I thought he was one of the actors
and that it was the beginning of the show, or the rehearsal rather,
I thought I'd interrupted the beginning. Where did you go?

Real Daniele None of the actors in this show play the piano.
Yeah sorry I just needed to talk to an actress for a second.
They're the technicians, they're sanitising the stage, you know, for safety.

Real Pietro Chopin's Waltz in C-sharp minor, he was playing it really well
I used to play that a lot a few years back.

Real Daniele I think we'll be a few minutes still
– can we have the table off to the side a bit? –
and anyway we were waiting for you,
we're basically doing it for you.

Real Pietro Of course.

Real Daniele Does that make you uncomfortable?

Real Pietro No no, quite the opposite, I'm just curious that's all.

Real Daniele What do you reckon? (*Points to the stage.*)

Real Pietro Is it
are we in a dream?

Real Daniele – just ever more slightly to the left? –
what do you mean?

Real Pietro Is the set drawn from a dream of yours?

Technician Like this?

Real Daniele – Better –
a dream of mine? No. It's your office.

Real Pietro My office?

Real Daniele Yeah. An imaginary reconstruction anyway.
I've never been to your office,
but this is how I imagined it.

Real Pietro Yeah you have.

Real Daniele Really?

Real Pietro Do you not remember? The summer before . . .

Real Daniele Ah in summer, yes. Maybe once
in the summertime?

Real Pietro Mm m.

Real Daniele Yeah yeah yeah now I remember.
But I wasn't mmm it didn't really stick somehow so
maybe I was a bit distracted.

Real Pietro Anyway it's nice,
even though it has a certain, I don't know
it feels quite closed in.

Real Daniele It's based on a Cattelan installation.

Real Pietro And the piano?

Real Daniele *Bidibibodibiboo* you know the one?
The one with the squirrel who's shot itself.

It's supposed to feel kind of open-spacey but sinister at the same time.

Real Pietro And the piano
is there
is there like, music in it?
Is it a musical?
I remember you saying you had a musical in mind.

Real Daniele No no. The piano's just part of the set really
it's like a sort of symbol of your
relationship with music, something like a dreamlike element
– can you say when we're good to go? We're running a bit tight –

Real Pietro A symbol, you know I just wanted to have a word with you about

Real Daniele In the end I'm not mentioning the company, you know
I mean apart from the whole legal thing
There's no need really.

Real Pietro Oh really?

Real Daniele Yeah.
It's just more elegant with no names somehow
less explicit

Real Pietro (*thinks for a second, a little perplexed*) Do you reckon?

Real Daniele – Let's check the trigger for the parcel can we? –

Lawyer (*entering from backstage with a script in his hand*) Dani! I know we're just about to run but I was thinking – I wonder if this whole section is just a bit overly explicit, a bit too much information.

Daniele (*looks at his script*) No no. It needs to deal with some central issues you see. And also trust me,
it has its own rhythm.

Lawyer Okay let's keep it for now, and then let's see.
I'm just suggesting a few cuts because when I'm actually speaking the lines it's – hi!

Real Pietro Hiya.

Real Daniele Let me introduce you to your lawyer.

Real Pietro Pietro.

Lawyer Hi Pietro, (*name of actor*), nice to meet you. You two look really alike.

Real Pietro (*looks a bit embarrassed*) We have different dads.

Lawyer (*also a bit embarrassed*) There's definitely something though . . .

Real Daniele I definitely look more like him than you look like his lawyer.

Pietro He's not actually *my* lawyer,
it was just on this occasion that he

Lawyer I know the whole story, don't worry.

Technician We're good to go here!

Real Pietro The whole story?

Lawyer Yeah, more or less.

Real Daniele – okay cheers! –
By the way,
did you hear from him?

Real Pietro From who?

Lawyer I'm going to get ready.

Real Daniele The lawyer.
Just to see if it's all
you know

Real Pietro No not yet
but I can't imagine there being any issues
at least not on that,
but on the subject of

Real Daniele Right exactly
I mean like no details, no names, no nothing
Nobody can come and say we're *disclosing*
or whatever the hell word they use.
Shit we could have invited him. I didn't think

Real Pietro Who, my lawyer?

Real Daniele Yeah.

Real Pietro I don't want him to come and see a rehearsal.
He's got nothing to do with it, it's not like he gets to decide.

Real Daniele Sure,
it's me who decides,
I just meant out of

Real Pietro It's not you who decides.

Real Daniele Well
Sorry, what do you mean?

Real Pietro Dani
I'd like to have a word with you

Real Daniele Let's chat afterwards,
now everybody's

Real Pietro I need to talk to you now,
before it's too late.

I'm not
the thing is I'm not so sure anymore

Real Daniele About what?

Real Pietro About the whole show
I'm not sure if
I know you've started working on it and

Real Daniele Started working on it?
Pietro we open next week
what do you mean you're not
you're not so sure anymore

Real Pietro You
you said we could just stop whenever
you
you wrote to me I won't do a thing without your consent

Real Daniele Yes at the start, sure
but
I'm doing it now I mean
it's work it's not a game – the parcel! –

Real Pietro I know I know I know
I'm not saying it's easy at this point but
I needed to tell you and the more
the more I say it out loud, the more I feel it's right actually
I don't want to
I don't want you to tell my story in
in this show

Real Daniele Did you talk to someone?

Real Pietro No honestly it's not

Real Daniele Did you talk to your lawyer?

Real Pietro What's my lawyer got to do with it?

Real Daniele Did he
Did he tell you it's a bad idea?

Real Pietro No, it's me who's saying this,
I don't need to speak to the lawyer.

Real Daniele Okay it was just a thought
I thought maybe he'd told you that legally speaking–

Real Pietro That's not the point!

Real Daniele But I've already said to you don't worry
whatever we say it's in
it's the realm of fiction, no-one will be able to tell it's your story, we're changing

what are you scared of?

Real Pietro I'm not scared.
What
What has *scared* got to do with it?

Real Daniele You are though.
They
all sorts of things happened to you
and you can't even
you can't even say what they did
because you're scared of what else they can do to you.

Real Pietro I hate you when you're like this.

Real Daniele Because I'm telling the truth.

Real Pietro Because you don't know what you're talking about.
First of all I'm not . . .
It's you who's doing the telling here,
not me.
Secondly
you know, you have no idea how it works
in a company
when a contract ends
you have no idea.
There are limits, there are things
things to respect.
Of course, it never happened to you.
You're the the idealist.
You don't know these things because you're not
you've never been in it
you just hang out,
you make your theatre,
you do your bullshit,
you have zero responsibilities
but you're not in it and you don't know what

Real Daniele My bullshit?

Real Pietro Yes your bullshit.
It's just game for you isn't it?
Oh my brother got fired from a corporation
I'll make a show about it so I
I can shock my friends.

Real Daniele Is that actually why you think I'm doing it?

Real Pietro Yeah
basically, yes.

Real Daniele Alright then I won't.

Real Pietro Great, that's what I'm asking you.

Real Daniele But how
how can you be so scared?

Real Pietro I'm not scared, please
don't be a
don't be a child
I'm not scared
I don't like it I'm telling you I don't like it
which is different.
It pisses me off that if I tell you I don't feel like it
you ask me if I'm scared.
You know, I'm I can
judge things too you know,
I do actually have a personality.
I'm not just the victim of a system of things
wallowing in some
some kind of unawareness

Real Daniele I never said you're a victim wallowing in unawareness.

Real Pietro You didn't say it but it's what you think
and I can tell you know? It's
it's in everything you do.
I can see it
the way you look at me
the way you talk to me
I can tell.

Daniele You're imagining this Pietro.

Real Pietro It's actually always there
in everything you do, it's as if you said it over and over
my poor brother poor thing who failed to
who wasn't able to whereas I on the other hand

Real Daniele I on the other hand?

Real Pietro Dani, come on.

Real Daniele I on the other hand what?

Real Pietro Do you actually want me to tell you?

Real Daniele No.

Real Pietro You on the other hand, you succeeded.
You did what you wanted to do and I didn't.
You tell me all the time

Real Daniele That's so not true
I'm
I don't know.

Real Pietro What?

Real Daniele I don't know what to say.

Real Pietro Maybe you had good intentions
but for me right now it's just not on.
I really don't want you to go ahead with this show,
I'm sorry,
I don't feel like it

Real Daniele You can't tell me this now.

Real Pietro Sorry.

Real Daniele You don't have to apologise but you can't fucking tell me this now.

Real Pietro So what shall we do?

Real Daniele I don't know
Don't you want to
Watch . . .

Real Pietro No.

Real Daniele For fuck's sake it just doesn't make sense.

Real Pietro Sorry.

Real Daniele I'm sorry, but in the beginning,
when I first asked you

Real Pietro In the beginning it was different.

Real Daniele How?
Sorry so what's changed?

Real Pietro It's changed
I don't know Dani
I don't think I'm
I'm asking you such a
we are talking about me here you know.

Real Daniele We're also talking about my play.

Real Pietro We're talking about my story in the first place
your
your play came later.
And you can't
you said to me once that you told
what you told your therapist
when she asked why you write your performances

Real Daniele   What does this have to do with anything?

Real Pietro   To engage with failure
right?

Real Daniele   It's not

Real Pietro   That's what you answered right?
To engage with failure.
I've been thinking about that
so what am I then
what am I,
a failure?

Real Daniele   What the fuck
What kind of fucked up reasoning is that supposed to be?
Failure

Real Pietro   You're not answering me.

Real Daniele   The aesthetics of failure
I engage with failure inasmuch as
I mean the failure
of representation
in itself

Real Pietro   I've seen your other performances.
Do you really think everyone is
I don't know
I don't particularly want to be in your failure collection
or help you engage

Real Daniele   Look, it's not a film
or a fucking musical
we're lucky if two hundred people come and see it.

Real Pietro   Mum will for sure.

Real Daniele   So?

Real Pietro   I don't want her to see this story from
from this point of view.

Real Daniele   Mum was there
you were there
I was there.
It's just a play! How can you think that she'll come and suddenly go
I don't know
oh yes our son the failure.

Real Pietro   So it is about my failure.

Real Daniele   No.

Real Pietro   What is it about then?

Real Daniele   It's not
it's the story, the whole story
failure or success has nothing to do with any of it
do we really need to even use these stupid
words? Because they are
they're stupid
and you're not.

Real Pietro   So what's it about?

Real Daniele   Pietro!

Real Pietro   Go on.

Real Daniele   First of all it's
it's about
the fact that you work
worked for a bunch of dickheads.

Real Pietro   How do you know?

Real Daniele   How do I know?
Oh so they're not dickheads now?

Real Pietro   Not all of them.

Real Daniele   Okay perhaps not all of them, but in general from the way they treated you

Real Pietro   You have no idea how they treated me
you don't know
you actually don't know

Real Daniele   I know what you told me.

Real Pietro   It's not enough.
It's not enough.
All you want is to fucking impress
this or that critic
or some director or other
so they can all be like
oh so clever, so charming, so sensitive

Real Daniele   Of course I want that
and? What the fuck is it to you?
What's that got to do with it?
Why wouldn't I want people to like my work?
I'm doing this for you as well you know.

Real Pietro   For me?

Daniele Yeah, definitely.
You're getting something out of it too.

Real Pietro I'm getting
I'm getting something out of it.
You actually have no fucking clue.

Real Daniele How
so what do you want from me then?

Real Pietro I want you to not do this show
I've been telling you in every possible way.
You asked me what I thought and I'm telling you
I don't think it's a good idea
and even if it was
I still don't want you to do it.

Real Daniele This isn't a joke you know
you can't just come in here
and start bossing people around bossing me around
doing whatever the fuck you want.
You don't get to decree whether I can talk about something or not.
I was there when you were sick you know,
when you were asking for help,
when you had scabs all over your face.
I went through this thing too.

Real Pietro You went through it?

Real Daniele Indirectly, yes I did.

Real Pietro How the fuck dare you?

Real Daniele I'm just telling the truth.

Real Pietro Tell me you're kidding.
Tell me you didn't just say that.

Real Daniele Alright look, I'm sorry but
I have to get on with this show now
I've made agreements with people
people give me money
to do my
my bullshit
as you call it.
It's my job
and this is how it works.

Real Pietro Your job.
Anyway at the end of the day you don't give a shit do you?
It's a brilliant story, and even better because you *went through it*!

So it's autobiography, it's about identity, which is so fashionable right now
a strong political topic for your shitty theatre activism
and bang, it's in the bag, right?

Real Daniele Fuck!   Fuck!
Can we please calm the fuck down.
What am I supposed to do?

Real Pietro I don't know.

Real Daniele Hold on a sec. I'm going to ask everyone to leave alright?
But please please please can we,
talk about it calmly, just for one minute?

Real Pietro Okay.

Real Daniele Sorry guys,
I have to ask everyone to leave us for a second,
we need a moment to ourselves please.
Thank you.

All the technicians leave, only **Real Pietro** *and* **Real Daniele** *remain on stage.*

Real Daniele Pietro, I don't know how else I can explain this
I need to do this show now.
There are no two ways about it.
I can't pull out anymore
everything is in place,
there are actors, technicians,
there's a production team behind it.
I can't just stop it like that, you know?
It'd be great if was that simple, but it's not.
If I pull out now, I'm going to get fucked over.
I'm not going to get any more work.
I mean no more work in general, not only on this occasion.
It isn't an easy environment you know, it's mega competitive,
everyone is just waiting for you to trip up.
If I cancel this show now, I'm going to feel it later.
You do understand that,
right?

Real Pietro Of course I understand.
That's why I came to talk to you now
before

Real Daniele Right before we open.

Real Pietro Exactly.

Real Daniele It's my job.
You can't put me in this position.

Real Pietro Your job.

Real Daniele Yeah, my job.

Real Pietro Work doesn't always come first.
I don't know if I thought that too at one point,
I can't remember,
but I promise you, it actually doesn't.

Real Daniele You know it was turning into a special thing,
it's a delicate piece of theatre.

Real Pietro That's not the point.
The point is I don't want you to talk about me.
You want my story,
but I'm not ready.

Real Daniele Okay.

Real Pietro Can you get your head around that?

Real Daniele Maybe.

Real Pietro I didn't mean it earlier when I said your bullshit,
I'm sorry.

Real Daniele I know.
It's okay.
I'm sorry too if I was cruel.
I can't actually remember the things I say,
when I'm cruel.

Real Pietro I know, I know you.
It's fine.

They're quiet for a while.

Real Daniele I'm sorry about all of this mess.
What are you thinking about?

Real Pietro I don't know.
You know, when I used to see things on TV about people losing their jobs
I used to think poor things, it's not fair.
But before it happened to me
I had no idea of
of what really happens to you,
when you're excluded from the workplace.
There is a certain violence and cruelty to it,
when it happens to you,
it's hard to explain.

Real Daniele I can't quite imagine it,
but I believe you. It was awful wasn't it?

Real Pietro   Yes.

Real Daniele   I've never been in that situation.
But when you were telling about this feeling of constant anxiety,
of always having to be on top of your game,
of always fighting because you never know what's coming next,
I get that.
I feel like that too.
I don't know if it's me
or if it's my field that's, I don't know, polluted by this kind of thing.
Sometimes I feel like a racehorse.
And time just wastes away,
there are so many things I wanted to do that I haven't done yet,
maybe I never will.
When are you getting married?

Real Pietro   September 11th.

Real Daniele   Oh yeah.
Hard date to forget.

Real Pietro   That's why we chose it.

Real Daniele   It makes me feel a bit weird you know.

Real Pietro   What does?

Real Daniele   That you're the first to get married, the youngest.

Real Pietro   Whatever, it just happened that way.

Real Daniele   Yeah.
Things happen a certain way, but you also shape them a bit.

Real Pietro   True.

Real Daniele   At first I thought I'd give you some money as a present,
but then I thought that's a bit sad.
A friend of mine gave me a plant once.
I thought that was quite beautiful, right?

Real Pietro   Very.

I'm responsible for all the choices I've made.
That's what scared me a bit,
that you were presenting me as a victim.
I decided to work there
because I wanted a career
and I decided to compromise for it.

Nobody forced me to do it,
I knew what was happening.
It's just that eventually I realised I was too unhappy.

I'm not sorry they fired me.
If they hadn't,
I would have never had the strength to leave.

And in the end they were right anyway,
I'm not suitable for that environment,
I'm not enough of a piece of shit.
What makes me angry is that deep down I already knew that from the start.

Real Daniele   Some things just take time Pie.
There's not always a shortcut.

Real Pietro   It feels a bit like someone didn't keep their promise.

Real Daniele   What promise?

Real Pietro   The promise that if you stick to the path,
you'll eventually be happy.

I did everything I had to do,
everything they told me to.
But I wasn't happy,
I'm not happy now even,
but before even less so.

A lot of my friends, a lot of my colleagues,
they won't say it out loud,
but they know it's like that.
Even if they're good and they hold on and they don't get fired,
that promise of happiness, it's just an illusion,
a myth from the past.

We can't really talk about these things,
only on the surface,
we complain but we laugh at the same time,
but if we talked about it seriously, I know,
I know it'd just be too much to deal with.
The realisation that the thing you do eight hours a day
doesn't make much sense,
to put it lightly.

You know almost everyone I worked with,
I saw them cry at their desks at some point.

Real Daniele   You never told me that.

Real Pietro   I didn't want you to write some heart-wrenching drama about it.

Real Daniele   I don't have it in me anyway.

Real Pietro   Do you like what you do?

Real Daniele   Sometimes.

A few days a year I love it.

Real Pietro I envy you.

Real Daniele Don't bother, there are also all the other days you know.
It's much more like other jobs than it seems.

Real Pietro You say that because you don't know what other jobs are like.
Your job and your passion coincide.
Looking back now I have to say I am a bit sorry,
that I didn't do what I wanted before it was too late.

Real Daniele It's never too late.

Real Pietro That's not true,
but thanks anyway.
I'm sorry I messed up your show.

Real Daniele Don't worry.

They sit in silence, lost in their thoughts.

Real Pietro You know what I was thinking?
Something both good and bad,
depending on how you look at it.

Real Daniele Tell me?

Real Pietro I was thinking that in spite of everything,
in spite of the choices I've made,
or where I've ended up as a result,
still when I wake up in the morning,
the very first thing I think about
is still, always, and only music.

A young music student enters the scene,
he is the age Pietro was when he could have made different choices,
the age that Pietro was when he should have taken his third exam.
He sits at the piano and plays Debussy's Clair de Lune.
The two actors on stage listen to him play.
Blackout.

The End

Big Fright

Grande spavento

By Valentina Diana

Translated by Margherita Laera

First staged at the Teatro Koreja, Lecce, on 27 October 2024.

Characters

Mr Lemon
Mrs Honeysuckle
Mrs Hydrangea
Mr Pomegranate
Mr Laurel
all middle aged

Voice of the journey

A centre for plant therapy. The space consists of a lounge area, with sofa and armchairs, a small table with wheels, a kettle and plastic cups for herbal teas. A formal space, vaguely shabby. The meditation area is a transparent plastic greenhouse, in the shape of a cylinder. This delimits the space where the plants are arranged on a table.'

CENTRE FOR PLANT THERAPY
The space consists of a lounge area, with sofa and armchairs, a small table with wheels, a kettle and plastic cups for herbal teas. A formal space, vaguely shabby.

The meditation area is a transparent plastic greenhouse, in the shape of a cylinder. This delimits the space where the plants are arranged on a table.

Content warning: violence and references to depression, alcoholism and child sexual abuse.

1

'**Mr Lemon, Mrs Hydrangea, Mr Pomegranate, Mr Laurel,** *and* **Mrs Honeysuckle** *are in the sharing lounge'.*

Mrs Hydrangea Last Friday, when I went to church, Father Thomas said, History has landed on our doorstep.

Beat.

He said, We were not ready, we couldn't believe that History had really made its way into our homes, just like this, so suddenly, into our lives, through our doors and windows, through the gaps, said Father Thomas. Beforehand, nothing bad ever used to happen, Father Thomas said, and we were used to it, everything always happened to others: in books, in newspapers, in the news we watched on TV. But now History has entered our homes – Father Thomas said – and there is no longer that very thin wall of protection, that thin and hard screen that made us spectators and the others fodder for slaughterhouses. Or for cannons . . .

Beat.

Mr Lemon *gets up from his chair, approaches her and makes a move to frighten* **Mrs Hydrangea**.

Mr Lemon Boom!

Mrs Hydrangea (*frightened*) Mr Lemon are you mad? You frightened me.

Mr Lemon I'm sorry Mrs Hydrangea, I didn't mean to frighten you, it's just that you were talking about cannons and so I thought of this little joke.

Mrs Hydrangea Yes, well, what I meant was that what Father Thomas told us, it made me feel a bit sick in the stomach . . . no, it was like I felt nostalgia for something that had suddenly gone.

Beat.

Mrs Honeysuckle Do you mean your husband?

Mrs Hydrangea No, Mrs Honeysuckle, not my husband, yes well he left but I didn't mean him, it was more like . . . a sense of nostalgia for . . .

Everything.

Mr Laurel A nostalgia for everything?

Mrs Hydrangea Yes, a nostalgia for everything.

Silence.

Mr Pomegranate This silence. I love it because very subtle things can be perceived in silence. In actual fact, silence is not really the absence of sounds. I once had the opportunity to access an anechoic room, thanks to a friend who's a researcher at the Institute of Metrology.

Mr Lemon Anechoic?

Mr Pomegranate It's a room where sound doesn't circulate. Any sound waves are absorbed by the surface. It's very odd. You can go crazy in there. That's true silence: the absence of any sound wave.

Mr Lemon Sorry, Mr Pomegranate, after all these months I'm still not clear – do you work in a university?

Mr Pomegranate I prefer to carry out my research at home. I am fifty-eight.

Mr Lemon You remind me of someone I met once in a castle in Austria, a beautiful castle, Hochosterwitz Castle, it's certainly one of the most beautiful medieval castles in the whole of Austria.

Mr Pomegranate I never go abroad. I promised myself never to go abroad.

Mr Lemon Not even Peru?

Mr Pomegranate No.

Mr Lemon You should! Peru is beautiful.

I remember that in Peru when you entered a club you had to put your gun on the counter. I didn't have a gun but, if I'd had one, I would've had to put it on the counter too.

Mrs Honeysuckle Why?

Mr Lemon It may be a form of politeness. If they kept guns in their pockets, who knows, they might inadvertently shoot someone while sitting down. Guns are dangerous sometimes.

Mrs Hydrangea Wow, Mr Lemon you've been to Peru, I didn't know you were . . . such an adventurer: Peru! Who would have thought it.

Mr Lemon Well, you do have to travel a bit if you work in tourism. My boss always used to say: how do you sell a cruise on the Nile, if you've never seen the Nile?

Mrs Hydrangea Yes. Yes. Yes. I remember now. I dreamt of something that got in through the draught and made us all become like numbers, just like figures in stats. We were numbers but we were ourselves. We could see each other, 1237, 1290, 3002, 3303, and we could also talk to each other, but we were made of numbers.

Mrs Honeysuckle Mrs Hydrangea, today you've popped open: first, Father Thomas' sermon, now this dream.

Mr Pomegranate *takes out a packet of crackers from his pocket.*

Mrs Hydrangea I hadn't expressed myself for so long.

Mr Laurel Mr Pomegranate, you can't eat here, didn't you know?

Mr Laurel *puts his coat on to go out.*

Mr Laurel I don't feel like sharing anything today. It's been four months since I requested a coat hanger, I wrote to them three times and got no answer, isn't that weird? I feel uncomfortable.

Seriously? (*Laughs.*) Well, it sounds a bit too much to say you are uncomfortable, just for a coat.

Mr Laurel   Don't you ever feel uncomfortable?

Mr Lemon   Actually, come to think of it, never. I'm always OK, I'm cheerful by nature.

Mr Laurel   Good for you.

Mr Laurel *leaves.*

Mr Pomegranate *takes the crackers out of his pockets and eats them.*

Blackout.

2

The sharing lounge.

Light.

Mr Lemon   Shall we go?

Mrs Honeysuckle   Let's go, let's go.

Mr Pomegranate   I can feel the vibrations, even from here.

Mrs Hydrangea   Do you? Tell you what, me too, today I feel like a little jolt in here, it's tiny but I can feel it.

They enter the meditation cabin.

Voice   Feel your body, feel your breath, feel that the air is good, feel the air that forgives you and cleanses you, feel the air that returns you to your soul, feel the world's soul, feel the world's roots pulling you, calling you. Inhale the light that turns into earth. Sink, sink, sink. Turn into sap, turn into centre, turn into leaf, turn into a leaf that flies in the wind and becomes yellow and crunches and dries up, feel the surrender that gives you to yourself. Feel how the matter, the dark matter with dark blood now becomes light: springing the limit between you melting and you becoming crystal and ice. Feel the courage to feel. Suck the sap and feed yourself with green-blue splendour, become chlorophyll and invent brightness, light up in light and be lighter, be water and rock, water that melts and water that nourishes roots, water that swells and fills breasts and is sucked by the soil, water that welcomes and collects, peace.

And now, repeat all together with your plants: I feel your vibrations.

All   I feel your vibrations. I feel your vibrations. I feel your vibrations.

Mrs Honeysuckle*'s mobile phone rings.*

Mrs Honeysuckle   Fuck.

Mrs Honeysuckle *comes out of the meditation cabin and takes her phone out of her bag.*

Mrs Honeysuckle Yes? Giulio! No not to worry, it's just that right now I'm not at work so I don't have access to the financial report. Of course, no problem. We can move everything to that bank account . . . yes that one, if you think it's more, as it were . . . Sure, sure . . . No, no, thanks for calling me even though, you know, I always have full confidence in your judgement. How much? Thee million? You decide, Giulio, I'm totally going to defer to your – what shall I call it? – your competence. After all, you know, I'm not that interested in money. No, no, come on, Giulio I was joking, go ahead and don't worry. I have to leave you now, I'm doing a . . . no, I'm not using the boat very much these days. Giulio, of course, let's have a drink and a barbecue, of course, say hi to Samantha, send my love to Samantha. I said: Say hi to Samantha.

The line drops.

Mrs Honeysuckle *returns to the meditation cabin.*

Mrs Honeysuckle I'm sorry, it was Giulio, my accountant, a very good chap, except he always rings me in the most . . .

All I feel your vibrations I feel your vibrations . . .

Voice Let's thank the leaves and flowers once again, let's thank all the branches, let's thank the sap, and finally let's all thank each other for this pleasant moment of connection.

And now continue your journey individually, repeating to your plants: I feel your vibrations.

They exchange thanks.

They all come out of the meditation cabin. They sit in the sharing lounge, everyone sits except **Mr Laurel** *who remains standing.*

Mrs Honeysuckle What's wrong, Mr Laurel?

Mr Laurel I feel uncomfortable in there with my coat, it's been a year since I flagged up the problem, and a year later no one deems us worthy of a coat stand.

Mrs Hydrangea If you fold it a little, like this, you can put it on the chair . . . Try it.

Mr Laurel It's too long, you see, it touches the floor, it's sweeping the floor.

Mr Lemon Ooooh. What a great session, huh.

Silence.

Mr Lemon It was . . . It was . . . Beautiful.

Mr Pomegranate *opens a packet of crackers and begins to eat them.*

Mr Laurel We've already had three warnings because of your crackers, I would not be surprised if they weren't giving us the coat stand as a form of a retaliation due to your flouting the rules.

Mr Pomegranate *looks at everyone, puts the crackers back in his pocket. He chews the cracker that was already in his mouth for a long time.*

Mr Lemon   Nice, really nice. Yes. Today it felt liberating.

Mrs Hydrangea   Very much so.

Mrs Honeysuckle   Did you really feel the vibrations Mr Lemon?

Mr Lemon   Of course. That's what we're here for.

Mrs Honeysuckle   Did you really feel them in your body?

Mr Lemon   Yes, of course.

Mrs Honeysuckle   I pretend to feel them, I've been pretending since the beginning of the journey, I think it's time to say this, frankly. I hope you won't judge me.

Mr Laurel   I feel something, I'm not sure if I'm making this up or not. I feel something funny in my foot, like it's itchy.

Mr Pomegranate   I think we shouldn't force ourselves. There's no rush. It's a process that takes time. The problem is that we're in too much of a hurry. We've been here for a year and we already want to achieve a result.

Mr Lemon   It takes a positive attitude, positive thinking. Towards the vibrations, towards ourselves, towards the plants. I think.

Mrs Hydrangea   Today, at times, I felt the vibrations, but as soon as I said to myself, 'Yes, I feel them', suddenly I couldn't feel them anymore.

Mr Pomegranate   In time . . .

Mrs Honeysuckle   Mr Pomegranate, you are right about the fact that we shouldn't be in a hurry, but this is also because out there you don't have, if I may, you are . . . how shall I put it, you don't have a real purpose. I have a job of my own, a husband and children of my own, Mr Laurel has his dog and his real estate agency, Mr Lemon too has his job in tourism, it seems to me his career is well underway – in short, we're all . . .

Mrs Hydrangea   What about me?

Mrs Honeysuckle   What I mean is, in short, I mean it's an investment. An investment must pay off.

Mr Pomegranate   There are populations who communicate without words, in the Amazon rainforest, I think. They don't need words, because in the forest they have to communicate over great distances. And so they use brain waves to say things to each other, to communicate positions and emotions to each other.

Mrs Hydrangea   Mr Pomegranate, it must be nice to study the universe. I always ask myself many questions about the world, and I can't find many answers. Except in the Gospel, of course. Sometimes, however, even in the Gospel there are things that are not easy to understand. Even Jesus sometimes speaks in a way that, well, I don't get it.

Mr Pomegranate I'm not a believer, my aunt isn't a believer and she taught me not to believe. As a child she used to say to me, if you want to believe, you can, if it helps you, but always remember that there is no god, it is we who have to create him within us, it's an immense effort. We humans are on earth to give birth to god. We hatch it like an egg, and eventually we give birth to it and this gives us relief, but god is still made up.

Mrs Hydrangea Did your aunt say these things to you?

Mr Pomegranate My aunt is a poet. She raised me, that's what she's like.

Mr Lemon Like Donald Duck. (*Laughs.*) That was a joke . . . in the world of ducks, in Duckburg, there are no parents but only aunts and uncles. Huey, Dewey, and Louie have no parents and uncle Donald also has no dad or mum, and uncle Scrooge? Well, better not think about it.

Mrs Honeysuckle No no, we should think about it: why all these uncles?

Mrs Hydrangea Jesus says: 'Foxes have their dens and sky birds their nests, but man's son has nowhere to lay his head'.

Mr Pomegranate Nice. Jesus was a poet too.

Mr Laurel I could use it with my clients: 'If you have nowhere to rest your head, buy a house'.

Mrs Honeysuckle Mr Laurel, what's the name of your estate agency?

Mr Laurel I no longer have an agency. Since my parents passed away, that is – I have no children, so I have no obligations, I'm only responsible for myself. I prefer to act as an intermediary: there's less bureaucracy, less effort. If someone has a house to sell I find someone looking for a house to buy, and I take a small commission. I do house viewings, I make them dream like Mr Lemon with his organised trips. I look at the clients, I study them, I try to understand if that house is for them, I don't believe in forcing a deal at all costs, I have my own professional ethics. Selling houses is like selling a backdrop in which an entire photo album will take place. A box of memories that are yet to happen.

Mrs Honeysuckle Why not? I have a friend, Amarilli, who changes house every three years, she says that after three years every house turns off, it stops shining in a way.

Mr Pomegranate What do you mean?

Mrs Honeysuckle I mean the energy of the house. All houses have a kind of energy, for example a house where someone committed suicide or where a girl was raped or something, well, this is all stuff that somehow remains in the air, in the particles.

Mr Pomegranate What particles?

Mrs Honeysuckle The particles! The particles of the house!

Mr Pomegranate Whatever.

Mrs Hydrangea For the first time today I managed to open up as I only do with God. Not with God, with Jesus actually. I don't know about you, but speaking to God directly, in prayers I mean, it feels intimidating, instead Jesus, I don't know, he seems friendlier to me. I imagine him as a handsome man, with a bare chest, who says, 'Mrs Hydrangea, Carla, tell me about you'. And I confide in him, I tell him, well, I'm not going to tell you what I tell him, I don't want to overshare.

Mr Laurel (*to* **Mrs Honeysuckle**) Your plant is so pretty.

Mrs Hydrangea *starts sobbing.*

Mr Laurel Did I say something wrong?

Mrs Hydrangea No, it's just that . . . you said that word: pretty.

Mr Laurel Pretty? I said that about the plant.

Mrs Hydrangea Yes, but even if you said it to the plant, it's as if . . . well . . . I'm not used to it, so.

Mr Laurel I'm sorry Mrs Hydrangea.

Mrs Hydrangea Forget it, it's OK (*blows her nose*) That's it.

(*To* **Mr Lemon**.)   MR Lemon I don't understand, why don't you want to leave your plant with the others at night, I really don't get this, Mr Lemon.

Mr Lemon I don't want to push her to socialise if she doesn't feel like it. She's a naturally shy plant.

Mr Pomegranate If you look closely, given the research I've been doing, your plant gives me the impression . . .

Mr Lemon Do tell us.

Mr Pomegranate Nothing, forget it.

Mr Lemon No, tell us. What's the matter with my plant?

Mr Pomegranate Nothing, if you don't want to see it, I don't want to force you.

Mrs Hydrangea I'm very happy with the relationship between my plant and Mr Pomegranate's plant. It seems to me that our plants have done a lot of bonding with one another, and I think it's very important to feel the energy of our plants, if we feel them socialise with each other. It's a good thing, isn't it?

Mr Laurel My plant has been socialising with Mrs Honeysuckle's plant above all.

Mrs Honeysuckle Thank you for your kind words, Mr Laurel, I'm a little down today. I feel frazzled. The truth is that I no longer see the meaning of all this. I too would like to open up a little but I don't know if I'm as good as Mrs Hydrangea. She talks to Jesus, I don't talk to anyone. It's like, I've made it as a woman, right? I've reached my life goals . . . a good marriage, polite children, a kitchen with a stand-alone island, induction hobs, my husband was very anti-induction hob at first, he's quite old-school, he doesn't like innovation in the kitchen, but I insisted and insisted, and in the end, I won so I . . . well, nothing.

I should be satisfied with what I've got.

One evening my husband opened a bottle of champagne, he gave me a small parcel, he said: 'Surprise'.

It wasn't really a surprise, I knew it was a diamond ring, because I'd asked him for one.

And in fact, in the parcel there was a solitaire diamond ring. I said thank you then I closed the box and I felt . . .

I felt nothing.

I felt nothing at all.

No joy.

It was as if life were flowing and I were somewhere else. And in the end I didn't feel like doing anything anymore: eating fucking shopping going to the cinema . . . Yes, Mrs Hydrangea, I said fucking.

Mrs Hydrangea   No no. I mean, yes. I understand.

Mrs Honeysuckle   I mean, it's not that at that time we weren't fucking at all, but it was something we did a bit like, because you have to, you get used to it and then you do it.

Mrs Hydrangea   Since my husband left me, I've been knitting a lot, I make these lovely slippers with leftover skeins, and it gives me great comfort.

Mrs Honeysuckle   Anyway, we were undecided between my journey with plants and a professional blast chiller. We'd been saying for a long time that a professional blast chiller would be quite useful, it wasn't just a whim, it was an investment, not just to make sushi, and also to give off a sense . . . a sense of social prestige. But this journey with plants was just for me, so my husband, it was a difficult period, I was always dragging my feet, and I wasn't really into it in bed, so he hugged me and he said to me: Paola, it's time to invest in your happiness, the blast chiller can wait. So I came here. But now I don't know, it's been a year now, and I sometimes think that if we'd bought that blast chiller we'd at least have something useful.

Mr Lemon *laughs.*

Blackout.

3

Mr Pomegranate   I must remember to go to the shop to buy cognac for my aunt, she's run out of it again and I promised her I'd go and buy it.

Mrs Hydrangea   Does your aunt drink cognac?

Mr Pomegranate　She drinks most things. These days she likes cognac, a while ago she used to like Eggnog. Do you know it? It's that egg liqueur.

Mrs Hydrangea　They're alcoholic beverages, they get to your head.

Mr Pomegranate　My aunt says it's an energy-booster.

Mrs Hydrangea　Well, energy-booster (*chuckles, embarrassed*) It might be.

Mrs Honeysuckle　I like Caipiroska.

Mr Pomegranate　My aunt usually makes Daiquiri, but these days she's became obsessed with cognac: there was a poet who died recently, who couldn't write poetry without cognac, and so my aunt, they were friends, I think she drinks cognac to remember him.

Mr Laurel　Is she an alcoholic, your aunt?

Mr Pomegranate　She's an artist.

Silence.

Mrs Hydrangea　'What a beautiful party, the party of your auntie!'

Mr Pomegranate　You made a rhyme! You're a poet too!

Mrs Hydrangea　No no, I was joking, it's just for fun. Do you ever write poetry?

Mr Pomegranate　No.

Mrs Hydrangea　That's strange! Perhaps it's because of the way you dress, *a little unkempt*, but I thought that you were a bit of an artist too.

Mr Pomegranate　My aunt buys me clothes. Maybe it's my aunt's poetry that pours onto my clothing.

Mrs Hydrangea　I didn't want to make you feel uncomfortable by saying you look shabby, maybe you felt . . .

Mrs Honeysuckle　Mrs Hydrangea that was a little insensitive, don't you see it's inappropriate to talk about Mr Pomegranate's sloppy clothes.

Mrs Hydrangea　I didn't mean to say that Mr Pomegranate wears scruffy clothes.

Mr Lemon　Mr Pomegranate is a little unkempt but that's also his style: an unkempt style. (*Laughs.*)

Mr Pomegranate *laughs*.

They all laugh.

Silence.

Mrs Hydrangea　Jesus loved the poor, he said: 'Let the poor come to me'.

Mr Laurel　The poor?

Mrs Hydrangea　Jesus said, 'Let the poor in spirit come to me'.

Mr Lemon Your aunt's not good for Jesus, Mr Pomegranate, because even if she is poor, she has a lot of spirit in her . . . (*laughs*) did you like my joke, I was playing on the word 'spirit', because your aunt drinks, glug glug glug (*laughs*)

Silence.

Mr Pomegranate (*to* **Mr Lemon**) We only know five percent of the matter that makes up the universe, we know nothing about the rest of the matter, so they call it dark matter.

Mr Lemon *laughs.*

Mr Pomegranate Even in the brain, only five percent is known, while the rest, it's not clear what it's for, so they call it grey matter.

Pause.

Mr Lemon Gray matter. Nice. (*Laughs.*)

Blackout.

4

The sharing lounge.

Mr Lemon How's the housing market going?

Mr Laurel Up and down. Do you own your house?

Mr Lemon Yes. But now I'm on my own, it's too big for me.

Mr Laurel I've got a couple of two-bedroom deals to hand if you're interested.

Mr Lemon There used to be two of us, me and Alice, then that damned accident happened. I don't want to upset you.

Mr Laurel No, that's OK.

Mr Lemon Have you ever lost someone you were very attached to?

Mr Laurel My parents.

Mr Lemon Ah, you lost your parents, I'm sorry.

Mr Laurel And my boyfriend.

Mr Lemon Boyfriend?

Mr Laurel My boyfriend, yes.

Mr Lemon Ah boyf . . . sorry, no I, no, sure, I have nothing . . . I just thought I'd misunderstood.

Mr Laurel How so?

Mr Lemon You know, I've travelled the world and I've seen a little bit of everything (*laughs*) I have a lot of gay friends.

Mr Laurel It's cool to say 'I have gay friends, I'm friends with a gay person'.

Mr Lemon No no, I mean it. We have a football game every Tuesday night, it's a mixed team, there are straight and gay people, but I can tell you that gay people look after their bodies, you can see that they don't let themselves go, they are fit, and they even play better, who knew. Everyone wants them in their team! (*Laughs, the laughter goes out.*)

Mr Laurel *laughs out of pity.*

Mr Lemon So you lost your boyfriend and I lost my Alice, we'd been together for almost eight years, we worked in the same tourist village, she took the car one evening to do some deliveries, I was busy and couldn't go with her, she was tired, she misjudged a bend in the road, ended up in a gorge, such a sad fate. And now, Mr Laurel, you and I find out that we share this sad fate, this loss. Had you been together for a long time?

Mr Laurel Two weeks.

Mr Lemon Ah. Ah so just like that, he flew away . . . flew away, just like that.

Mr Laurel Yes.

Mr Lemon Just two weeks and fate took him from you . . .

Mr Laurel I threw him out.

Mr Lemon From where?

Mr Laurel From my house.

Mr Lemon Ah, so he wasn't dead, you meant that he was dead for you.

Mr Laurel He's not dead, I don't think he is.

Mr Lemon I thought that . . .

Mr Laurel He kicked my dog.

Mr Lemon Poor Foofi, I'm sorry Mr Laurel, I hope he didn't hurt him too much.

Mr Laurel Luckily he was OK, he barely hurt him. But now Foofi is very ill, he's got something in his stomach, the vet said I should get ready.

Mr Lemon Eh, one gets attached to dogs too.

Mr Laurel He was my parents' dog.

Mr Lemon Must be a big blow for you.

Blackout.

5

THE GREENHOUSE.

Everyone.

Voice It is important for each of you to pay close attention not only to your own plant, but also to other people's plants. During the past two years the plants have become very similar to you and now they are trying to communicate their truth to you. It is of the utmost importance that, at this advanced stage, everyone focuses on nothingness. You have done so much to get to this point of the journey and you will be rewarded: today we will work together on high frequencies, don't cross your fingers or arms or feet, as it could cause reception issues.

Let's take a deep breath and make a high-pitched sound, but without making a sound. The sound should be in your imagination. Push upwards with the strength of your pelvic floor muscles, your vocal cords should vibrate without making any noise. This is because your plants are able to perceive high-pitched vibrations more than low ones, and they will respond by producing a very intense inner light that, in many cases, can give rise to an actual orgasm. Don't be scared if this happens, the orgasm is directly proportional to the intensity of your silent cry.

On the count of three, let's take a deep breath . . .

All I feel your vibrations, awareness brings happiness.

Voice I feel I feel I feel your vibrations, awareness brings happiness.

All I feel I feel I feel your vibrations, awareness brings happiness.

Mrs Honeysuckle's *phone rings. She leaves the meditation cabin upsetting everyone. She answers the phone while the others try to regain their concentration.*

Mrs Honeysuckle Oh Jesus fuck. (*Comes out of the greenhouse.*)

Hello? Yes, Carlo, no, not a problem at all, yes I can talk, I was just here, I was having a session of your plant thing, remember? Yes (*laughs*) yes it's crazy we got to the second year, almost the third. Carlo? No, no worries, we're free now, we found our balance . . . You think it's bullshit?

Why? No.

I trusted you so much, you told me so many good things about your journey with the plants, didn't you? A more intensive one? I don't know, Carlo, it's just that right now I'm so involved in this thing, I feel something's moving . . . no, I've never felt the vibrations. Never. Not even close. Cramp therapy, did you say?

I don't know, never heard of it. I'll think about it, thanks Carlo. Your friend . . . Maybe in spring, I have to hang up now they're all waiting for me. Of course, of course. Batten down the hatches, as they say. (*Laughs.*)

Mr Lemon Unfortunately I have to go now, I have a football match, they're waiting for me.

Mr Lemon *leaves with his plant.* **Mrs Hydrangea**, **Mr Laurel** *and* **Mr Pomegranate** *get out of the greenhouse and go sit in the sharing lounge while* **Mrs Honeysuckle**, *having finished with her phone call, returns inside the greenhouse, determined to feel the vibrations.*

Mr Pomegranate   Oh well.

He takes a packet of crackers out of his pocket and is about to eat.

Mr Laurel   A-a-a-a

Mr Pomegranate *looks at them with a cracker in his hand, undecided.*

Mrs Hydrangea   I just don't get it: how can one person cause any damage to our plants by eating a cracker? (*Takes out her rosary.*) I beg your pardon. (*She prays.*)

Mr Pomegranate   I like listening to you.

Mrs Hydrangea (*hands him the rosary*)   Do you want to try?

Mr Pomegranate   I'm not a believer.

Mrs Hydrangea   But we all believe in *something*.

We don't know what destiny holds in store for us and (*to* **Mr Laurel** *and* **Mr Pomegranate**), if you wanted to come to our parish . . . every Saturday afternoon we have a meeting with Father Thomas. He is a simple person, like us, we all sit in a circle and sing . . . it's nice to hear all the voices together, you know, it's emotional. And then in turn, each of us says a prayer for someone else, for their neighbour. I think it might be a nice surprise for you to come to these Saturday meetings with Father Thomas.

Mr Laurel   No.

Mrs Hydrangea   From 3 to 4pm. An hour. Only an hour, it's very quick.

Mr Laurel   On Saturdays at that time I always take Foofi for his walk, we're so used to it and I can't destabilize him.

Mrs Hydrangea   At church we also have a corner where our pet friends can be together. There are dogs of every species, they're all together in harmony while their owners share advice on how to look after them properly, you know, there's always a lot to learn. That's on Wednesday afternoons, this meeting with pets. It's on Wednesdays from 1pm to 2pm, during your lunch break. It's specifically designed for those who work.

Mrs Honeysuckle *is in the greenhouse. She has an orgasm.*

Mr Laurel   I never take lunch breaks. Ever.

Mrs Hydrangea   If you'd like to come sometime just to eat a bite, from 12 to 1pm. Our church is also open for those (*to* **Mrs Pomegranate**) who are hungry.

Mr Pomegranate   I have my crackers, I'm fine.

Mrs Honeysuckle *has an orgasm in the greenhouse.*

Mrs Hydrangea   We have all sorts of volunteers! There's also an African man, with very dark skin, a handsome chap, very young. There's also a Chinese guy . . . or maybe he's Japanese. Everyone's very keen and kind, they also speak quite good English. We always need volunteers.

Mr Pomegranate I might come one day or another, but I can't guarantee that.

Mrs Hydrangea That would be very lovely, Mr Pomegranate. Do you know that the canteen volunteers are given a white gown and even latex gloves, we mustn't touch the food. We also have a mask, a hat, all white. We're like white angels.

Mrs Honeysuckle *has an orgasm in the greenhouse.*

Mr Pomegranate What do you think, Mr Laurel?

Mr Laurel I'll think about it.

Mrs Hydrangea If you come on a Wednesday, you can stay with your dog and we can all have lunch together.

Mr Laurel My poor Foofi is dying actually.

Mrs Hydrangea I'll pray for him.

Mrs Honeysuckle *has an orgasm in the greenhouse.*

Mr Laurel It's getting late. Will you excuse me.

Mr Laurel *goes out, but forgets his coat on the chair.*

Mrs Honeysuckle *has an orgasm in the greenhouse.*

Mr Pomegranate Mrs Hydrangea, if it's not a problem for you, I would take advantage of the fact that Mr Laurel has gone to finish my crackers. I'm very hungry.

Mrs Hydrangea You eat, Mr Pomegranate, I won't say a thing.

Mr Pomegranate *takes out his packet of crackers.*

Mr Pomegranate Please, take one.

Mrs Hydrangea It's the last one.

Mr Pomegranate We can divide it in half.

Mrs Hydrangea Okay, just a little bit, just to taste it.

Mr Pomegranate Is it good?

Mrs Hydrangea *nods. She is moved, she cries.*

Mr Pomegranate Are you OK, Mrs Hydrangea?

Mrs Hydrangea No, sorry, it's just that it's been a long time, since my husband dumped me I always eat alone. Now, the sound of us munching together, you and I, sitting close together, I don't know, it made me quite emotional.

Mr Pomegranate Mrs Hydrangea, you are too sensitive.

Silence.

Mrs Hydrangea Have you noticed that Mr Lemon is the only one who has been taking his plant home? He says she's shy, but I really don't understand this reluctance.

Mr Pomegranate   Mr Lemon's plant . . . (*with solemnity*) is sterile.

Mrs Hydrangea   What did you say? Why did you use that word?

Does Mr Lemon know that it's sterile?

Mr Pomegranate   He knows, he knows. I talked to him about it. It was his choice: symbolically, for him, it's like a wild plant.

Mrs Hydrangea   Wild! (*Restrained laughter.*)

Mrs Honeysuckle *comes out of the greenhouse looking overwhelmed.*

Mrs Honeysuckle   Fuck me. I felt a kind of warmth, a kind of fire, that surrounded me all over.

Mrs Hydrangea   Did you feel the vibrations?

Mrs Honeysuckle   No.

Mrs Hydrangea (*to* **Mrs Honeysuckle**, *excited*)   Mrs Honeysuckle, did you know that Mr Lemon's plant is sterile?

Mrs Honeysuckle   Eh?

Mrs Hydrangea   Mr Pomegranate just shared this with me, isn't that right Mr Pomegranate? (**Mr Pomegranate** *doesn't answer, he is distracted by something.*) I don't know what he meant, but Mr Pomegranate knows his stuff, right? And he told me word for word: Mr Lemon's plant is sterile.

Mrs Honeysuckle   Is it really sterile?

Mrs Hydrangea Well, quite, it's . . . it's the first time I hear of a sterile plant. (*She starts to chuckle, embarrassed.*)

Mrs Honeysuckle   Mrs Hydrangea, I don't think it's any of our business if Mr Lemon's plant is sterile.

Mrs Hydrangea   You're right, I don't know why I felt like laughing, that was silly of me, I think it's a very serious matter, sometimes God is so hard, so . . .

Mr Pomegranate *faints and collapses on the sofa, with his body straight and rigid.*

Mrs Hydrangea   Mr Pomegranate has collapsed.

They help him up on the sofa.

Mrs Honeysuckle   Mr Pomegranate, are you feeling better? I kind of need to go.

Mr Pomegranate   All good.

Mrs Honeysuckle   I have to dash.

Mrs Hydrangea   I can't stay either, I have so many things . . .

Mr Pomegranate   You can go, I'll stay here a little longer.

Mrs Honeysuckle   Are you sure you're OK alone? You should not be left alone in your state.

Mr Pomegranate   I'm sure. I'm fine.

Mrs Honeysuckle   Are you sure? You're very pale.

Mr Pomegranate   I'm fine, I'm fine.

Mrs Honeysuckle   OK, take care Mr Pomegranate.

She leaves.

Mrs Hydrangea   So many emotions today, Mr Lemon's plant is sterile, and then you faint, Mr Pomegranate. So many emotions.

She covers him with the coat that Mr Laurel forgot on the chair. While covering him, she falls on him, for a moment they are in this position, one on top of the other, we understand that **Mrs Hydrangea** *wants to stay in this position but that she is completely shocked by what just happened. She gets up, she settles down, she looks for a way to leave.*

Mrs Hydrangea   Are you OK?

Mr Pomegranate   All good, all good.

Mrs Hydrangea   Be well, Mr Pomegranate.

Blackout.

6

The following morning. **Mr Pomegranate** *is lying on the sofa covered with* **Mr Laurel**'s *coat.*

Enter **Mr Laurel**.

Mr Laurel   Good morning.

Mr Pomegranate   Good morning.

Mr Laurel   I came by for the coat.

Mr Pomegranate *hands the coat back to* **Mr Laurel**, *who smells it, and doesn't wear it.*

Mr Pomegranate   Does it stink?

Mr Laurel   According to my parameters yes, according to yours probably not. Are you feeling OK?

Mr Pomegranate   I fainted last night, I slept here.

Mr Laurel   Did you sleep well?

Mr Pomegranate   I had a dream. I dreamt that I was flying.

Mr Laurel   It must have been a good dream, I always dream of things that are realistic, I'm used to giving myself boundaries, not only in real life, but even when I sleep, that's the kind of person I am.

Mr Pomegranate You like to hang your coat, you like tight schedules . . . how's your dog doing?

Mr Laurel He's sick. There's nothing more to be done. He barely walks and he smells.

Mr Pomegranate Like me.

Mr Laurel That's right. Only I'm very attached to him. Sorry, Mr Pomegranate, I didn't mean, I mean, I am fond of you too. Your unauthorised crackers, your poetic licences . . . I'm fond of you, a little bit. But with Foofi the matter is more upsetting. The vet says he should be put down but . . . He is the last thing, the last bond I have left, I'm on my own otherwise. My folks are gone and, as for the rest, well. I'm unable to make a decision, Mr Pomegranate. He looks at me with his eyes, as if nothing but good could come from me, do you know what I mean? How can you decide life or death, he trusts me completely.

Mr Pomegranate I have my aunt, but the situation is different, she's still fine. She's tough, that's why she's still healthy. She drinks, she writes, she swears, she talks all the time, she says: 'toilet, shit, rot, screw you all', she's angry with me, she says I'm weak, a failure, sometimes, sometimes, Mr Laurel, I feel like putting my fingers around her neck and squeezing slowly, slowly, squeezing. To make her understand that sometimes, every now and then, it's best to shut up.

Mr Laurel Tell me about your dream, what's it like to fly?

Mr Pomegranate It's something that comes from water.

Mr Laurel Flying in water?

Mr Pomegranate Yes. It's like the sensation of moving the air with your arms, with your fingers, like when you swim. It's just about feeling the air between your fingers, moving in a clear fluid, it's amazing.

Mr Laurel I would love to feel like that.

Mr Pomegranate You can try, you just have to spread your arms wide, like when you swim.

Mr Laurel I can't swim.

Mr Pomegranate Try it.

Mr Laurel How?

Mr Pomegranate *takes a coffee table and makes him lie on his stomach on it.*

Mr Pomegranate Place yourself like this.

Mr Laurel Like this?

Mr Pomegranate Yes. And now move your arms and legs, arms and legs, arms and legs, and breathe . . . Can you feel it?

Mr Laurel Yes, it's very nice.

Gets up on his feet again.

Thank you, Mr Pomegranate.

Mr Pomegranate   What for?

Mr Laurel   You taught me how to fly.

Mr Pomegranate   It's nothing, it's just a matter of coordination.

Mr Laurel   Yesterday while I was walking around the block with Foofi I felt this desire to die, maybe I had been thinking about it for some time without even knowing it. In the morning I went into the bathroom to wash my hands and I tripped, I don't know how I did it, on a slightly uneven tile. I fell on my face and stayed there, lying down, with my cheek on that cold tile feeling that cold surface, just breathing. I don't know how long I was there for. It seemed to me as if someone had slapped me to teach me a lesson and had knocked me down. In the end, it was almost nice to be there feeling my cheek pressed against that cool tile, it seemed to me that the tile, with all its coolness, was telling me that there was nothing that could hurt me anymore. I thought, 'I'm safe here, I can't fall any further than this'.

Mr Pomegranate   I see.

Mr Laurel   I'm so sorry, Mr Pomegranate, you've been unwell, you will have slept very little and I'm here talking rubbish to you.

Mr Pomegranate   We're also here to talk about stuff.

Mr Laurel   Shall we have a coffee? There's a bar out here, they make excellent coffee.

Mr Pomegranate   If it's on you, I won't object, I would also like a slice of cake, I really like chocolate cake with whipped cream on top.

Mr Pomegranate *and* **Mr Laurel** *go out.*

Blackout.

7

A plastic Christmas tree has appeared on stage.

Mrs Honeysuckle *and* **Mr Laurel** *decorate the Christmas tree.*

Mrs Honeysuckle   That watch? It's nice.

Mr Laurel   It was my dad's. I always keep it with me. I always keep it a quarter of an hour ahead to be on time.

Mrs Honeysuckle   Well I, on the other hand, happen to have stopped looking at the time lately. I was always so attentive to my commitments, my tight schedule, my meetings, it had become an obsession.

Mr Laurel   I was also thinking of the idea of suspending time, since my dog Foofi became ill.

Mrs Honeysuckle Ah, how's he doing by the way?

Mr Laurel I don't want to talk about this, tell me about yourself, Mrs Honeysuckle.

Mrs Honeysuckle I don't like dogs that much. I prefer cats actually.

Mr Laurel Some prefer cats, some prefer dogs. I didn't choose myself. If it'd been up to me, I wouldn't have had pets. They give you too much love and eventually they die. I prefer to stay away from such things.

Mrs Honeysuckle Which things?

Mr Laurel Love. Death.

Mrs Honeysuckle Why?

Mr Laurel I just don't like it.

Mrs Honeysuckle My uncle had a dog, a bulldog, Alfred. One day I thought about poisoning him.

Mr Laurel Was he aggressive?

Mrs Honeysuckle No, on the contrary he was a sweet dog.

Mr Laurel Then why did you want to poison him?

Mrs Honeysuckle Don't you ever have violent thoughts?

Mr Laurel I don't know. Maybe just once. I wanted to, I would have wanted to smash my boyfriend's head against the kitchen tiles. But it was a moment. I saw him kick my dog for no reason at all. A sixteen-year-old dog who hadn't done anything to him. When I asked him why he did it he shrugged: 'he stinks, he's old', he said, 'I don't like him coming near me'.

And at that moment I wanted to hurt him. But my instinct held me back. I asked him to leave. I put his things in a backpack and handed it to him. So he went. End of story.

Mrs Honeysuckle It's so easy to have violent thoughts sometimes. Yes, I held back too, in the end.

Mr Laurel Was your uncle fond of Alfred?

Mrs Honeysuckle Very. Yes. (*Pulls out a gun.*)

Mr Laurel (*remains impassive*) A toy gun?

Mrs Honeysuckle It looks like a toy, doesn't it?

Mr Laurel I never had anything to do with guns, I didn't play with them, even as a child.

Mrs Honeysuckle (*pretends to shoot* **Mr Laurel**) Bang bang!

Mr Laurel Why do you carry a gun with you, Mrs Honeysuckle?

Mrs Honeysuckle When I was fourteen my uncle, the owner of the dog, raped me.

Mr Laurel It's quite a big thing, what you're telling me, Mrs Honeysuckle, we've known each other for some time now but we're not that close.

Mrs Honeysuckle I don't know why, Mr Laurel, maybe it's precisely because we are not that close, I feel I can talk to you about this. I never spoke to anyone about this before. The way it happened was so idiotic, I adored my uncle, he was older than me, I was fourteen at the time, he was fun-loving, he had a lot of passions and was full of surprises. He was the one who taught me to sail, you know? I often went to visit him in his villa. One night I told my parents that I was going to see him and they had no objections. It was normal for us to spend time together, we'd eat pizza and then we'd watch a movie, on the sofa, on his big screen. That evening my uncle stroked my hair and then on the sofa . . . well Mr Laurel, my uncle took me. I wasn't able to say anything. I stayed there like that, as if it were something that had to happen, something normal.

I realize this is a bad moment for you, with your dog Foofi and all . . . but maybe this is the first time I feel I can open up. My life went on as if nothing had happened. My folks, I don't know whether they knew or not, but I think so. I think they'd sensed something, but they preferred to avoid conflicts. Our entire family life was a farce, and I think the only thing I learned from them was to pretend, just as well, that everything was fine.

Mr Laurel Mrs Honeysuckle, have you ever dreamt of flying?

Mrs Honeysuckle I never dream.

Mr Laurel Mr Pomegranate taught me. Do you want to try?

Mrs Honeysuckle Why not!

Mr Laurel *takes the same coffee table he used earlier.*

Mr Laurel So you have to place your body like this, no, not like this, lying down, and then you have to feel the water, a lot of water, all around you and then you have to move your arms and legs like this.

Do you feel it?

Mrs Honeysuckle Yes.

She swims / flies.

Thank you, Mr Laurel.

Mr Laurel You're welcome, like I said, Mrs Honeysuckle, this is something I learned from Mr Pomegranate.

Mrs Honeysuckle Mr Pomegranate. What a strange person, is he not?

Mr Laurel Yes, maybe. Maybe we're all strange.

Mrs Honeysuckle We're all very strange.

Mr Laurel Even this thing, perhaps you missed it, that Mr Lemon . . .

Mrs Honeysuckle What?

Mr Laurel   Maybe it's just a rumour . . . it appears that Mr Lemon's plant is . . . sterile.

Mrs Honeysuckle (*laughs*)   Mr Laurel, I didn't think you were such a gossip.

Mr Laurel   You're right, Mrs Honeysuckle, I don't know what happened to me, I usually mind my own business, it's just that this thing about Mr Lemon's plant being sterile really struck me, I don't know why.

Mrs Honeysuckle   Don't think about it Mr Laurel, our plants already have their own problems.

Blackout.

8

Mrs Hydrangea *is alone in the greenhouse. She talks to her plant.*

Mrs Hydrangea   I need someone to touch me, someone to speak to me kindly. I ask for nothing, just a tight handshake, a stroke, with respect. Sometimes I feel so alone that I almost feel like I don't exist. When I feel alone I scratch the kitchen wall with my house keys, each time I made deep marks on the wall, and all these marks, these scratches, one day I looked at them and it seemed like a tiger had been locked up in my house, in my kitchen. It frightened me, what I'd done, I was sorry to have messed up the wall. It's a sign of something that's not right, I thought, not right at all. I will hide all the things about me that aren't right, cover them in soap and become clean – would anyone love me then?

Blackout.

9

THE LOUNGE.

Mrs Hydrangea   Lately I've discovered that I do a lot of new things. I shouted at my daughter Michela last night, for instance.

Mrs Honeysuckle   I've always shouted a lot.

Mrs Hydrangea   Really?

Mrs Honeysuckle   With my husband we scream our heads off. Lately we even hit each other, perhaps that's because we don't fuck, you know what it's like.

Mrs Hydrangea   No.

Mrs Honeysuckle   I'm sorry, Mrs Hydrangea, I didn't mean to embarrass you, I always forget that you're an old-fashioned woman.

Mrs Hydrangea   No, that's OK, these are things that happen. What happens in the world pleases the Lord. After all, I think, if the Lord hadn't wanted us to do the deed, so to speak, he would have made us all smooth, you know, the way dolls are made sometimes, have you noticed, they don't have, how shall I put it, they don't have, even male dolls, they have nothing down there.

Mrs Honeysuckle   Do you mind if I take off my shoes? I need to let myself go.

Mrs Hydrangea   I love your shoes, they're so stylish . . .

Mrs Honeysuckle   Keeping them on all day, though . . . my feet, my toes are a bit . . . Mrs Hydrangea I've been meaning to tell you something for a while . . . Have you noticed that Mr Lemon was looking at you a bit like . . .

Mrs Hydrangea   What, that's rubbish . . . Really?

I don't think so.

Mrs Honeysuckle   But of course! You're still a beautiful woman, you should just brush yourself up a little bit, Mrs Hydrangea. A tight dress, a nice neckline highlighting your generous breasts, if only I had a couple of boobs like yours, Mrs Hydrangea, my goodness.

Mrs Hydrangea   Oh Lord no, why would I? I have no reason to . . .

Mrs Honeysuckle   There doesn't need to be a reason, Mrs Hydrangea, just do it for yourself.

Mrs Hydrangea   You think? What would I wear then?

Mrs Honeysuckle   If I were you, I would show a bit more flesh . . . you have beautiful legs, you're tall, slender, why not? Why not show off your goodies.

Mrs Hydrangea   Are you serious? I never thought about it, really.

Mrs Honeysuckle   For example, what's your underwear like?

Mrs Hydrangea   I have a V-neck vest. They are quite good, they keep my tummy warm.

Mrs Honeysuckle   Oh my goodness, those woolly vests? Please, Mrs Hydrangea!

Mrs Hydrangea   Why? They're good, they're warm.

Mrs Honeysuckle   What about a nice bra, a nice pair of culotte panties . . .

Mrs Hydrangea   Culotte?

Mrs Honeysuckle   Cu-lotte, Mrs Hydrangea.

Mrs Hydrangea   Well, I have a pair of panties with a slightly high waist that keep everything in place . . . don't make me say too much.

Mrs Honeysuckle   Tell me Mrs Hydrangea, tell me, it's just us two girls, the boys haven't arrived yet, we can talk freely.

Mrs Hydrangea   Well. Sometimes I imagine . . . I imagine being in the middle of an empty room, dancing one of those dances, you know, where everyone moves towards one side and then there's like a change of direction and everyone goes the other way, and . . . it's a whole movement, a movement of bodies.

Mrs Honeysuckle You're talking about group dances.

Mrs Hydrangea Yes. I would love that.

Mrs Honeysuckle Well, Mrs Hydrangea, I myself would really like to have a good fuck, if you don't mind me telling you? (*She takes off her coat.*) I can't take this anymore. Last night I had a date with a man, a guy I met a few weeks ago on a dating app, yes (*undresses*), and look, look what I was wearing last night. What do you reckon?

Mrs Hydrangea Quite subtle.

Mrs Honeysuckle I was there all saucy on the sofa, I was ready, ready to receive his cock and what did he do?

Mrs Hydrangea I don't know, did he give you his shirt?

Mrs Honeysuckle He fell asleep, Mrs Hydrangea, like a moron, like a moron, Mrs Hydrangea. I can't even think about it.

(*Showing her underwear*) Do you like it?

Mrs Hydrangea Maybe . . .

Mrs Honeysuckle He didn't even make me a compliment.

Mrs Hydrangea It's a bit audacious . . . it's bold!

Mrs Honeysuckle I'd like to see you wearing it, why don't you try it on?

Mrs Honeysuckle *undresses* **Mrs Hydrangea**, *she has five layers of clothes.* **Mrs Hydrangea** *raises her arms each time to take off her shirts and all the following lines are uttered while* **Mrs Honeysuckle** *undresses* **Mrs Hydrangea**, *until she finally takes off her bra.*

There is no one here, Mrs Hydrangea, don't be shy . . .

Mrs Hydrangea But I don't have your figure . . .

I don't think this is appropriate, I'm not used to these things . . .

Mrs Honeysuckle There is always a first time. We came here precisely to free ourselves and feel the vibrations, Mrs Hydrangea.

Mrs Hydrangea Well, I don't know, I mean I, do you think . . . I don't know (*laughs*) I mean . . .

Mrs Hydrangea *is topless and* **Mrs Honeysuckle** *takes her dress off too, then gives it to* **Mrs Hydrangea** *to wear.*

Mr Pomegranate *enters, sees them, goes out, makes a noise, enters a second time.*

Mr Pomegranate I brought a little something to put on the Christmas tree.

Mrs Hydrangea What a nice thought, Mr Pomegranate.

Mr Pomegranate It's nothing, it's just a star to put on the tip, that's all.

He places the star on the tip.

Mrs Honeysuckle Mrs Hydrangea, do you know that Mr Laurel taught me to fly?

Mrs Hydrangea To fly?

Mr Pomegranate nods and smiles.

Mrs Honeysuckle Mr Pomegranate taught Mr Laurel to fly and he then taught me.

Mrs Hydrangea Can I learn too?

10

The sharing lounge.

Mr Pomegranate Are the girls not coming today?

Mr Laurel They must have met for a coffee, I've noticed those two have become best buddies lately.

Mr Lemon Best buddies or best bunnies? (*Laughs.*)

Mr Laurel I'm sorry Mr Lemon but I don't feel like having a laugh today, sorry, I'm not in the mood. I had to call the vet to get my Foofi to sleep. For some days he hadn't eaten anything and he was wailing a lot. The vet said: if he doesn't complain it means that he's not in pain, but if he complains he's in pain, and you must call me. And so, I had to do it.

Mr Lemon I'm sorry Mr Laurel, my thoughts are with you.

Mr Pomegranate My thoughts are with you, Mr Laurel.

Mr Laurel That's life.

Mr Pomegranate The other day I was coming here to bring Christmas decorations and I heard Mrs Honeysuckle say to Mrs Hydrangea, 'I'd really like a fuck'.

Mr Laurel Mrs Honeysuckle?

Mr Pomegranate Mrs Honeysuckle . . . I found them both topless.

Mr Laurel Both.

Mr Pomegranate Yep.

Mr Lemon What did they do when you got in?

Mr Pomegranate They got dressed.

Mr Lemon You could've taken advantage.

Mr Pomegranate   They were swapping bras.

Mr Lemon   Indeed, well, it was quite an adventure because (*laughs*) I mean, Mrs Hydrangea's bosoms are quite the knockers.

Mr Laurel   Mr Lemon, it's not very polite to make such statements about the bodies of others.

Beat.

Mr Laurel   And so you, Mr Pomegranate, you saw Mrs Honeysuckle and Mrs Hydrangea . . . swapping bras?

Mr Pomegranate   Mrs Hydrangea is well equipped but Mrs Honeysuckle, I must say, isn't doing that bad at all either.

Mr Laurel   Mrs Honeysuckle is very glamorous.

Mr Pomegranate   Yes.

Mr Laurel   Mrs Honeysuckle takes care of all the details.

Mr Lemon   But I really can't picture Mrs Hydrangea taking off her bra like that.

Mr Laurel   Sometimes I think she smells, she smells of church, or of the church canteen, it's a smell of loneliness.

Mr Pomegranate   She's had three children. She too must have tasted the pleasures of life.

Mr Lemon   I think all this modesty, this restraint, makes Mrs Hydrangea quite attractive.

Mr Laurel   Mrs Honeysuckle has a gun in her bag.

Mr Pomegranate   A gun?

Blackout.

11

Christmas party. Lights up. The party has already begun, a few bottles have already been opened, there is a warm and over-excited atmosphere. Some unwrapped presents are on the floor.

Mr Laurel *unwraps a tall object which turns out to be a coat hanger.*

Mrs Honeysuckle   You didn't expect it, huh?

Mr Laurel   Thanks! (*He finally hangs up his coat.*)

Mr Lemon   Better late than never. (*Laughs.*)

Mr Pomegranate   I hadn't celebrated Christmas for years.

Mr Lemon *and* **Mrs Honeysuckle** *unwrap a parcel containing a pair of* **Mrs Hydrangea**'*s hand-knitted slippers, they look at each other and show them to each other.*

Mrs Honeysuckle   I love the colour.

Mr Pomegranate   My aunt and I never take ours off, not even to sleep.

Mrs Hydrangea *has received a Nivea hand cream from* **Mr Lemon**.

Mrs Hydrangea   How did you guess it was my favourite cream?

Mr Laurel *takes a large shell out of a box.*

Mrs Honeysuckle   I hope you like it, Mr Laurel.

Mr Lemon   A shell from the Antilles.

Mr Pomegranate   My guess is . . .

Mrs Honeysuckle *shushes him because* **Mr Laurel** *is listening to the sea through the shell.*

Mr Pomegranate   Three or four hundred years.

Mrs Honeysuckle *shushes him again because* **Mr Laurel** *can't hear.*

Mr Pomegranate   From the measurement you understand how long the shellfish worked to create its shell.

Mrs Honeysuckle *shushes him.*

Mr Pomegranate   It's a mollusc . . .

They all want to hear the sea through the shell.

Mr Pomegranate (*reads the note*)   Dear Mr Pomegranate, by chance I found a pair of shoes that I had given my husband some time ago, I think he didn't like them because he wore them very little. They are made of excellent plastic material, light and breathable.

Mrs Honeysuckle   I hope you like red.

Mr Pomegranate *shows the shoes.*

Mrs Hydrangea   How lovely.

Mr Pomegranate *takes off his own shoes and wears the new ones happily, paces back and forth in disbelief at the comfort.*

Mr Pomegranate   They're non-slip!

Mrs Hydrangea   Mrs Honeysuckle can you top me up – just a drop.

While **Mr Pomegranate** *walks back and forth,* **Mrs Hydrangea** *walks behind him, a little embarrassed, with her present for him in her hand, and gives it to him timidly.*

Mrs Hydrangea   Hurray!

Mr Pomegranate   Hurray!

Mr Pomegranate *opens* **Mrs Hydrangea**'*s gift, it's a small notebook.*

Mr Pomegranate (*reads*) 'I'm a light and sensitive soul, a modest butterfly flying in the snowy sky' (*repeats approvingly*) 'A modest butterfly'.

(*He resumes reading.*) 'Last Christmas I gave you my heart, but the very first day . . .'

Mrs Hydrangea   Hurray!

Mr Lemon   Hurray! A toast to the new poet. (*Laughs.*)

Mr Lemon *gives* **Mr Laurel** *and* **Mrs Honeysuckle** *a drink.*

Mrs Honeysuckle   Let's have a toast for the bottle of cognac that belongs to your auntie!

Mrs Hydrangea   Which rhymes with party!

Mr Pomegranate *starts walking back and forth to try his shoes while* **Mr Lemon** *invites* **Mrs Hydrangea** *to dance, they dance.*

Music starts. It's Tom Waits' All the word is green.

Mrs Honeysuckle *is on the sofa between* **Mr Laurel** *and* **Mr Pomegranate** *who is sitting on the arm of the sofa,* **Mrs Honeysuckle** *has* **Mrs Hydrangea**'s *slippers on her eyes and is laughing like crazy.* **Mrs Hydrangea** *is dancing with* **Mr Lemon**. *When he gets too close to her, and is almost about to kiss her, she withdraws and goes to sit on a chair. For a moment* **Mr Pomegranate** *tries to invite* **Mrs Hydrangea**, *but* **Mr Lemon** *returns on the offensive and* **Mr Pomegranate** *then goes to the table, fills a bowl of snacks, and begins to nibble eagerly, while watching* **Mrs Hydrangea** *and* **Mr Lemon** *dance.*

From the sofa, **Mr Pomegranate** *shouts to* **Mrs Hydrangea**, *making a sign of complicity towards her.*

Mr Pomegranate   Hurray!

Mrs Hydrangea *unties herself from* **Mr Lemon**'s *grip. She begins to dance alone facing the audience, doing the steps from the group dance she was talking about with* **Mrs Honeysuckle**. *She laughs.* **Mr Pomegranate**, *who up to now was looking at her while standing next to the table, is appreciative and begins to follow her footsteps. Progressively the others join in and the group dance takes shape. At a certain point* **Mr Laurel** *detaches himself from the group and begins to fly on the table where* **Mr Pomegranate** *had taught him to fly. The game is successful and, little by little, they abandon the group dance and begin to fly.*

The image of a whole group flight is established: everyone moves their arms as if they were swimming. This must make one think of falling skydivers, but also of slow-moving cockroaches.

The MUSIC goes from Tom Waits' into Rosemary Stadley's cover of All the word is green.

END OF MUSIC.

Blackout.

12

Mr Lemon's *Death.*

Everyone is asleep. **Mrs Honeysuckle** *is lying on the sofa with her head on* **Mr Laurel**'s *lap,* **Mrs Hydrangea** *and* **Mr Pomegranate** *are slouching on the armchairs.* **Mr Lemon** *is awake in the greenhouse.*

Mr Lemon (*in the greenhouse*)   I feel the vibrations I feel the vibrations.

He goes out, claps his hands.

Mr Lemon   Hey it's time to wake up! Merry Christmas everyone (*laughs*)

Makes coffee with the kettle.

Mr Lemon   Would you like some coffee, Mr Pomegranate?

Mr Pomegranate   Yes please.

Mrs Hydrangea   I have a headache.

Mr Lemon   You drank a lot of cognac last night.

Mrs Hydrangea   I have a headache.

Mr Pomegranate   All night you were like, 'I feel the vibrations, I feel the vibrations', you didn't let us sleep for a moment.

Mrs Hydrangea   I have a headache.

Mr Pomegranate   He didn't let us sleep for a moment.

Mr Lemon   I had a great experience, I really felt the vibrations, big time.

Mrs Hydrangea   Shhh, I have a headache.

Mr Lemon *goes to take his plant from the greenhouse and takes it into the main space and sits next to* **Mrs Hydrangea**.

Mr Laurel   I slept really badly.

Mr Lemon *puts down the plant and prepares to feel the vibrations.*

Mrs Hydrangea   Again?

Mr Pomegranate   Excuse me, Mr Lemon, may I ask you a question.

Mr Lemon   Are you talking to me?

Mr Pomegranate   Has your plant spent the night with ours?

Mr Lemon   She was with the others (*he starts to feel the vibrations again*), you should try it too Mrs Hydrangea, in the morning you can feel stronger vibrations, you too, Mr Pomegranate, take advantage of it.

Mr Pomegranate *gets up, goes into the greenhouse, comes out with his plant,* **Mrs Hydrangea** *gets up, goes into the greenhouse, comes out with her plant in her hand. They both look at their plants with concern.*

Mr Pomegranate   There's something odd, Mr Lemon, did you notice anything odd last night?

Mr Lemon   No. Apart from last night's party.

Mrs Honeysuckle   Good morning.

Mr Pomegranate   Something's wrong. My plant is awkward, I feel it's not well.

Mr Lemon   It must be the cold, there is no heating in the greenhouse at night.

Mr Pomegranate   Our plants are used to being in the cold. They're not used to being next to a sterile plant.

Mrs Hydrangea *and* **Mr Lemon** *with their plants in hand feel the vibrations.*

Mrs Honeysuckle (*stunned, looking around, sees the tree, recovers her sense of reality*)   Ah, indeed, it's Christmas.

Mr Pomegranate   It's as if my plant had had a chlorophyllic apoplexy, it can be lethal for plants.

Mrs Hydrangea   Mine looks asphyxiated, as if she couldn't take a good sip of oxygen.

Mr Pomegranate   It's got the same symptoms as mine, in fact, you see, yours has a different colour, look at it carefully, it's not the usual colour.

Mrs Hydrangea   Some little white veins have appeared.

Mr Lemon   Your leaves have always been like this.

Mrs Hydrangea   These white veins are normal?

Mr Pomegranate   Don't be ridiculous Mr Lemon, you're trying to clutch at straws.

Mr Lemon   What straws? There are no straws (*laughs*)

Mrs Honeysuckle *enters the greenhouse.*

Mr Pomegranate   Lesson number two, touch the leaves to evaluate their consistency. Mrs Hydrangea, touch the leaves.

Mrs Hydrangea *touches the leaves.*

Mrs Hydrangea   They're rough.

Mrs Honeysuckle   Mr Laurel, come here.

Mr Laurel *gets up and joins* **Mrs Honeysuckle** *in the greenhouse.*

Mr Pomegranate (*with a professional voice*)   Try and break a leaf, what's it like? Does it feel like it's lost lymph? Does it feel dry?

Mrs Hydrangea   What?

Mr Pomegranate   Crush it, do you feel the sap or not?

Mrs Hydrangea   I don't know, it seems like . . .

Mr Pomegranate Too little sap?

Mrs Hydrangea Not much. Too little sap.

Mr Pomegranate Indeed. That's what I feared. Precisely what I feared. Shock-induced chlorophyllic apoplexy.

Mrs Honeysuckle *runs out of the greenhouse, goes to her handbag on the sofa, takes a handkerchief and runs back into the greenhouse.*

Mrs Honeysuckle (*To* **Mr Laurel**) Did you see?

Mrs Hydrangea *sits next to* **Mr Pomegranate**.

Mrs Hydrangea Even the smell, can you smell it?

Mr Pomegranate The smell is gone.

Mr Laurel *and* **Mrs Honeysuckle** *come out of the greenhouse, dismayed, carrying their plants.*

Mr Laurel It looks dehydrated.

Mrs Honeysuckle Mine has something too, it's not the same anymore. Looks like it's shrunk, doesn't it?

Mr Pomegranate Crazy. One night was enough.

And the strange thing is that your plant, Mr Lemon, seems to be doing very well.

Mr Lemon Mine is fine, yeah.

Mr Pomegranate Mr Lemon, what happened last night? What did you do to our plants, tell us the truth.

Mr Lemon Nothing, I felt the vibrations.

Mr Pomegranate All night feeling the vibrations, you're a maniac.

Mr Lemon Yes, it seemed like a good moment.

Mr Pomegranate You and your *sterile plant* have raped our plants.

Mr Laurel Do you realise?

Mr Lemon What should I realise?

Mrs Honeysuckle Look at my plant, see?

Mr Lemon It seems in good health.

Mrs Honeysuckle It's shrunk, you sucked up its sap. It's shrunk, even the leaves are smaller than they were.

Mr Laurel It looks like a bonsai.

Mr Pomegranate You knew very well that our plants had never had the experience of being together with yours at night, and despite this you and your sterile plant vibrated all night at the expense of our plants, you should be ashamed.

Mr Lemon   My plant isn't sterile, it's a Cyrenaica lemon, this is what it's like.

Mr Pomegranate   It has thorns, it's sterile.

Mr Lemon   Cyrenaica lemons have thorns.

Mr Pomegranate   Don't make me say things I don't want to say, Mr Lemon.

Mr Lemon   Cyrenaica lemons have thorns, they reproduce with thorns.

Mr Pomegranate   Thorns are a clear sign of sterility.

Mr Lemon   Mr Pomegranate, you're airing a lot of nonsense, stop it now.

Mr Pomegranate   I've been studying quantum physics and plant biology for fifteen years, fifteen years, so I think I can speak as an expert, I think.

Mr Lemon   And are you also a boob expert? Since you came to tell us about Mrs Honeysuckle's and Mrs Hydrangea's breasts?

Mr Pomegranate   Don't you dare say things that have nothing to do with the issue of our plants.

Mrs Honeysuckle   What did you say about Mrs Honeysuckle and Mrs Hydrangea?

Mr Pomegranate   What did I say?

Mrs Honeysuckle   Mr Lemon said you said something about me and Mrs Hydrangea.

Mr Pomegranate   Yes. I said you were playing at swapping bras and he, I don't want to report what he said because his depravity has no limits.

Mr Lemon   But they never swapped bras, you made that up in the loo while you were wanking.

Mr Pomegranate   Ah, I was wanking, was I, and what were you doing last night?

Mr Lemon   I was feeling the vibrations.

Mr Pomegranate   You used your sterile plant to rape our plants.

Mr Lemon   I felt the plants' vibrations.

Mr Pomegranate   You used your *sterile plant* to rape our plants. All night long.

Mr Lemon   I just felt the plants' vibrations. That's all I did.

Mrs Honeysuckle   You have . . . Yes, yes, yes, you were trying to fuck our plants, tell the truth.

Mr Pomegranate   Perverse.

Mrs Honeysuckle   Yes, your plant was trying to fuck mine. You think I haven't noticed that you've been checking me out with your horny eyes since I arrived?

Mr Lemon   Who, me!?

Mrs Honeysuckle   Yes, you.

Mr Pomegranate I didn't say anything, I didn't say anything! I just said the truth, that I saw your bra-swapping game, but he immediately started making indecent jokes about you, about your . . .

Mr Lemon Don't be ridiculous.

Mr Pomegranate He said that Mrs Hydrangea has two big boobs like this.

Mr Lemon I've never seen them, you're the one who said you saw them.

Mr Pomegranate I simply described what happened.

Mr Lemon What did you describe? You made it up with your ardent imagination, grey matter, black holes, women swapping bras . . . just try to be a little sensible instead of having your head stuck in the clouds.

Mr Pomegranate Mr Laurel.

Mr Laurel It's true. He said that Mrs Hydrangea has 'quite the knockers'. But did you really take off your clothes?

Mrs Hydrangea It's her fault! I didn't want to, it's all her fault. I'm astounded, Mr Pomegranate, I thought you were a good person, I've also given you my . . . beloved notebook . . . with those words that I'd never told anyone, 'I gave you my heart' . . .

Mr Pomegranate I didn't say anything, I reported a small event with child-like innocence. It was him! He was the one who put those words in my mouth.

Mrs Hydrangea Those words that I'd never told anyone, 'I gave you my heart' . . .

Mrs Honeysuckle And you! You need to cut it out with these pathetic scenes, pretending you're a virgin.

Mrs Hydrangea You need to wash your mouth before you talk about me.

Mrs Honeysuckle Give me a break.

Mrs Hydrangea It's all your fault, it's all her fault!

Mrs Honeysuckle You put on airs and pretend to be a saint, my church here, my church there, and then . . . don't make me say things . . .

Mr Lemon Say it.

Mr Pomegranate I didn't do anything wrong. I lost a plant and I also lost a loved one.

Mrs Hydrangea I'm astounded, Mr Pomegranate, I could have expected it from Mr Laurel who killed his dog, and maybe I could have expected it from Mrs Honeysuckle who wanted to lead me to perdition.

Mrs Honeysuckle I was only trying to help you look inside yourself, you're always out, you're fake, and you're always judging everything, you're disgusting.

Mr Laurel What the hell does my Foofi have to do with it, I don't understand, it was the vet who told me to put him to sleep.

Mrs Hydrangea   You killed him. You're a killer.

Mrs Honeysuckle (*to* **Mr Pomegranate**)   Leave my bag alone.

Mrs Hydrangea   You killed your dog.

Mr Pomegranate   I wanted to see the gun.

Mrs Honeysuckle   How do you know I have a gun?

Mr Lemon   Mr Laurel said so.

Mrs Hydrangea   Mr Laurel is a scaremonger.

Mr Lemon   For three years I've been attending a congregation of lunatics, one has a gun in her handbag, and the other pretends to be a church-loving woman but goes out topless.

Mrs Honeysuckle (*to* **Mr Laurel**)   I trusted you.

Mr Pomegranate   I'm sorry, Mr Laurel, I didn't want to . . .

We are losing the plot here, the problem is with our plants, the plants have been raped, he's the culprit, he wants to pit us against each other and he's doing it on purpose.

Mrs Honeysuckle   You are robbing us of our dignity!

Mr Pomegranate   It's him!

Mrs Honeysuckle   It's all his fault!

Mr Pomegranate   I'd never been so happy.

Mr Lemon   Mr Pomegranate, I've done nothing.

Mrs Honeysuckle   You're denying the evidence.

Mr Lemon   What evidence?!

Mrs Honeysuckle   Why did you come here? Why did you infiltrate our group? Who sent you?

Mr Lemon   To do what?!

Mrs Honeysuckle   Spy on us.

Mr Lemon   Do you think this so interesting?

Mrs Honeysuckle   And what about your life?

Mr Lemon   An ordinary life.

Mrs Honeysuckle   A shit life, if I may say so.

Mr Lemon   Like yours Mrs Honeysuckle, and that of Mrs Hydrangea, Mr Laurel and Mr Pomegranate. If we're here it's because our lives are shit.

Mrs Hydrangea   You feel deeply guilty because you killed your girlfriend who was running away from you because you were too superficial.

Mr Lemon She wasn't running away from me, she wasn't . . .

Mrs Hydrangea Yes, she was running away because you wouldn't give her anything, you had misunderstood her and disappointed her and she . . .

Mr Lemon No!

Mrs Honeysuckle I'd opened my heart to you, Mr Laurel, why did you betray me like this?

Mr Lemon She wasn't running away.

Mr Laurel You never told me not to tell anyone!

Mrs Hydrangea Yes Alice was running away, it's your fault! You killed her.

Mr Lemon I'm only guilty of . . .

Mrs Hydrangea You bring your sterile plant here to kill everyone else around you.

Mr Lemon I'm only guilty that I wasn't able to save her, I couldn't go with her.

Mrs Hydrangea You had never intended to go with her.

Mr Lemon Yes I did! I wanted to go with her but then . . . it was late, she left, we drove down that road every day, that evening she was a bit strange, I couldn't go with her (*he cries*), I told her, 'rest before you go', then she fell asleep at the wheel.

Mrs Honeysuckle *gets up, takes her handbag, approaches* **Mr Lemon**, *takes his plant and places it far away from him.* **Mr Lemon** *takes off his glasses, wipes his eyes, gets up, goes to his plant.* **Mrs Honeysuckle** *takes a few steps away and points the gun at him.*

Mr Lemon Let's get it over with at this point, if it has to end like this . . .

Mrs Honeysuckle *shoots,* **Mr Lemon** *collapses slowly.*

Mr Lemon Merry Christmas (*he falls to the ground*)

Mrs Honeysuckle *passes the gun to* **Mr Pomegranate**.

Mrs Honeysuckle Will you deal with it?

Mr Pomegranate *takes the gun, shoots at* **Mr Lemon**'*s plant.*

Everyone looks at **Mr Lemon**'*s body.*

Blackout.

13

Light. Morning. All lying in the morning position. A jingle wakes them up.

Voice Good morning, everyone, and happy awakening. You will find your participation and value certificates in parchment paper under the tree. A certificate of attendance will be sent to you within four working days in digital format with the following identification codes: 1237 Mrs Honeysuckle, 1290 Mr Lemon, 3002 Mr Pomegranate, 3303 Mr Laurel, and 4422 Mrs Hydrangea, it will need to be digitally signed to guarantee authenticity and returned to management for archiving.

The management hopes that the journey has been to your liking. Happy Christmas.

They all get up, tidy up their clothes, get their diploma. They greet each other with a simple handshake.

They all leave the room, except **Mrs Hydrangea**, *who remains alone with her handbag. She looks at the audience, then leaves.*

Blackout.

Carbon

Carbonio

By Pier Lorenzo Pisano

Translated by Atri Banerjee

First staged at the Piccolo Teatro, Milan, on 23 June 2022.

Characters

A   her
B   him
—   a voice

place   a dark room with a source of light from above
time   a week from today

Content warning: strong language and themes of child loss and bereavement.

1.

A *and* **B** *are seated on either side of a table in the centre of the room.*

A Tell me.

Silence.

B What should I tell you?

A Tell me the details of the Encounter.

B Everyone saw it.

A It's important.

B There are videos . . .

A I need a first-hand account. What did you feel, what was it like, what did you see, what did you hear . . . consider, please, all five of your senses, and tell me what you thought, too.

B It happened a week ago . . .

A You've forgotten?

B No, it's not that, but . . .

A Tell me.

B What exactly do I need to tell you?

A Tell me what you saw.

Silence.

B There were plenty of people around.

A But you were the one who encountered it.

B Yes, but others saw it better, they saw it more clearly. There's the video.

A We've seen the videos and the photos and the recordings. We've seen all the digital material there is. We're just missing one thing: your account. We're missing you.

Tell me.

B It went by really quickly. Really fast.

A Yes.

B And I can't exactly describe . . . I mean, it was something . . . new.

A Yes.

B Something that's never happened before, like I don't have anything to compare it to, does that make sense?

A Yes.

B It's as if . . . it wasn't one of us. Like it came from somewhere else. And somehow I knew that, that it was . . . I felt that instinctively, I think everyone must have felt that.

A Yes.

B Which is why I'm saying . . . maybe someone else nearby, who also saw it, can be more helpful.

Silence.

A Carry on.

B I don't know what else to say.

A Carry on, please.

B I've thought all sorts of things, but I don't . . .

Silence.

A Keep going, please. Tell me some more.

Silence.

B I've thought about it so much that I've lost track of the actual feeling. Whatever I felt in that moment.

Silence.

B And maybe I made a mistake.

A What mistake?

B I watched all the videos, everything I could find online.

A And?

B Something strange happened. I watched so many, to try and understand, to understand what had happened, that now when I think back . . . it's like I'm seeing it from the outside.

A Meaning?

B Meaning it's like I've overwritten my own memory. I remember the videos more than what really happened. Looking back on it now, it's the videos that come to mind.

A Concentrate. What did you see. Tell me.

B Nothing. There's just the videos.

A That's not possible.

B I watched them hundreds of times, to try and understand, I know them off by heart. The sounds too, the voices . . . I remember those from the videos.

Silence.

A What was it that you couldn't understand?

Silence.

A What were you thinking?

Silence.

B I . . . don't know exactly what I was thinking in that moment. I can tell you what I thought afterwards . . . Later . . . I don't know how much later, I realised something. I don't know if it's an explanation I gave myself, or what really happened. But I realised that thing was messing with my head.

A Was that because of its physical appearance?

B No, no. It was symmetrical in its own way.

A A particular smell? You can't smell on video.

B I don't remember any smell in particular.

A Was it cold? Did it give off heat?

B No.

Silence.

A What was destabilising about it?

B Yeah, sure, that's the right word, perhaps. I looked at it and I felt like I had lost my balance. But I don't know if I really felt that in the moment, or if that's what I thought afterwards, like a feeling in hindsight, you know?

A Carry on.

B We had nothing in common. Nothing. And every tiny particle of my body knew that, somehow.

A That its life form wasn't based on carbon?

B I didn't know anything about that, but it's like I knew it, yeah.

Silence.

A So that's how it made you feel? Unwell, unbalanced, in pain?

B A lack of balance, yes. And a sort of . . . pain.

Silence.

A I need you to be more specific. What did you feel during the close encounter?

B This pain and . . . and fear, too.

A You wanted to run away?

B No. It was a different kind of fear.

A Tell me about it.

Silence.

B I feel like . . . everyone, even kids, have some kind of idea of how they appear to others. Even when you look at, I don't know, a dog, you imagine for a moment how it sees you, from down below, wagging its tail . . . in some way, you put yourself in its place. But when I encountered this thing, this creature, I felt for the first time like I didn't know how it might perceive me. That I wasn't able to put myself in its place, nor it in mine. That I couldn't identify with it. That we were worlds apart. I immediately felt certain, somehow, that I and that thing would be different, forever.

A Do you think there's any potential for communication?

Silence.

B No.

A This question is very important. Consider it carefully. You don't believe there's any potential for communication?

Silence.

A You don't have to answer right away. We can come back to it later.

B No.

A You don't want to come back to this question?

B No, there isn't any potential for communication. They're different.

A They're different?

B They're something other.

A We could try.

B I don't know. It's like it wasn't even really there.

Silence.

A *makes a note.*

A Why are you so uncertain of everything, apart from this one point?

B It's like a hunch.

A Tell me about it, please.

B The moment I encountered that being, and I perceived it as something so far away, so distant, I also felt like the rest of us - our team - for the first time, was one.

A What team?

B Us. Team Carbon. The animals and the plants.

A Life on Earth.

B Yes. I felt like all life on Earth was united in an instant against that creature. That there's a thread, something in common, that really does exist.

2.

First trace of carbon on Earth

(carbon's self-portrait)

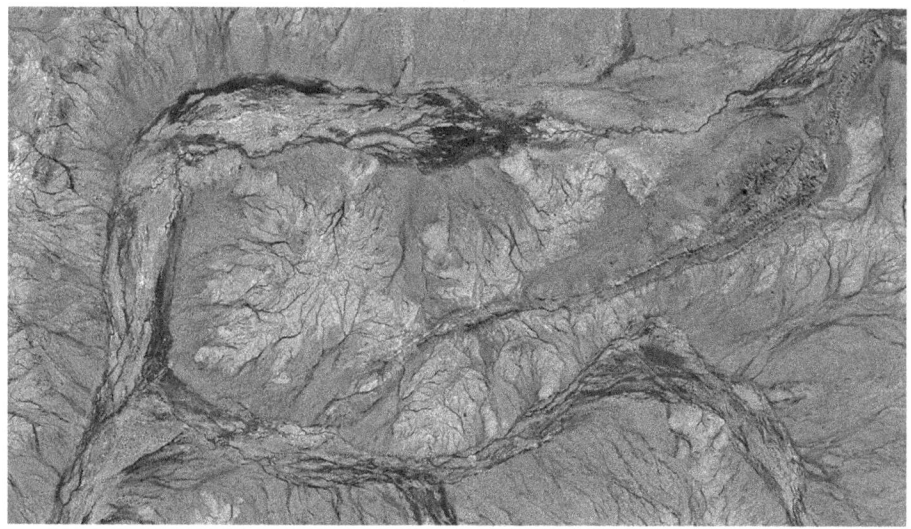

2 'Western Australia's Jack Hills'. Image by Robert Simmon, based on data from the University of Maryland's Global Land Cover Facility, captured by the Landsat satellite on July 27, 1999. © NASA's Earth Observatory.

Blackout.

An image appears with the title, projected.

A voice on a microphone.

— Four and a half billion years ago, a photo of the first trace of carbon on Earth, the very first appearance of a jagged element, an extreme close-up on what is essentially a face of Trump; an interesting feature of these carbon-based life-forms is their construction of meaning, it's their construction of meaning at random, out of anything, the obsessive quest to find purpose in every movement, in life, in images, so here's Trump laid out, looking down, with his quiff towards the bottom left, there, now you see him, there, desperate construction of meaning, it's so sweet, look, the construction of meaning in a universe that is altogether cold, indifferent, and uncontrollably expanding, but without any grand designs; please we're not asking to be at the centre, we understand we're only peripheral, so please don't crush us with your random machinations; a little prayer turned towards a plurality, a royal 'we', 'we are not amused', but we are amused, just don't kill us; a little, personal obsession on carbon's part to survive at all costs; just an idea or two, a little bit of brainstorming here on Earth, free snacks to nibble on while we try and figure out how not to be destroyed, how not to destroy ourselves, how to pass the time without getting bored, how to have sex with the other person in the room without everyone else in the room noticing, exploring in detail how to live in a nice flat one day, but also figuring out how to pay the rent on said flat; all in all these are carbon's typical problems, little ideas tossed into the suggestion box of the universe, into a bottomless pit that can't read and actually doesn't even exist, all our transmissions go further away from Earth and don't go anywhere, are of no interest to anyone; understand this, nothing you do interests anyone at all, so why all this effort to come forth and develop multi-cellular life, all this stress of detaching from this rock and bonding with other elements to eke out self-consciousness, if ultimately there's no conversation with any other elements, if ultimately carbon talks to itself and no-one replies?

3.

A Did you experience any other sensations?

B Not as strongly.

A But there were some?

B Maybe . . . yes.

A Tell me about them.

B I felt a great anger.

A Did you feel threatened?

B I don't know. But it's . . . it's like when you're a kid you want to squish things.

A What things?

B Like when you squash a bug, when you're little.

A You wanted to squash it?

B I couldn't move, I couldn't do anything. These are . . . sensations that came to me later.

A As if all your reactions were delayed?

B That's right, yeah.

A Or maybe you were processing them later.

B Perhaps.

A As a way to overcome a great fear.

B I don't know . . . I don't know.

Silence.

A If you could have hurt it, squashed it . . . if you had had a weapon, would you have attacked it?

B   No.

A   But you did feel a strong sense of aggression.

B   Yes. You can see that in the video too, and also later, when they came to get me . . .

A   You attacked the doctors.

B   Yes. I'm sorry. I've said that to them too, I'm sorry.

A   Did you think they might harm you?

B   I didn't think anything. I wasn't well and that's it.

A   But during the Encounter you didn't suffer, you weren't unwell, is that right? Can you confirm that for me? I'm just asking again to be sure. All your fear, your anger, they came later?

B   Yes. I don't even remember much of the Encounter.

A   Too stressful to remember it properly? As if you'd repressed it?

B   I reckon so.

Silence.

A   Was there ever a moment when you thought it wasn't real, that maybe it was a hallucination, or a prank?

B   No.

A   Never, not even for a moment?

B   No.

A   Why not?

B   Because I had goosebumps for no reason. Not because of the cold. It was like a warning from my body. There, that's something I remembered watching the video.

A   You can't see goosebumps in the video.

B   Yeah but there's a moment when I bend my legs a bit and tense up, that's the moment.

A   You were ready to fight?

B   Or to run away.

A   But you didn't.

B   No, I just stood there.

A   You couldn't move.

B   Yes, it was awful.

A   Did you feel powerless?

B   I felt unable to control my body.

A Perhaps that's also part of the 'lack of balance' you described?

B Yes. I've thought about it a lot.

A Can you explain it?

B Maybe.

A Tell me, please.

B It's just that . . . maybe we're not meant to have anything to do with these . . . non-carbon-based life-forms. And I think that instinct decides more than we imagine. My body got ready to react like when there's a dangerous animal, as if I'd seen a lion. And then it felt that this thing was not of this world, and it froze. Like it didn't know what to do.

Silence.

A Do you often talk about your body in these terms?

B What terms?

A As if it were something separate from you.

B What do you mean?

A As if you don't have full control over it.

B I don't believe anyone would have had full control of their body in a situation like that.

A *makes a note.*

A Have you ever had an out-of-body experience? A moment in which you could see yourself from the outside? Seeing yourself from above, perhaps?

B No, not that I remember, no.

A Are you sure? Maybe as a child. Maybe you thought it was a nightmare.

B I don't think so, no.

A And that hasn't happened to you recently either.

B No.

A I mean since the Encounter.

B No, no.

Silence.

A Usually people who report close encounters have actually had experiences of this kind. Often episodes of alien abduction can, in reality, be attributed to phenomena of this sort.

B Doesn't seem to be the case for me.

A (*smiling*) Admittedly not.

4.

Carbon's group photo

3 'Diagram of vertebrate evolution' © John Lomberg.

Blackout.

An image appears with the title.

— 1977, Carbon gets tired of talking to itself and fires a golden disc full of images, the Voyager Record, into space, to attest to its achievements in front of a universe that is, for the most part, unimpressed; and here we are, here's one of the pictures sent out to the aliens and the cosmos, here we are all together, three fish, a toad, a crocodile, an eagle, a goat and two people; and really, it was 1977, perspective had been around since the Renaissance, and colour existed too, but for some reason this task has been assigned, apparently, to a seven-year-old boy, figures suspended in thin air, proportions out of whack; the aliens will think we're two dimensional, maybe it's a tactic to misdirect them; really, the initial idea, the real key to understanding, is that this image was meant to explain evolution, taking us from those shapeless fish there, through to the first unfortunate amphibian that ever put on legs and then through the 'classic' evolutionary route: eagle, goat, man and woman, with the woman at the top of the evolutionary tree, although looking at it like this it looks more like an ad for creationism - look at those losers waving, waving hello, hi we're here, here we are, we're all here together in the same moment, newly created, here we are, silhouettes yet to be coloured in, yet to be properly defined, details yet to be invented, it's us, we're Team Carbon, and we're probably all going to be ripped to shreds by that crocodile.

5.

B Can I ask you a question?

A We haven't finished yet, but yes, of course.

B Where did it go?

A The creature?

B Yes. Do you know where it is?

A I can't answer that.

B But I need to know.

A Why?

Silence.

B I'm scared it'll come back.

A Do you think there might be a connection between the two of you?

B I don't know. But I'd like to be sure it's far away.

A I'm sorry but I can't answer you.

B But do you know?

A   I'm not at liberty to say. We're waiting for results.

B   You don't know. I can't believe this. You don't know where it is. Here you are torturing me while that thing is roaming the planet.

A   Do you think of these questions as torture?

B   I didn't mean that. No. But the fact that no one knows anything is driving me mad.

A   That's not what I said.

B   You don't know what it was like.

A   I'm trying to understand.

B   Yes. Yes.

Silence.

A   Why did you ask me this question?

B   Because I'm afraid.

A   You could have asked me something about yourself. About whether there will be any consequences for your health. Whether you're safe here. You could have asked me anything, but the first question you asked me was, 'where is that creature?'

Silence.

B   Because I feel like it's still there.

A   You can feel it?

B   Yes.

A   As part of that feeling you described earlier, of being connected to everything on Earth?

B   I think so.

A   But you don't know where it is.

B   No.

A   Why didn't you tell me this straight away?

B   Because it isn't real. It's an instinct.

A   Sure, but we need to know everything. We don't know anything about how these things behave. You're the first one in history.

B   How have you not worked out its path? Where it came from, where it was headed?

A   Why do you keep asking me these pointless questions?

B It's what everyone wants to know. The whole world wants to know.

A The whole world wants to know what you went through. That's why we're here.

B I felt like shit. There you go. That's what I went through. Now the whole world knows. Go tell the whole world.

A Are you tired?

B I'm tired of going round in circles. I'm tired of talking about those two minutes of my life that I can barely remember.

A *glances at her notes.*

A When you saw the video . . . the many videos . . . did you read any of the comments, across the various platforms?

B Each one I could.

A Were there any in which you recognised your own experience? Someone who had experienced that same feeling of unity against a common enemy? Your anger? Your fear?

B Don't think so. Half was New Age stuff about the Age of Aquarius. The other half was quotes from the Book of Revelation and conspiracy theories.

A Nothing interesting, then.

B No.

A I have a list of comments, written material and new sightings. Can you help me by pointing out which ones resonate most with your experience?

B Do we have to do it now?

A If you don't want to do it now, we can do it in a bit.

B I can't right now. I don't feel like reading.

A *makes a note.*

A Are you having trouble reading?

B No, I'm just tired.

A Do you find reading more tiring than usual?

B Yes. Just like everything else.

A But reading in particular tires you out?

B I don't know.

A Let's try something.

A *writes something on a piece of paper and hands it to* **B**.

A Are you struggling to read what I've written?

B A bit, yeah.

A Why?

B The words are dancing back and forth.

A Can you be more specific?

B I don't know, it looks like it says one thing, then another.

A Like two different sentences?

B Two similar sentences. A few letters are changing. The shape of the letters.

A Do you have any problems with your eyesight?

B No. Never have.

A And now, right now, your vision is blurry, a little out-of-focus?

B Some things look a bit blurry sometimes.

A For example?

B I don't know. The edges of things. The edge of your arm. Things like that.

A And this started after the Encounter?

B Yes. They already asked me about this at the military hospital.

A But you're still experiencing these symptoms?

B From time to time.

A Ok. Are you up to reviewing some video material? You don't have to read, just watch some footage.

B Maybe later.

A Are you having trouble watching videos too?

B Maybe later.

A Ok.

Do you want some water?

B Yes.

A *hands him a small bottle of water.*

She takes one too.

6.

Carbon's inefficiencies

(the drawbacks of having an 'always improvable' design)

4 'Sprinters' © History of the Olympics, Picturepoint, London.

Blackout.

An image appears with the title.

— We are made of water; this is demonstrated by the fact that if you poke holes in us we explode in cascades of blood, and also by the fact that we have to drink constantly, in order to then sweat the water out; and finally that we stink, these are all highly advanced processes, the result of millions of years of evolution, the fact that we stink; millions of years to come up with solutions that, in trying to please everyone, end up pleasing no one; here, in this other photo taken from the Golden Record, there are four guys who are sweating, and there are several odd details; for starters the white man is winning, this might be the only existing photo of a white guy winning a race, so of course it was immediately sent, express delivery, in this universal golden disc, and what are the aliens possibly meant to understand from this picture? Even if they perceived depth as we do they would think we were a race of one-legged marionettes floating telekinetically over the red earth, plus, runner 932 is a Soviet, and it's strange if you think about it because the Americans (the temporary administrators of carbon in the '80s) chose which photos to send, so perhaps the real meaning of this photo is actually to demonstrate not a sport, running, specifically, but sportsmanship itself: so that the aliens might known that even though the moon is ours, and the rocket, and the planet, and everything else, we Americans are attaching a photo of this Russian sweating harder than anyone else, in glorious Technicolor.

7.

B *takes a sip of water.*

A   You know we spoke to everyone involved. To all the people who were in the area during the Encounter. Including the people who filmed the videos, to be clear. In order to collect their accounts, their versions of events. And they didn't feel what you're describing. No one felt at one with life on Earth. No one felt their aggression rising.

B   You don't believe me?

A   Hang on, that's not what I said. Let me finish. Nobody else reported such strong experiences. Apart from two people.

B   Who?

A *looks through her papers. She finds a photo. She shows it to* **B**.

A   Do you know the person in this photo?

B   I don't believe so.

A   Have you ever met? Can you think of any occasion where you might have met?

B   I have no idea who she is.

A   Alright. I'm going to show you another picture now.

A *shows* **B** *another photo.*

B   Nothing.

A   Picture him without a beard. Are you sure you've never seen this man before?

B   I don't think so.

A   Maybe in a different context. A few days earlier?

B   No, no.

A *makes a note.*

A These are the two people who were closest to you in the moment of the Encounter. Physically closest. The girl filmed the first video.

B I don't remember seeing her.

A And the man was behind you. A few metres away. He threw himself on the ground to protect himself.

B I didn't . . . I didn't look around much.

A These two people testify to something very similar to what you reported. Feeling a sort of sudden bond with the Earth. Probably not as intense as yours. But these are two people who have never had contact with you, yet they felt the same things you did.

B So that means I'm not the only one?

A It means that what you felt is more than just a sensation. It was a new experience. Something that exists within us, buried somewhere in our DNA, something that's required for our survival and was suddenly awakened. And you felt this more intensely because you had contact. Physical contact. And your body rejected it. At a very profound level, an almost molecular level. As if there were an incompatibility. You're right when you say it's new. It's like when you burn yourself for the first time. It's a warning.

Silence.

A I think it's important that we talk more about this 'burn.' Does that description work for you, a 'burn'?

B Yes. Whatever.

Silence.

A May I see your hand?

B They examined it all over.

A Can I see it, if you don't mind? For my own personal curiosity?

B *raises his right hand.*

A May I see the palm?

B *shows her the palm of his right hand. It's trembling slightly.*

A I know they didn't find anything unusual with your hand. What do you make of that?

B I think it could be worse. It could have fallen off.

Silence.

A Why did you touch it?

B I don't know.

A You were frozen with fear yet you raised your hand to that being?

B I don't know.

A Was it only after the contact that you felt hostility?

B I don't know what order things happened. I've already told you, everything happened all at once.

A Do you suppose it felt something similar? That its entire molecular system, its whole world, had united against our own? Against our team, like you were saying earlier?

B No.

A Why not?

B Because I don't think it reasons like we do. I don't believe that at all. I told you, I wasn't able to identify with it then, and I can't now.

A *makes a note.*

Silence.

A I have a theory. I don't know if it would be helpful to share it. Do you want to hear it?

B Let's hear it.

A I think you touched that being because you were curious.

B That's it? That's your theory?

A Yes.

B That doesn't seem like such a complex theory.

A It doesn't have to be complex.

B I don't know. Was I curious? Yes, maybe. I don't remember.

A You saw something no one had ever seen before. Something that every atom in your body perceived as foreign. A life form based on principles different from our own. And you did what children do. Out of curiosity, you held out your hand. You were curious, because in front of you was the most incomprehensible and most bizarre thing that ever existed on Earth. And you just had to touch it. At all costs. Out of curiosity, that's all. Because that's how human beings work. And then, your instinct warned you of the danger. There's nothing strange about it. Curiosity. It's human nature.

Silence.

A Does this idea reflect your experience?

B I'm a human being, that's for sure.

8.

Carbon's need for meaning

(and a ruthless absence of meaning)

5 'Demonstration of licking and eating' © Cornell University.

Blackout.

An image appears with the title.

— Here are three human beings: there's a girl licking her ice-cream while looking straight at the guy in front of her; then there's some other guy in the middle who has decided the best way to eat a toastie is to take a bite out of one side, turn it around, and crunch! take another bite from the other, all while using one hand, actually just three fingers, which forces him to use his mouth as a key point of support, and then to the right - guess what - there's some maniac drinking from a glass jug, and there don't seem to be any tables so it looks like he's in the habit of carrying it around with him, and this whole scene, their positions, their relationships, is an enigma: what does it mean? It's incredible how even though this image has no meaning, we can't help but look for some connection between them. Are they related? Are they enemies? Is it a middle school reunion? Is it a ritual? Why's the one on the right wearing sunglasses? What exactly is the meal in which ice cream and a toastie are eaten together, and also, ice cream and toasties can be eaten standing up, but the jug? The guy on the right is the hardest to understand, but luckily carbon's sixth sense for making sense comes in handy here, like an irrepressible impulse, and here's the deal: the woman on the left and the man on the right are a couple, she's seducing him by licking the ice cream, he's demonstrating his virility by lifting the jug with one hand and pouring water all over his face, the man in the middle has turned his toastie around because he dropped it earlier but then he picked it up within the famous five second rule and turned it around and it's still good, and anyway he stands there and observes the sexual tension between the couple like some sort of voyeur and takes it all out on the sandwich; alternatively, we can choose to consider the reality of the photo, there probably wasn't much time to take the shot because the ice cream was melting and the guy on the right could only hold that pose for so long, maybe they took the shot on the second attempt, that's why the one in the middle has taken the bite on the other side, because it's the second bite he's taken, and this could be a rational, simple explanation for the meaning of the photo, but a lame one too, because carbon doesn't like rational explanations, it doesn't really care about them, carbon wants to be amazed, it wants wonder, carbon wants awesome, magical things, tectonic shifts, ice ages, explosions of stars, spiral galaxies and Big Bangs.

9.

A When is the precise moment your memories stop?

B I don't know.

A What's the last thing you're certain of?

B I was crossing the road.

A In the video you can see you were wearing headphones, earbuds. Were you listening to something, a voice message?

B No. No message. Maybe I was listening to something . . . Yes, I think I had a song stuck in my head.

A Do you remember what it was?

B *whistles a nursery rhyme.*

A Did you look around while you were crossing the road?

B I don't remember.

A And nothing after that?

B Nothing after that.

A It almost looked like an appointment. It looked like you were there for a reason.

B Everyone keeps trying to make sense of it, when if there's anything to make sense of it's that it doesn't make sense. I've been saying that since I got here. We can't understand it, we can't empathise with it. That's one thing you can get out of me. I'm telling you, that creature doesn't reason the same way we do.

A Maybe you're right, maybe that creature doesn't make sense. Maybe it's a creature of pure survival that moves randomly through the universe. But that's impossible for us to accept. What if it has a motive? That's too great a risk to take. We can start with the things we understand. Why were you there? Shall we retrace your steps that day?

A long silence.

A *is about to say something but stops herself. Then she resumes:*

A Is this a route you always take?

B Yes.

A Always on foot?

B Yes.

A When did you realise something was off?

B My phone didn't have any signal.

A When did it stop working?

B They've already asked me all these questions.

A Maybe going over them again will reveal something new.

B They've asked me a thousand times. I know them off by heart. I know this story by heart, too. It's always the same.

A You don't think it could be useful?

B I think earlier on I had doubts about the timings, the details, what I had eaten, what the creature was like. Gradually I got over them all. They made me retell the same story so many times over and over, so I chose one version and didn't change it again.

A So let's focus on one thing.

B Alright.

A Something I'm interested in.

B Ok.

A Your accident. Three years ago, correct?

B I don't want to talk about that.

A Please. It's important.

Silence.

A Please.

Silence.

A When you passed out underwater. In your car. When you passed out from lack of oxygen. I read that since then you sometimes have respiratory problems. You feel like you're out of breath. Do you still suffer from these attacks?

Silence.

A I know it's not easy to think about. But listen to me. Try to listen. You just have to answer a question, yes or no.

Silence.

A Was this one of your respiratory attacks, or was it something different? Were you having trouble breathing for some other reason?

B I don't know. Is there a difference?

A   It's an important distinction. Try to remember. You froze. Ok. Then what happened? Did you have an attack, or did something else happen?

B   I don't know.

A   Listen to me. I believe there was no oxygen in the area around the creature. I think you felt unwell because there was no oxygen for you to breathe, there was nothing, you were plunged into a vacuum. Can you answer me, please?

Silence.

B   There was air. I had the beginning of an attack but it passed. I was just scared to take a breath.

A   This is very important. I'm sorry I brought up the accident. But it's necessary . . .

B   It's necessary?

A   Yes.

B   I think it's sadistic.

A   I'm sorry you feel that way.

B   I think that taking me back . . . making me think about the accident is cruel.

A   I didn't want to. But it's an important date in your history. We would have had to talk about it sooner or later.

B   You could have asked that question a thousand other ways.

A   I'm sorry.

B *stands up.*

A *remains seated.*

B   How long have I been here?

A   Not long.

B   What time is it?

A   It's been about half an hour.

B   How much longer do I have to stay?

A   Only as long as it takes.

B   To do what?

A   To understand what happened. To protect you from that thing.

B   You're not able to protect me. No one is able to protect anyone else.

A slight tremor goes through the room. Almost imperceptible. The table shakes a little.

A   If you help us . . .

B   I am helping you and you've only hurt me. You've filled me with bullshit and useless theories. None of you are able to protect me. You're all just scared. Even more than I am. At least I've seen it. I know what it is.

A Yes, you do. You know what it is. And we're trying to understand it.

B But I've already told you. There is nothing to understand. It is something else entirely.

A Nothing is entirely different.

B That thing, yes. That thing is.

A We have to try and understand the creature.

Silence.

B Is that why you call it a 'creature'? You're all twisting your words to avoid saying 'alien'. Because if it's an alien, it's over. Isn't it? If it's an alien we've lost.

A Yes. 'Alien' means something different to us. Irrevocably. There's no hope in that word. But we have to try to understand it in order to survive.

B Curiosity.

A Yes. You tried to touch it, which means there's something to discover.

Silence.

A Let's take a break.

10.

Carbon's pig-headedness

6 'The Great Wall of China' © Dana Andreea Gheorghe.

Blackout.

An image appears with the title.

— Even carbon's name itself sounds like something that gets stuck, that sticks to you and won't let go, and indeed carbon has a sort of nagging quality, a biting of the nails until they bleed, an obsession with geometric shapes, regular shapes, with cleaning, with sweeping the floor, with fighting against dust, against itself, against dead skin, and against the end of things; a tendency to tidy things up, to break shapeless things into pieces and then to put them back together again, cataloguing them, giving them meaning, for example by smashing rocks to build roads (usually near a river, so carbon can wash and drink, wash and drink compulsively), and with those roads come houses and communities and cities and then there are so many of them, they multiply, which means walls are needed, and here, in this photo, is the longest wall in the world, and it's the most useless too, it's obsolete, by now nothing more than a tourist trail, but it suggests something, it speaks of the will to contain: to contain enemies, cities, the whole world outside; it's an ancient dream, after all, that of containing everything outside, it's a cellular dream, the nucleus from inside the membrane wants the external world to never be able to touch it, its organelles, the Golgi apparatus and all the other things it holds most precious, most holy, and the DNA in the centre, a tiny dictator in a forbidden palace surrounded by walls; we're at the mercy of a mad dictator who is made up of, of course, carbon, five atoms of protectionist folly, five terrified atoms that make you put on slippers when you enter, or rather they don't let you in at all, and if you *do* enter the cell it explodes, five atoms of a typical mad dictator barricaded within his bunker, who understands nothing of reality outside - knows nothing of the inorganic world - yet believes he has to command it, so he carves stone and builds kilometres of walls, and goes so far as to tell you that the wall is one of the Seven Wonders of the World (in his opinion, as always).

11.

A *is sitting at the table, looking through her notes.*

A You want a cigarette?

B You can smoke in here?

A (*laughing*) This *is* the smoking area.

A *lights a cigarette.*

B How's the world outside?

A The world is different from what you remember. People are locked away inside their houses. Everyone's looking up in case something falls from the sky. It's all they talk about on the news. I don't know when we'll get through this. And you wouldn't believe how often you see your face. I think you must be more recognisable than Jesus right now.

B So not great, then.

A No. What do you think?

B I hope it all blows over. I hope this turns out to be the most elaborate prank ever. I'm half expecting any moment now you'll look at me and say 'you've been framed!' and someone in an alien costume will walk through that door. I know it's not that, but it would be nice if it was.

A I'd like that too.

A *pushes her papers aside and stands up.*

She leans against the wall.

A Sorry about earlier. Sorry about all these questions. I imagine it's exhausting.

B I've lost track of time. The days are all the same, they blur together. Like one long endless day.

A I'm sorry.

B What more do we have to talk about?

A I just have a couple more things to ask you. Then I think you'll have to do some more tests. And then they'll let you go.

B You're pretty clear on everything. You already know how it ends.

A That's my job. To try and figure out how it's going to end.

A *sits back down.*

B And what will happen to me, do you think? Out there.

A Nothing. You'll live your life as before. Try not to get eaten alive by the media, if you can. Go on holiday somewhere far away.

B You seem like a reasonable person. The first I've met since I got here.

A There are different ways to get results.

B And have you found what you're looking for?

A Not yet.

B Maybe we already know everything. We can't know more than this. We can't go any further. You've squeezed me dry.

A There's always something else to discover. And I think deep down, you also want to know what happened. You need someone like me, to take you by the hand and guide you towards the truth. Towards whatever happened that day.

B I don't know anymore. Right now I just want to get out of here.

A You're curious. You'd like to forget but you can't. Because first you have to know, you have to understand.

B No. No.

A Then why did you touch that being?

B I wish I never had.

A You feel regret?

B I don't feel anything. If I don't remember it, it's as if didn't have a choice. I don't remember the moment I decided to touch it.

A If we were able to get you back to that moment, we might understand something.

B I don't want to go back to that moment. I want to move on. I want to go to the beach. To the park. To the mountains. I don't know. I need my daughter. All I know is that I need her.

A *scribbles something on a piece of paper.*

B Do you have kids?

A I have a daughter, yes.

B Are you close?

A She's an only child. She's used to always getting her own way. She always has to be right. To be the smartest person in the room. I mean, you get it.

B She's grown up?

A She's a research assistant at the university. Economics. Children are always a worry, but she seems happy. It seems her life is going well.

B Does she know you're here?

A No, I had to sign a lot of paperwork before coming into this room with you. You can't even imagine what's beyond these four walls. The whole world is waiting for something.

B Waiting for what?

A An answer.

B I don't think I have anything else to tell you. I don't feel like the most famous man on the planet. I feel like the unluckiest man on the planet.

A *makes another note.*

B You're still writing. I thought we were on a break.

A You're right.

B What did I say that was so interesting? You made a note earlier too.

A Sorry, you're right. It was a private moment.

B Will my whole life be like this from now on? Will they study everything I say and do?

A I'm sorry.

12.

Carbon's conversation

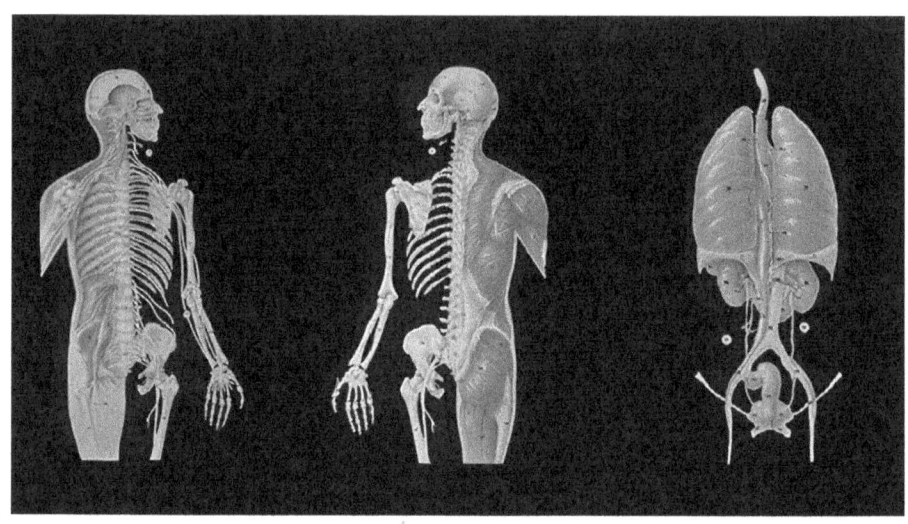

7 'Skeletons' © unknown.

Blackout.

An image appears with the title.

Three voices:

1 Good morning.

2 Good morning to you.

1 How's it going, how are things at home?

2 Splendid, thank you.

1 We're on the same page, right?

2 Absolutely, totally transparent I'd say.

1 Indeed, hands outstretched towards one another, man to man.

2 Or woman to woman, I can't tell the sex.

1   Yes, well, totally open, physically too, I open my ribcage to you.

2   I appreciate that very much and I open mine to you.

1   I'm a bundle of nerves these days.

2   And I'm a bundle of muscles.

3   And I'm the monstrous mass of things we have inside. I'm the unspoken subtext of the conversation.

1   What's that?

2   I didn't say anything.

3   I am the unspoken, I'm a monster floating above you and everything else. I'm everything that's left behind inside your lungs and I float through the air spreading anxiety.

1   So everything's good at home, how's work?

2   Work is splendid, I was promoted.

1   Again?

2   Again.

3   His wife left him.

1   Did you say something?

2   No, nothing.

1   Oh, I thought I heard something.

2   No, no.

3   And he had a fight with his father about the mortgage, they haven't spoken since.

1   Well, that's that, it's always a pleasure to bump into you doctor.

2   Professor.

3   You'll go back home where nobody is waiting for you, you'll go home and you'll think about every single world you said, and you'll regret it all; your fake politeness, your self-interested sociability, the systematic dismantling of any real ties in your lives to reach positions of middle class pseudo-power, the doctor and the professor, a life thrown away. On days like these you want to kill yourself, but you end up watching cat videos on YouTube and getting drunk to pass the time until the evening, how cute you are, how very cute. But you used to have dreams, you had aspirations, and above all you had people who loved you, and what was the name of that girl, you don't even remember her name, how pathetic, my God, how pathetic.

13.

B You think they've been here before?

A I don't know. Probably not. But there are some theories regarding the being you saw.

B The usual rubbish about the pyramids?

A No. Something more serious. Are you familiar with the Kardashev scale?

B What's that?

A It's a system of classification. A scale that ranks the development of civilisations. By type. It goes from one to four. Type one is a planetary civilisation. Type two is a civilisation that controls an entire solar system. Type three civilisations have an infinite amount of energy, they're able to travel the universe beyond their own system, they can move around, establish colonies . . .

B Do such civilisations exist?

A The scale is just hypothetical. We don't know anything about civilisations built by other forms of life. We rely on the only metric that seems objective.

B Which is?

A The consumption of energy. According to this classification, type ones can harness the energy of their home planet. Type twos have access to the the energy of their home star, and thus their entire system. Type threes can draw on the resources of an entire galaxy. And type fours control multiple galaxies. As you grow, you need more energy. Just like in life. In high school you just need pocket money. The bigger you get the more money you need.

B And which level of development do you think this thing could belong to?

A Type one, or type two. That's the only thing we're sure of.

B Why not higher?

A Because if a more advanced civilisation were to exist, capable of moving structures in space to harness the energy of the stars, we'd already have been aware of its presence. It would be visible. The existence of this being, and the lack of traces of more advanced civilisations, means that it must be a type one or a type two. Which is good news. They're not much further ahead than us.

B What type are we?

A We're type zero.

Silence.

B We don't even register on a scale we invented ourselves?

A We only just about manage our own planet's energy resources, and not very efficiently at that. Type zero. In a few hundred years, assuming we haven't self-destructed by then, we'll be at one. But I wouldn't count on it. The universe could be full of type zero civilisations that will never get to one. Maybe the transition to one is impossible for a species like ours.

B   Are we in danger?

A   Maybe we are. If we're not able to identify with them. If we can't work out what they want from us, we might be.

Silence.

B   Have there been any other sightings?

A   No. Nothing verified, anyway. You're the only certainty we have. You're the only thing that makes us sure it wasn't a collective delusion.

B   And the videos.

A   All those videos, yes.

Silence.

A   You said that at first, when you gave your statement the first few times, you had some doubts about timings and details.

B   Yes, I did.

A   So you gave approximate answers, right?

B   I think so, yes.

A   I read every version of your story and compared them. I studied your expressions. Your tone of voice. You could say that when you got here, it's like I already knew you. And I realised your uncertainties, what you call doubts, are actually very precise. You didn't give me figures at random. If you compare the statements, you do get many different versions, it's true, at least seven of them. But these same seven versions repeat themselves. It is as if the same details were scattered across various versions. But the details themselves always stay the same. As if you have seven versions of the same event in your head. Do you follow?

B   Well, maybe there's some kind of statistical law, something like that. That says if we're unsure between two numbers we always default to the same one.

A   Yes, but we're talking about little things here. Things you described using the same words, with the same intention. We're talking about details. Anomalies.

B   So what does that mean?

A   I don't know. I haven't figured it out yet. That's as far as I got. I'd like to know what you think.

B   What do I know. I think it's a coincidence. I think you're out of your depth and so you're finding a thousand non-existent connections. I think you're in pieces. And I'm in pieces now too. I'm tired. I want to go home, or to the hospital, wherever you want. In any case, I want to go. I've told you everything you wanted to know. Now let me go.

14.

Carbon's self-destructive tendencies

8 'Climber' © Gaston Rébuffat Archive, Cinémathèque d'Images de Montagne.

Blackout.

An image appears with the title.

—   Here is the most tiresome suicide in history, at the summit of an impossible mountain ledge, here is a man depicted in the moment before falling and smashing into the rocks, by now it's already too late, his chest is leaning too far back to be able to stop, it's a terrible thing, he had the courage to climb a mountain with his bare hands and – apparently – without any equipment, which means he must be a man in peak physical condition, and nevertheless he has decided to end it all, what a disaster, imagine the frame that follows this one, frame by frame, he's falling, he's thinking back to when he was a boy, when every door was open to him; his relationship with his five brothers, his mother's disappointment, the convent school, caning on his hands, tangerines stolen from the neighbours' garden, he's falling and at last, he's happy; he hears the wind whistling past his ears like when his parents would throw him back and forth laughing and saying fly, fly, fly, so now fly little mountaineer, fly towards your peace at the bottom of the mountain, because the fact is, one of the main facts about carbon is that it hates itself, that by its nature it is never satisfied, there are brief flashes of joy, but they're over in a instant, you're on the first mountain you ever climbed with your father, and a second later you're on top of K2, and the next second you don't want to live any more, because unfortunately our nature is such that we're constantly seeking improvement, whilst also being fundamentally lazy, we don't feel like doing anything, we'd just like to sit in the same position, but after a while our physical posture starts to make us sore, after a while our culture makes us feel guilty, and even if we achieve some form of happiness, it's never enough, if it had been we'd still be fish, and so we all more or less follow the same path, we scale the most absurd peaks, we reach the top, we say to ourselves: I mean, is that it? And so of course we jump.

15.

A I have one last question for you, then we're done.

B Good.

A It's something you've already been asked. Three times, to be precise. And each time you've flown into a fit of rage.

B I don't want to talk about it. I was told before I came here that . . .

A We're on the same team, remember?

B I don't care.

A If you answer my question now, nobody will ask you again.

B They told me that before.

A Yes, but those were people who didn't have the authority to make that promise to you. I do. If you trust me, no one will ask you ever again.

B But I don't trust you. People are going to keep asking, keep asking me questions.

A It'll be a lot, that's true. But at some point it will be over. Maybe you won't be the only one anymore. Who knows, maybe the Earth will explode and we'll all die. Nobody knows what's going to happen. But if you answer me, you will have done your part. Just by answering this one question. Talk to me. Don't worry. Take a deep breath. And tell me.

B What do you want me to tell you?

A Tell me about your daughter.

B She's at home.

A She's not at home. Don't you remember? Where were you going that day you had the close encounter?

B I was going to pick her up from school.

Silence.

A What do you remember about your accident three years ago?

B I skidded. The guardrail broke. My car went into the water.

A And your daughter?

B They rescued her. She was about to die, but they pulled her out.

A No. She didn't make it out. Don't you remember? She stayed underwater. They didn't get to her in time.

B That's not true.

A It was an accident. There was a funeral. Remember the funeral?

B No.

A Do you remember who was there? Do you remember if you were crying?

B Stop it.

A Try to remember. Please.

B I remember her coming home. I remember that bloody day I saw the alien all I kept thinking was: who's going to pick her up now, I hope she doesn't get scared when she sees me on TV, I hope she doesn't get scared.

A There are news articles from when it happened. It's in the paper. I can find them for you. They say 'fatal accident'.

B It's not true. And if there are newspapers, *you've* written them. You've done this all on purpose for some reason that I still don't understand. I'm trying to help you. I thought there was a mistake, that you had misunderstood. And yet everyone keeps telling me that Emma's dead. Because you need her for God knows what fucking reason. Because you think that if you torture me I'll tell you more things. But I don't know anything else.

A Were you happy, when you were going to pick her up?

B Enough with the questions. Enough.

Silence.

A Alright. No more questions. Now listen to me.

Silence.

A Your daughter is gone. But you think she's still alive, that she's still at home waiting for you. And that's not the reality. Do you understand? It's not true.

B Yes, it is reality!

A vibration shakes the table and the room.

A *takes a quick look around. Then she continues:*

A You understand this is crucial, because you had no other reason to be there that day. Your close encounter only happened because you went to pick up your daughter from school. But she wasn't at school. The teachers said you never showed up there again. So it was the first time. The first time you woke up convinced that she was still with you.

B I . . . . no.

Another vibration.

A *and* **B** *stay still, as if to work out whether it's the beginning of an earthquake.*

Calmly, **A** *resumes:*

A You must understand what the reality is. Your daughter is gone.

B I . . .

A The others have been understanding with you. They tried to console you, they pretended in order to indulge you. They thought you were in shock. It's understandable. It's normal to call for your loved ones when you're in shock. But I want you to stay with us. I want you to realise that this is reality. That your daughter is gone.

Silence.

B Yes . . .

B *stands up. There is a jolt, the whole table shakes.*

A *stands up too, alarmed.*

They both stay standing, their breathing shallow, listening. **B** *looks down, distraught.*

B I tried not to understand how it was possible that . . . I don't know how to explain it, but to me, she's still here. She's at home waiting for me. Then sometimes, she's gone. But when she's here, she's really here, you understand? I remember her laughing and joking. I remember us having breakfast together. And I remember the funeral too. And that day at school, I was going to pick her up. And she *was* at school. She was there, you hear me? She was there because I had taken her that morning.

A That's impossible.

B Yes, but that's how it is. I remember both things: I remember the accident where she died. And I remember the accident where she survived. But these are real, concrete memories, understand? I'm not making it up. It's not fake. It's real. This is reality too.

Silence.

A Stay with me. There is only one reality. And it's the most painful one. Stay with it. It happened. It cannot be erased.

B You don't understand. I'm not making it up, both things are real, they really happened.

A Focus on reality. On the pain.

B No!

Another sudden, extremely strong tremor.

A I think we need to get out of here. Something's not right.

B You think I'm crazy? You think this Encounter thing has made me lose my mind?

A I don't know what's happened. But I believe if we were able to understand what's happened, we'd know why you went there. Why the Encounter took place. What will become of us. The ability to predict the future is the greatest expression of intelligence. We need to see as far ahead as we can. And right now, we're blind. You, on the other hand, are looking backwards. You're creating a past that doesn't exist.

B Maybe it's true, maybe I'm losing my mind. It wouldn't be the first time . . .

A The first time what?

B The first time something like this has happened to me.

A What's happening to you?

B Everything seems to be shifting, nothing's stable. In the hospital too. And earlier, when I first got here.

A What is happening? Please, tell me.

B I don't know what's happening myself either. I don't know what's going on anymore.

A Tell me. If you tell me we can work it out together.

B Even now. Even now. At this very moment.

A What are you feeling?

B You're standing now with your arms crossed.

A I don't understand.

B (*breathing heavily*)   I don't . . . I don't . . . .

A Calm down.

A *takes the chairs and moves them closer. She sits down next to* **B** *and looks at him, worried.*

B Now you're standing . . . and you're sitting.

A Explain what you mean. Explain yourself more clearly.

B I can see. I can see both things. I don't know how to explain it. It's getting stronger, it keeps getting stronger. It was less intense before.

A What was? These visions?

B It was just small things. The edges a little blurred. Now . . . Now it's . . . more intense. It doesn't make sense.

A Describe it to me. How you see me now.

B Now you are talking. You're telling me to calm down. And you're also leaving the room. You're afraid of the tremors. You're talking about an earthquake.

A I am afraid of the tremors. But we're not leaving.

B You're leaving, you're leaving now.

A Stay with me. Talk to me, the me that is here. I am here.

B I don't know what's real . . . I don't know . . .

A I am real. This is reality. I'm your reality.

16.

Carbon's delusions of grandeur

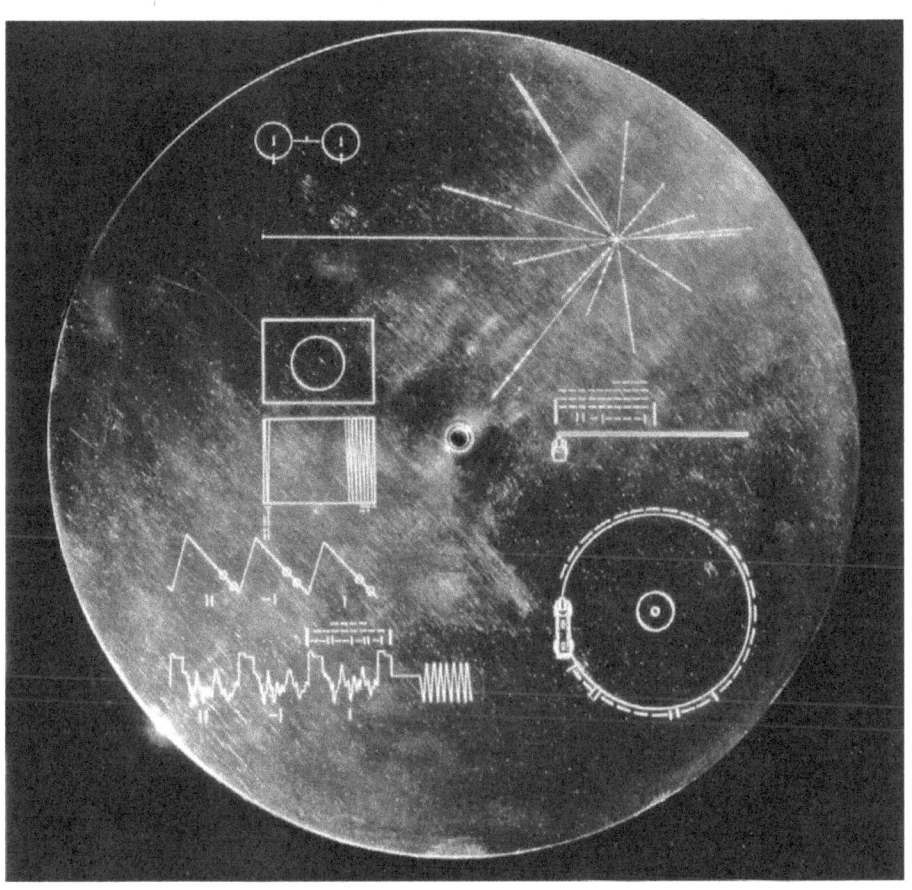

9 'Golden Record' © NASA / Alamy Stock Photo.

Blackout.

An image appears with the title.

— Here it is at last, the Golden Record: the madness of our people to send into space a golden disc with all our business engraved on it, the object we've created that is now the furthest away from us, 22 billion kilometres, you could say that it's out of sight, out of mind, because we've kept everything else close at hand, but love is proved in the letting go, and we're in love with this little cosmic disc, this jewel in space's crown; if you think about it, It's an act of unparalleled egocentrism – the pyramids you can see from space, yes, but we're shoving this right in your face, like galactic salesmen, here's our Golden Record, it's free, inside you'll find every display of our marvellous intelligence, and you better start getting to know us because, here's the most important thing, carbon wants to stay, wants to resist at all costs, it dreams of making the great leap, of transferring consciousness from organic life forms to inorganic ones, carbon dreams of silicon, it dreams of artificial intelligence, dreams of an organised world, wants to transform the universe into a kindergarten playground – everything under control, everything softened, no more supernovas, no more nebulous clusters, no more dark matter, nothing but an enormous garden with those few people in it that it really cares about, because carbon, in the end, only cares that its loved ones are happy, for there to be as little suffering as possible, and for life to carry on, this stubborn, mindless fixation on the part of organic matter to carry on existing, against all the hardships of an inhospitable universe that is practically built to destroy it; but nevertheless carbon persists, and here you go, we've explained it all in the Golden Record, we're made of carbon and nonsense, of matter and useless thoughts, of matter we consume and thoughts that consume us, little things, I hope my daughter is happy, that she isn't treated badly at school, that that boy smiled at me, tiny things that we kill ourselves for over and over again, and I hope the record is exhaustive enough, and not so insufferable that it makes you want to come look for us in order to extinguish us; in our defence, we are multi-faceted and we find all sorts of meaning in life, we try with all our might, it's not possible that it's meaningless, so we invent some meaning, we have so many different possibilities of meaning that we don't know what to do with them all, we have so many that one of them must be correct, at least one – please check the Golden Record and let us know, compare it with whatever you've discovered yourself and then get back to us, we'll be here, immersed in our stupid everyday things, on the blue planet, at the bottom right.

17.

A What does that mean? What you just told me?

B I don't know.

A What does it have to do with your close encounter?

B I don't know. But it never happened to me before.

A   Are you sure?

B   I don't feel well.

A   Let's try something together.

A *takes a sheet of paper and places it on her right.*

A   Where is the paper?

B   On your right.

A   Do you see it on my left too?

B   No.

A   I'm going to pick it up now. Ok?

A *picks up the paper.*

A   Am I about to put it down on the right or on the left?

B   I don't know.

A   Think of a side. Ok? I want you to think hard. I want you to visualise my movement, my hand putting the paper to the right or the left. Ok?

B   Yes . . . yes.

A   Have you decided?

B   Yes.

A *puts the paper to the right.*

A   Is that where you thought it would go?

B   Yes.

A   Now picture me putting it on the left.

A huge vibration. The lights flicker.

When the lights go back to normal, the paper is on the left.

B   It moved.

A   Are you sure?

B   Yes.

A   It hasn't always been on the left?

B   No. It was on the right and now it's on the left.

A   You're absolutely certain?

B   Yes.

Silence.

A That's . . . that's . . . not possible. But it's happening. It's not possible.

B What's happening?

A You can . . . you can change things. Things . . . the past, too. You can change everything.

B What do you mean?

A I think that . . . everything you told me. The blurred vision. You said you saw letters as if they were smudged.

B Yes.

A The edges blurred, as if multiple letters were on top of each other.

B Yes.

A And the edges of things. Small variations.

B Yes, yes.

A These aren't defects in your sight, these are overlaps. You're seeing possibilities. You can see two, three, four possibilities. You're seeing multiple realities one on top of another. Do you understand what I'm saying? In your memories too. You see more than one reality, you can . . . can experience more than one reality.

B Are they real?

A I believe . . . I believe they are real. They are real and you can . . . choose. You can choose to change your reality. You've changed . . . you've changed . . . who knows how many things you've already changed without even knowing it. Have you only changed small things?

B I don't think I . . .

A Have you only changed small things? The video?

B I think so.

A But you're trying to change something big. You're doing it without even realising. Something . . . are you trying to bring your daughter back?

B I . . . no. I just. It's like . . . sometimes it's real for me. I have like a vision . . . -and when I have it, then that's the only thing that exists for me - I have like a vision of a . . . road.

Silence.

A Listen to me. This Encounter you had. This alien you saw. That you touched. I think that. I think it did something. I don't think it's a good thing, I think it's . . .

B If my daughter were to come back . . .

A Wait. Wait. Listen to me, please, listen to me.

B What harm could there be. Maybe they chose me. They chose me to give me a gift. It's a gift.

A No, wait. Listen to me. These changes, these things, they can't be without a cost. Do you understand? You cannot alter reality without consequence. If these beings . . .

B It's a form of love. Maybe I was wrong to judge them. Maybe they're not so different.

A But they are! They are! Listen to your gut. Don't forget what you said to me. They are something else. It's true, they are. Listen to the defences you have within yourself, against evil. They are evil. They are something else. They're incompatible with us.

B But they're giving me back my daughter.

A No, they . . . I don't know what they're doing. But if they are able to manipulate space, to bend light, they're also able to modify reality, do you understand? They are . . .

B Yes. But this reality isn't right.

A This reality is real.

B No, this is the wrong reality. What's right about a little girl dying? How can something like that happen? And they're offering me the chance to change it. To fix things.

A Yes, but at what cost? Please wait. Listen to me. Listen. These beings don't reason like we do. We cannot understand them. They are too advanced. We cannot know if they subscribe to our notions of right and wrong. Maybe they're parasites, maybe they've worked out you don't need to wage war, that all it takes is a trap, all it takes is one person, just one person to destroy a planet . . .

B It's you who need to listen to me. There is only one possible reality, and it's the one where I'm with my daughter.

A But it hasn't happened yet, so far you've only had visions of this reality, you've had some mental pictures, memories, you've done little things, but if it were to become the true reality, if she really were to come back, do you realise what could happen? It's too great a change.

B You know I don't have much choice. There's not a second when I wouldn't bring her back to me.

A huge earthquake begins.

A Wait. Just wait a moment. That feeling of hate, of aggression, you felt it because it felt it too, that being also felt it. That thing hates us too . . . and it wants to kill us. It'll kill us all. They can do that. These tiny changes, these things, they've already created disruptions in reality. I don't even know what's happening, but these tremors, these . . .

B I'm listening to you . . . and I'm sorry. But I cannot do as you say. I can't stay in this unfair world.

A Maybe you don't realise now the consequences your decision could have, but wait, please, maybe it's our salvation. Maybe we can change things, save ourselves from these beings. Or maybe not. Maybe . . .

B Or maybe not. Maybe something capable of manipulating space and time doesn't make mistakes. Maybe this is how it has to go. Maybe we can't understand them, but they can understand us. It's as if someone had sent them an instruction manual. They know us. They know this the only choice I can make. They know that we are small, selfish, and that we will only ever choose the people we love. That's us, Team Carbon, a team of cannibals.

The earthquake intensifies.

A An entire planet, an entire civilisation, is it worth putting our whole world at risk? It's a trap, do you understand? It's a trap.

B You're afraid, you're just afraid. From the first moment we met, you've been afraid. But not me. I don't care about the world at all, about all the people in the world. If it's like you say, then there will be consequences. But I don't care about everyone, I just care about one person. And I can already see that person. I'm starting to see her. She's getting closer, we're going to the park together, the park near our house. She has little coloured shoes with soles that light up. I can see her perfectly, do you understand? I'm not imagining her, I can see her. She's right here with me, in the park. We're on our way to the merry-go-round, it's a beautiful morning. There's a bit of a breeze. There's no one on the horses, so she's running to her favourite one, the red one with the long mane. All the others have damaged manes, she doesn't like them. And I follow her, I sit on the steps of the slide. There's no one around. We're alone, her and me. Hey, she's got a big smile on her face. She rocks back and forth on the horse and starts to sing a little song. It's one of those nursery rhymes, la la la la laaaa . . . . .

An immense, unnatural vibration.

B And she carries on singing, then the breeze picks up, it blows so hard that I can't even hear her voice anymore. It sends her hair flying, so she stops a moment and fixes it, and then she keeps humming, and she keeps rocking back and forth on the little horse, but I can't hear anything anymore, there's this incredibly strong wind that turns the merry-go-round, and it keeps blowing, blowing, blowing . . .

Blinding light.

20.

Carbon squares the circle

(B-side of the Voyager disc – end credits)

Blackout.

An image appears with the title. The disc begins to spin.

A song:

— And here, surprise, the B-side of the Golden Record: the Sounds of Earth. Here, you place it in the gramophone, included in the delivery, and it starts to spin and you start to hear, to hear a song, yes, yes, Johnny B. Goode, and then it's gone, the record keeps spinning and now you hear voices, children yelling, children playing with clay, children raising their hands to ask questions, your daughter asking you to tie the laces on her light-up shoes, you can hear her, then it's gone, the record keeps spinning and you hear it now, that sound, the sound of water boiling, and cutlery scraping against plates, the sounds of Earth, the sounds of a block of flats, windows open and everyone eating on their balconies, the sounds of the room – you hear them – on a Sunday afternoon, your head being caressed, your breath on the pillow, you hear hands closing your eyes, sleep darling, sleep, right in your ear, little shivers on your arm, you hear it, the needle gets stuck and then starts again, and that's gone too, everything goes, the record keeps spinning and you hear the sound of the sea, inside a shell, you hear it, you're so young, you hear the waves lapping at the sand, getting your towel wet, you hear the towel swelling with salt, and all the voices calling you, voices of kids calling you to play, there's a castle that needs building, can you believe it, a whole castle, and then it's gone, the waves, the castles, youth, everything is gone, the needle keeps eroding the gold and you hear the wind, the wind on your bike, the tyres on the asphalt, the mud on your knees, you can hear it, do you remember your first bike, maybe not, but it's in there, it's in the sounds of the Earth, everything is, everything is in there, can you hear it, that song, how did it go, too late it's already gone, the record spins fast and you hear it, the soft pop of a kiss, and then another, and then another, and then it's gone, and the record is spinning and you can hear the voice of your mother as a young girl, that's in the record too, your mother calling your name, saying your name for the first time, and then it's gone, and the record runs on, you can hear the bricks, crunching on top of each other, incredibly fast, it's the first ever house, the first stone hut, and you can hear the fire, the fire destroying the wood, you can hear it, and everything around it is trembling, and the ice melting everywhere, across the whole planet, the ice is melting, finally, the cold is over, the Ice Age, finished forever, and the flesh, you hear flesh against iron, against arrows, against teeth, you hear it, it's tearing apart, you hear the ground beneath your feet, the desert, the rocks, you smell burning, you can hear it, the whole world burning, the volcano erupting, your feet on the ashes, you hear them, you hear the animals, their cries in the night, you hear them and you're afraid, but everything goes, the record spins so fast, it keeps going back, further back, and you can hear the water covering the still-incandescent earth, the water covering the hills, filling up the sea and the ocean, you hear the Earth forming, it's a young planet, you're so young too, you hear the atmosphere being formed, you hear the air slotting into place, the tornadoes breaking everything apart, the sky going from red to blue, you can hear it, the world being born, you realise that your memories begin with the creation of the world, that your consciousness is born with the first molecule of carbon, the whole world is etched inside you, recorded within this disc, you hear it and then you stop the record, you hear everything, and you put the needle back, you keep going back to those few things, the whole world, the whole universe is in there, and you just listen to that summer, that day, that kiss, that Sunday, those voices, that sea breeze and sandwiches and bees, you didn't even think they still existed but things don't disappear, they remain etched in gold, they move away from you at the speed of light but they don't disappear, that's right, it's not possible for everything to happen just once and then never again, it's not right, you hear them calling you to the table, you hear them racing down the corridors of the house, everything goes, everything goes, but you keep putting the needle back to the start, there's the whole universe within this record, but what do you care about the universe, you keep putting the needle back to the start again, and again, and again.

Biographies

Francesco Alberici is an actor, author and theatre director. Alongside his work with his company Frigoproduzioni, he collaborates with other artists too. With the company, Deflorian/Tagliarini, he took part in five shows as an interpreter and co-author: among them the Italian version of the monologue *Chi ha ucciso mio padre* [*Who Killed My Father*] by Edouard Louis, for which he won the 2021 UBU Award for best actor under 35. Among other important collaborations are those with Liv Ferracchiati and with Babilonia Teatri, winners of the Silver Lion at the Venice Biennale. In 2022, together with Enrico Baraldi, he authored the dramaturgy of the piece, *Non tre sorelle* [*Not Three Sisters*], which was awarded the ANCT Prize by Italy's National Association of Theatre Critics. His play *Bidibibodibiboo* was a finalist at the 56th edition of the prestigious Riccione Award and opened at the Piccolo Teatro in Milan in 2024.

Emanuele Aldrovandi is an Italian writer, playwright, screenwriter and director. He is the recipient of the most important Italian playwriting awards (Riccione/Tondelli, Pirandello, Hystrio). His plays have been translated, performed and published in English, German, French, Spanish, Polish, Slovenian, Czech, Croatian, Romanian, Catalan and Arabic. As a director he has worked with the Emilia Romagna National Theatre and Turin's Teatro Stabile, directing his own plays. He wrote and directed three short films that have been presented in many Italian and international festivals (*Bataclan* won the Silver Ribbon 2021 for best Italian short film) and he's now working on his first feature film. In 2024 his first novel, *Il nostro grande niente*, was published by Einaudi. He teaches writing for the stage and cinema at Civica Scuola Paolo Grassi in Milan and Holden School in Turin.

Ubah Cristina Ali Farah is a Somali-Italian poet, novelist, playwright and librettist based in Brussels, Belgium. She grew up in Mogadishu but fled to Europe at the outbreak of the civil war. In 2006, she won the Lingua Madre National Literary Prize. She is the author of three novels: *Madre piccola* [*Little Mother*], published by Frassinelli in 2007, and winner of the Vittorini Prize; *Il comandante del fiume* [*Commander of the river*], published by 66thand2nd in 2014. Both titles came out in English published by Indiana University Press as part of their Global African Voices series. Lastly, *Le stazioni della luna* [*Stations of the Moon*], published by 66thand2nd in 2021. She also wrote the ekphrasis *La danza dell'orice* (Juxta Press, 2020) and the collection of short stories *Le ceneri della fenice* [*The Phoenix's Ashes*], published by Hopefulmonster in 2022. She holds a PhD in African Studies from the University of Naples, L'Orientale. *Antigone Power* is her first play.

Atri Banerjee is a theatre director and translator based in London. He grew up in Oxford and Florence, read English at Cambridge, and completed an MPhil in Medieval & Renaissance Literature at Cambridge and an MFA in Theatre Directing at Birkbeck. Atri has directed productions at venues including the Royal Shakespeare Company, the Almeida and the Royal Exchange Theatre, and is currently Creative Associate at the Gate Theatre. In 2019, Atri won *The Stage* Debut Award for Best Director for *Hobson's Choice* at the Exchange in Manchester. In 2022, he received a Peter Hall Bursary from the National Theatre and was named by *The Stage* as one of '25 theatre-makers to watch out for over the next quarter-century'. On screen, Atri directed *HARM* for the BBC and Bush Theatre. As translator, Atri has been commissioned by the Royal Court, RSC, and Fabulamundi. His translation of Pier Lorenzo Pisano's *Carbon* was selected for a 2023 honour by Eurodram, the European network for drama in translation.

Magdalena Barile is a playwright, screenwriter and teacher. As a playwright she has worked with prestigious venues and producers in Italy, such as Milan's Teatro dell'Elfo, Turin's Teatro Stabile, Venice Biennale of Theatre, and Milan's Piccolo Teatro. She has been a member of Fabulamundi Playwriting Europe network since 2012. Her plays have been translated into French, English, Catalan, German, Swedish and Russian. For the past ten years she has been working as screenwriter for the Italian Swiss Television (RSI) and for major Italian broadcasters, authoring successful shows such as *Camera Café* and *l'Albero Azzurro*. Since 2020 she is the programme leader for the playwriting course at the Civica Scuola di Teatro Paolo Grassi in Milan. She also teaches screenwriting at the European Institute of Design in Milan. Her latest book, *Gentleman Anne and Other Feminist Plays*, published by Vanda Edizioni, is a collection of plays about queer identities such as Anaïs Nin and Janis Joplin. Her new play *The Collector is* freely inspired by Peggy Guggenheim.

Davide Carnevali is an author and director. He is an associate artist at the Piccolo Teatro di Milano. He holds a PhD in Theatre Theory from the Universitat Autònoma de Barcelona with a year at the Freie Universität Berlin. He teaches playwriting and theatre theory at the Civica Scuola Paolo Grassi in Milan, at the Institut del Teatre in Barcelona, at the Universidad de Castilla y León and Universitat Autònoma de Barcelona. He is the editor of the journal *Estudis Escènics* and collaborates with many international publications. He is the recipient of the Theatertreffen Stückemarkt (2009); the Prix de les Journées des auteurs de Lyon (2012); the Premio Riccione per il Teatro (2013); the Premio Hystrio alla Drammaturgia (2018). His plays have been translated into 15 languages and staged internationally. His work is published by Einaudi and Il Saggiatore in Italy, by Actes Sud and Les Solitaires Intempestifs in France. He has published the academic study, *Forma dramática y representación del mundo en el teatro europeo contemporáneo* [Dramatic Form and Representations of the World in Contemporary European Theatre], published in Ciudad de México by Paso de Gato (2017) and the collaction of short stories *Il diavolo Innamorato*, published in Rome by Fandango (2019).

Valentina Diana lives in the Piedmont countryside with a dog named Orlando. She has been active in the Italian literary scene for many years as a writer of poetry, fiction and plays. Her production stands out for an authentic and original voice, capable of exploring the complexity of the human soul with ironic, intimate and deeply reflective tones. Her plays include: *I tre monologhi* [The Three Monologues] (Einaudi, 2022), a collection of monologues; *La palestra della felicità* [The Happiness Gym] (Cue Press, 2016), a play on the search for happiness combining drama and irony. Her novels include *Smamma* (Einaudi, 2014), treating family dynamics with a sarcastic and irreverent vein; and *Mariti* [Husbands] (Einaudi, 2015), in which she explores the nuances of couple relationships with a sharp eye. She has published the poetry collection, *Uno [One]* (Perrone, 2022), where her observations of the world become more introspective.

Dr Margherita Laera is a Senior Lecturer in Drama and Theatre in at the University of Kent in Canterbury, UK, where she serves as Deputy Head of the School of Arts and Architecture. Her research and impact work explores the many intersections between theatre, migration and modern languages. She has published widely on contemporary Italian and European theatre, theatre translation and adaptation. She is the author of *Playwriting in Europe: Mapping Ecosystems and Practices with Fabulamundi* (Routledge 2022); *Theatre & Translation* (Bloomsbury, 2019) and *Reaching Athens: Community, Democracy and Other Mythologies in Adaptations of Greek Tragedy* (Peter Lang, 2013). As an editor, she published *Theatre and Adaptation: Return, Rewrite, Repeat* (Bloomsbury, 2014). Since 2024, she is the co-editor of the book series *Theatre &* for Bloomsbury Methuen Drama. Margherita regularly translates plays from English to Italian and vice versa. She serves as a Trustee of the London-based theatre company, Actors Touring Company.

Nalini Vidoolah Mootoosamy is a Mauritian-Italian playwright and writer. After completing a PhD in French Studies, focusing on the narratological study of fictional characters, Mootoosamy founded Ananke Arts Association in 2018, where she leads theatre training workshops and performance events as a playwright. Mootoosamy collaborates with the Teatro Utile project at the Accademia dei Filodrammatici in Milan, offering drama training to second-generation migrants in Italy. In 2021, she joined the Fabulamundi Playwriting Europe network, participating in several theatre projects across Europe. Mootoosamy's works for theatre include: *The Dance of the Kabootar* (2019), *The Foreigner's Smile* (2020, winner of the Fabulamundi Call for Second-Generation Migrant Playwrights in Italy), *Now is Forever* (2021), *Bleach Me* (2022), *Lost & Found* (2022 – selected as a finalist for the prestigious Theater Award Premio Riccione 2023), *Eleven Days: What Happened to Agatha Christie?* (2023) and *Ban Ban Kaliban* (2024).

Pier Lorenzo Pisano is a director and author of films, plays and novels. He graduated as a film director at Centro Sperimentale di Cinematografia (Italy's National Film School). His debut short film *Così in terra* was selected in competition at the 71st Cannes Film Festival and in more than fifty international festivals. The following year his second short film *Antiorario [Anticlockwise]* was produced and presented at the 72nd Locarno Film Festival. He was author in residence at the New York Theater Workshop (NYC) and at the Royal Court Theatre (London). He has received the most prestigious Italian awards for new writing, including the Riccione Award, the Solinas Award, the Tondelli Award, the Hystrio Award. He published *Il buio non fa paura [The dark isn't frightening]* (NN), *Carbonio [Carbon]* (Il Saggiatore), *Per il tuo bene [For Your Own Good], Semidei [Demi-Gods]* (Einaudi). His plays have been translated into 14 languages and performed worldwide, including international venues like the Avignon Festival and FIBA (Buenos Aires). He is currently an associate artist of Piccolo Theatre in Milan.

Flora Pitrolo is a scholar, curator and translator, currently teaching History of Theatre and Performance at the Academy of Fine Arts in Palermo and a Research Fellow at Birkbeck, University of London. Her work investigates the problems of the postmodern through experimental music and performance archives, mostly in Italy and South-Eastern Europe, from the 1980s to the present. Her most recent books are *Taroni-

Cividin: Performance, Video, Expanded Cinema 1977-1984 (Silvana 2023, co-edited with Jennifer Malvezzi) and *Global Dance Cultures in the 1970s and 1980s: Disco Heterotopias* (Palgrave 2022, co-edited with Marko Zubak). Flora's work as a curator and programmer currently includes co-directing the festival Teatro Bastardo and the collective Nuova Orfeo, both in Palermo, Italy, and acting as a consultant on larger EU and national cultural projects.

Marco Young is a British-Italian actor and translator. He trained at Bristol Old Vic Theatre School and the University of Cambridge, and has worked onstage as an actor in London and across the UK. Translated productions in the UK with his theatre company Riva Theatre include *Utoya* by Edoardo Erba (Arcola Theatre, August 2024, published with Bloomsbury Methuen), *Scusate se non siamo morti in mare* [*Sorry We Didn't Die at Sea*] by Emanuele Aldrovandi (Park Theatre, September 2023, published with Salamander Street Press). His translation of *Miracoli metropolitani* [*Suburban Miracles*] by Gabriele Di Luca was showcased at Camden People's Theatre in January 2023, and his translation of *Allarmi [Alarms]* by Emanuele Aldrovandi received a rehearsed reading at Omnibus Theatre in July 2023. He has translated texts by Stefano Massini, Davide Enia, Fabio Pisano. He was a mentee on the 2022-23 Foreign Affairs Theatre Translator Mentorship Programme, and a member of Mercury Theatre Colchester's Producer Development Programme 2022-2023.